Cambridge Elements

Elements in Quantitative Finance
edited by
Riccardo Rebonato
EDHEC Business School

HYDRODYNAMICS OF MARKETS

Hidden Links between Physics and Finance

Alexander Lipton
ADIA Lab

CAMBRIDGE
UNIVERSITY PRESS

CAMBRIDGE
UNIVERSITY PRESS

Shaftesbury Road, Cambridge CB2 8EA, United Kingdom

One Liberty Plaza, 20th Floor, New York, NY 10006, USA

477 Williamstown Road, Port Melbourne, VIC 3207, Australia

314–321, 3rd Floor, Plot 3, Splendor Forum, Jasola District Centre, New Delhi – 110025, India

103 Penang Road, #05–06/07, Visioncrest Commercial, Singapore 238467

Cambridge University Press is part of Cambridge University Press & Assessment, a department of the University of Cambridge.

We share the University's mission to contribute to society through the pursuit of education, learning and research at the highest international levels of excellence.

www.cambridge.org
Information on this title: www.cambridge.org/9781009503112

DOI: 10.1017/9781009503129

First published 2024

A catalogue record for this publication is available from the British Library.

ISBN 978-1-009-50311-2 Hardback
ISBN 978-1-009-50310-5 Paperback
ISSN 2631-8571 (online)
ISSN 2631-8563 (print)

Hydrodynamics of Markets

Hidden Links between Physics and Finance

Elements in Quantitative Finance

DOI: 10.1017/9781009503129
First published online: November 2024

Alexander Lipton
ADIA Lab

Author for correspondence: Alexander Lipton, alexander.lipton@adia.ae

Abstract: An intriguing link between a wide range of problems occurring in physics and financial engineering is presented. These problems include the evolution of small perturbations of linear flows in hydrodynamics, the movements of particles in random fields described by the Kolmogorov and Klein–Kramers equations, the Ornstein–Uhlenbeck and Feller processes, and their generalizations. They are reduced to affine differential and pseudo-differential equations and solved in a unified way by using Kelvin waves and developing a comprehensive math framework for calculating transition probabilities and expectations. Kelvin waves are instrumental for studying the well-known Black–Scholes, Heston, and Stein–Stein models and more complex path-dependent volatility models, as well as the pricing of Asian options, volatility and variance swaps, bonds, and bond options. Kelvin waves help to solve several cutting-edge problems, including hedging the impermanent loss of automated market makers for cryptocurrency trading. This Element is also available as Open Access on Cambridge Core.

Keywords: affine processes, Kelvin waves, Kolmogorov equation, Klein–Kramers equation, stochastic volatility

MSC2020 Classification: 34A34, 35A22, 42A38, 60H10, 76E99, 91G20

ISBNs: 9781009503112 (HB), 9781009503105 (PB), 9781009503129 (OC)
ISSNs: 2631-8571 (online), 2631-8563 (print)

Contents

6accdae13eff7i3l9n4o4qrr4s8t12ux
Letter from Isaac Newton to Henry Oldenburg, 24 October 1676[1]

Bob Montagnet: Yeah, good choice, Vlad.
Get back to the security system. How does it work?
Vlad: The way everything works. Mathematics.
"The Good Thief," screenplay by Neil Jordan, 2002

1 Introduction

1.1 Background

Newton's discovery of differential equations and calculus was crucial in developing classical mechanics because it allowed for the mathematical description of the motion of objects. This discovery took a groundbreaking step in unifying mathematics with physics, enabling the prediction of planetary orbits, the motion of objects under various forces, and much more, and marked the beginning of a new era in mathematics and science, laying the cornerstone for over three centuries of advancements.

Newton understood the immediate impact of his discoveries and their potential to transform the understanding of the natural world. To establish and protect his intellectual property rights at the same time, he concealed his discovery in the fundamental anagram of calculus, which he included in his 1676 letter to Oldenburg. This anagram contained a Latin statement describing the method of fluxions (his term for calculus) when decoded. The need for an anagram reflected that Newton was competitive and cautious in equal measure by balancing the desire for recognition with the fear of disclosure. The number of occurrences of each Latin character in Newton's sentence agrees with his anagram, thus proving that the actual sentence was written in 1676.[2] The original letter is shown in Figure 1.

The fact that differential equations are instrumental in mathematics and physics alike was firmly established in the late seventeenth century. However, methods for solving these equations remained ad hoc for more than a

[1] *Data aequatione quotcunque fluentes quantitae involvente fluxiones invenire et vice versa.* – "Given an equation involving any number of fluent quantities to find the fluxions, and vice versa." Vladimir Arnold paraphrased the statement as follows: "It is useful to solve differential equations." Cambridge University Library, Department of Manuscripts and University Archives. ItemReference Code: GBR/0012/MS Add.9597/2/18/56.

[2] Newton's anagram is an early example of a one-way hash function. An anagram is easy to calculate, provided the message is known, but not vice versa. Hash functions are indispensable in modern cryptography, including its applications to cryptocurrencies such as Bitcoin; see, for example, Lipton and Treccani (2021).

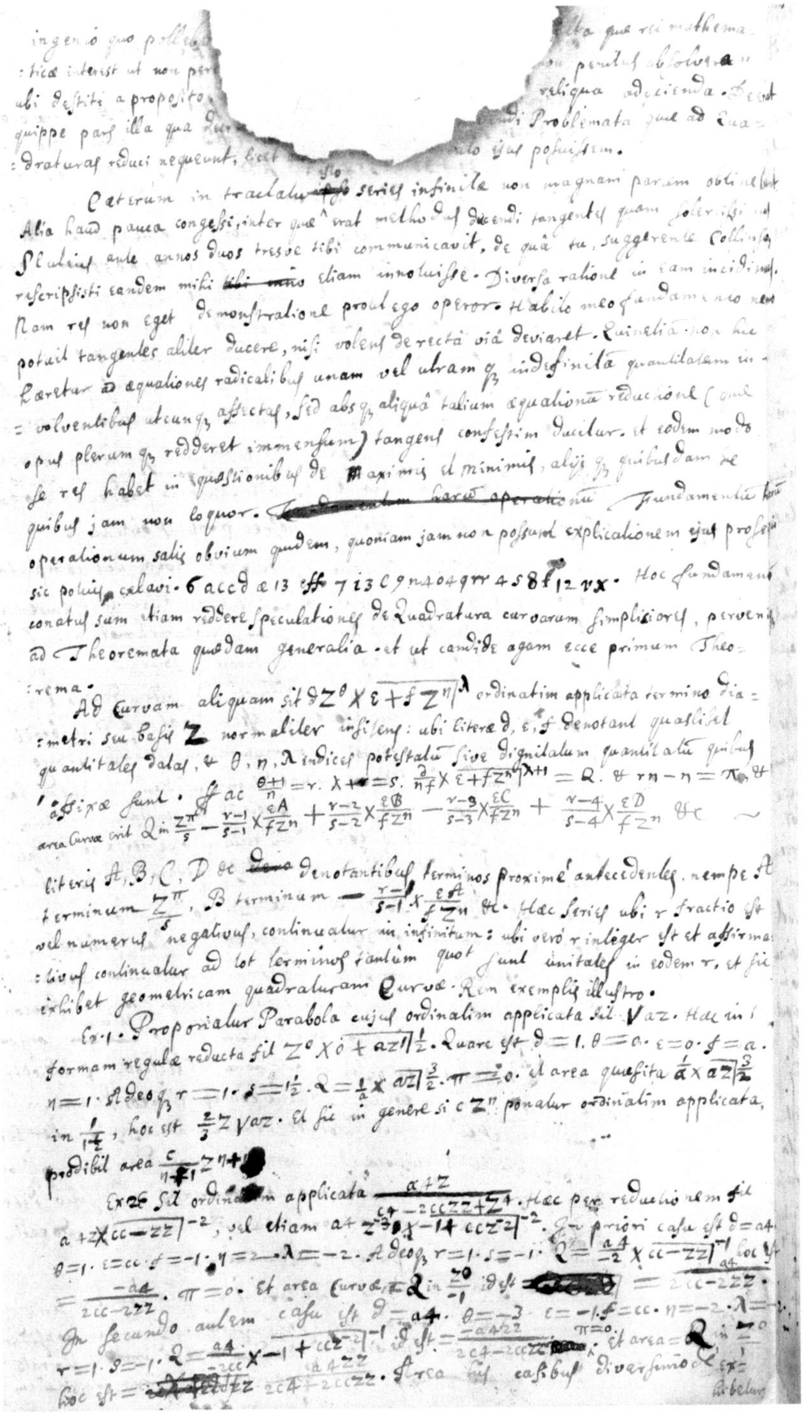

Figure 1 Newton's letter to Oldenburg, 1676. Reproduced by kind permission of the Syndics of Cambridge University Library.

century until the work by Lagrange, Laplace, Fourier, and many other mathematicians and physicists. In particular, the Fourier transform stands out as the most potent tool in an applied mathematician's toolkit, enabling the solving of linear partial differential equations (PDEs) and partial pseudo-differential equations (PPDEs) with spatially constant coefficients; it is also invaluable for analyzing time series and tackling other critical tasks (Fourier (1822); Morse & Feschbach (1953)).

At the heart of the n-dimensional Fourier method are wave functions, expressed as follows:

$$\mathcal{F}(t, \mathbf{x}, \mathbf{k}) = \mathsf{a}(t) \exp(i\mathbf{k} \cdot \mathbf{x}), \tag{1.1}$$

where $\mathbf{x}$ and $\mathbf{k}$ are n-dimensional vectors, $\cdot$ denotes the scalar product, $\mathsf{a}(t)$ is the amplitude, and $\mathbf{k} \cdot \mathbf{x}$ is the phase. Depending on the particular problem at hand, the amplitude $\mathsf{a}(t)$ can be a scalar or a vector, hence the notation. Substituting $\mathcal{F}$ into a PDE with spatially constant coefficients, one reduces the problem of interest to a system of ordinary differential equations (ODEs) or a single ODE when $\mathsf{a}(t)$ is scalar. Of course, this system parametrically depends on $\mathbf{k}$.

This Element studies PDEs and PPDEs with coefficients linearly dependent on $\mathbf{x}$, which are called affine. Hence, one must use a more general approach and consider wave functions with time-dependent wave vectors:

$$\mathcal{K}(t, \mathbf{x}, \beta(t)) = \mathsf{a}(t) \exp(i\boldsymbol{\beta}(t) \cdot \mathbf{x}). \tag{1.2}$$

Kelvin (1887) and Orr (1907) were the first to use such waves to analyze the stability of the steady motions of an incompressible fluid.

Affine problems are not artificial constructs. They appear organically in several situations, for example, when the linear description of the underlying physical mechanism is either exact or provides an excellent approximation to reality or when the evolution in the phase space is studied; see Section 3.

Subsequently and independently, affine PDEs and the associated wave functions were used by many researchers in various areas, including the theory of stochastic processes, physics, biology, and mathematical finance, to mention a few. The Ornstein–Uhlenbeck (OU) and Feller processes are the simplest but extremely important examples of affine processes; see Uhlenbeck and Ornstein (1930), Chandresekhar (1943), and Feller (1951, 1952). For financial applications of affine processes see Duffie and Kan (1996), Duffie *et al.* (2000), Dai and Singleton (2000), Lipton (2001), Duffie *et al.* (2003), Sepp (2007), Lipton and Sepp (2008), and Filipovic (2009), among others.

This Element uses Kelvin waves of the form (1.2) to study transition probability density functions (t.p.d.fs) for affine stochastic processes. These processes can be either degenerate, namely, have more independent components than the sources of uncertainty, or nondegenerate, when every component has its source of uncertainty. Recall that the t.p.d.f. for a stochastic process describes the likelihood of a system transitioning from one state to another over a specified period. Knowing the iterated t.p.d.f. is fundamental for understanding the dynamics and behavior of stochastic processes over time and is tantamount to knowing the process itself.

In this Element, Kelvin waves are also used to solve several essential and intricate problems occurring in financial applications. These include pricing options with stochastic volatility, path-dependent options, and Asian options with geometric averaging, among many others.

The main objective is to link various financial engineering topics with their counterparts in hydrodynamics and molecular physics and showcase the interdisciplinary nature of quantitative finance and economic modeling. Finding such connections allows us to understand better how to model, price, and risk-manage various financial instruments, derive several new results, and provide additional intuition regarding their salient features. This Element continues previous efforts in this direction; see Lipton and Sepp (2008) and Lipton (2018), chapter 12.

There are several approaches one can use to solve affine equations efficiently. For instance, Lie symmetries are a powerful tool for studying certain classes of affine equations. Numerous authors describe general techniques based on Lie symmetries; see, for example, Ovsiannikov (1982), Ibragimov (1985), Olver (1986), and Bluman and Kumei (1989), while their specific applications to affine equations are covered by Berest (1993), Aksenov (1995), Craddock and Platen (2004), Craddock (2012), and Kovalenko *et al.* (2014), among many others. However, Lie symmetry techniques are exceedingly cumbersome and might be challenging to use in practice, especially when complicated affine equations are considered.

Laplace transform of spatial variables can be used in some cases, for instance, for Feller processes; see, for example, Feller (1951, 1952). However, they are hard to use for solving generic affine equations.

Reductions of a given equation to a simpler, solvable form is another powerful method that can be successfully used in many instances; see, for example, Chandresekhar (1943), Carr *et al.* (2002), Lipton *et al.* (2014), and Lipton (2018), chapter 9. Although the reduction method is quite powerful, experience suggests it is often hard to use in practice.

Finally, the affine ansatz based on Kelvin waves provides yet another approach, which is the focus of the present Element; see also Duffie and Kan (1996), Dai and Singleton (2000), Duffie *et al.* (2003), Lipton and Sepp

(2008), Filipovic (2009), and Lipton (2018), chapter 12. Undoubtedly, the affine framework, also known as the affine ansatz, is the most potent among the abovementioned techniques due to its comprehensive nature, versatility, and (relative) ease of use, even in complex situations. In practice, applications of Kelvin waves consist of three steps:

- Effectively separating variables for the evolution problems with pseudo-differential generators linearly dependent on spatial coordinates;
- Solving ODEs parametrized by time-dependent wave vectors; see (1.2);
- Aggregating their solutions together to get the solution to the original problem.

However, despite being a ruthlessly efficient tool, Kelvin waves have limitations – using them to solve evolution problems supplied with external boundary conditions is challenging. This exciting topic is being actively researched now; it will be discussed elsewhere in due course.

1.2 Main Results

This Element develops a coherent, unified mathematical framework using Kelvin waves as a powerful and versatile tool for studying t.p.d.fs in the context of generic affine processes. It discovers previously hidden connections among large classes of apparently unrelated problems from hydrodynamics, molecular physics, and financial engineering. All these problems require solving affine (pseudo-) differential equations, namely, equations with coefficients, which linearly depend on spatial variables. The Element discusses some classical results and derives several original ones related to:

- small wave-like perturbations of linear flows of ideal and viscous fluids described by Euler and Navier–Stokes equations, respectively;
- motions of free and harmonically bound particles under the impact of random external white-noise forces described by the Klein–Kramers equations and the hypoelliptic Kolmogorov equation, which play an essential role in statistical physics;
- Gaussian and non-Gaussian affine processes, such as the Ornstein–Uhlenbeck and Feller processes, which are the archetypal mean-reverting processes, and their generalizations;
- dynamics of financial markets, particularly derivative products.

To solve some of the more complicated problems, one must augment primary processes by introducing subordinate processes for auxiliary variables, such as integrals over the original stochastic variable, and develop a uniform mathematical formalism to construct t.p.d.fs for the abovementioned processes.

Quite unexpectedly, the analysis identifies and rectifies an error in the original solution of the Kolmogorov equation. The rectified solution is dimensionally correct, properly scales when the process parameters change, and agrees with numerical results.

Furthermore, this Element derives many original results and extends and reinterprets some well-known ones. For instance, it develops a concise and efficient expression for t.p.d.fs in the case of processes with stochastic volatility. Moreover, the analysis reveals an unexpected similarity between the propagation of vorticity in two-dimensional flows of viscous incompressible fluid and the motion of a harmonically bound particle, which is used to find a new explicit expression for the vorticity of a two-dimensional flow in terms of the Gaussian density.

Finally, the Element applies the new methodology to various financial engineering topics, such as pricing options with stochastic volatility, options with path-dependent volatility, Asian options, volatility and variance swaps, options on stocks with path-dependent volatility, and bonds and bond options. In contrast to the classical approach, the Element treats primary fixed-income products, such as bonds and bond options, as path-dependent, allowing us to gain additional intuition regarding such products' pricing and risk management. It also highlights the flexibility of the interdisciplinary framework by incorporating additional complexities into the picture, such as jump-diffusion processes and, more generally, processes driven by affine pseudo-differential processes frequently used in financial applications.

1.3 Element Structure

Section 2 introduces Kelvin waves. Section 2.1 introduces the Euler equations, which describe the dynamics of a perfect fluid, alongside the Navier–Stokes equation for viscous incompressible fluids. Section 2.2 discusses the exact equilibria of these equations, focusing on states where velocity varies linearly and pressure quadratically with spatial coordinates, referred to as linear flows. Section 2.3 illustrates that the renowned Kelvin waves provide solutions to the linearized Euler and Navier–Stokes equations for small perturbations of the linear flows. This section also explores the use of Kelvin waves in analyzing the stability of these flows.

The Element uses Kelvin waves as a fundamental tool in the analytical arsenal, demonstrating their applicability across various study areas. For instance, they allow one to discover profound and surprising links between the viscous two-dimensional vorticity equations and the Klein–Kramers equation, a cornerstone of stochastic physics; see Section 6.6. This connection results in a novel formula representing vorticity as a Gaussian density and the stream function as the solution to the associated Poisson equation.

Section 3 investigates the degenerate stochastic process introduced by Kolmogorov in 1934, alongside the associated Fokker–Planck equation and its solution proposed by Kolmogorov. Further connections between the Kolmogorov and Klein–Kramers equations are explored in Section 4. To start with, Section 3 summarizes Kolmogorov's original findings. Surprisingly, the Fokker–Planck equation, as used by Kolmogorov in his seminal paper, is inconsistent with his initial assumptions regarding the underlying process. Moreover, his proposed solution has dimensional inconsistencies and, as a result, does not satisfy the Fokker–Planck equation and initial conditions. However, there is a silver lining; Kolmogorov's solution can be corrected via several complementary methods, which the section outlines. It concludes with an example of a representative corrected solution to the Kolmogorov problem.

Section 4 explores a selection of representative affine stochastic processes in statistical physics. First, it introduces the Langevin equation, which describes the dynamics of an underdamped Brownian particle in a potential field. Following this, it derives the Klein–Kramers equation, capturing the probabilistic aspects of the motion of such a particle. It turns out that the Kolmogorov equation derived in Section 3 is a particular case of the Klein–Kramers equation. The section presents Chandrasekhar's solutions to the Klein–Kramers equations describing free and harmonically bound particles. The Klein–Kramers equation is inherently degenerate, with white noise impacting the particle's velocity but not its position. It is shown in Section 8 that many path-dependent problems share this characteristic in mathematical finance. For instance, financial variables like the geometric price averages, which serve as the underlying instruments for a particular class of Asian options, can be conceptualized as path integrals, fitting into the category of degenerate stochastic processes.

Section 5 describes backward (Kolmogorov) and forward (Fokker–Planck) equations for t.p.d.fs of multidimensional stochastic jump-diffusion processes. The section explains the significance of studying t.p.d.fs. It sets up the general framework for Kolmogorov and Fokker–Planck equations and identifies the subset of affine stochastic processes amenable to analysis using the Kelvin-wave formalism. Subsequently, the section introduces an augmentation technique, providing a natural approach to tackle degenerate problems. Finally, it illustrates methods for transforming specific nonaffine processes into affine form through coordinate transformations, enhancing the scope of problems accessible by the Kelvin-wave methodology.

Section 6 studies Gaussian stochastic processes. It introduces a general formula for regular Gaussian processes, accommodating both degenerate scenarios and nondegenerate cases, as in Kolmogorov's example. It expands this formula to address the practically significant scenario of killed Gaussian processes, followed by several illustrative examples. Then, the section presents the derivation of the t.p.d.f. for the Kolmogorov process with time-varying coefficients and explores the OU process with time-dependent coefficients and its extension, the augmented OU process, which models the combined dynamics of the process and its integral. Although the results are classical, their derivation through Kelvin-wave expansions provides a novel and enriching angle, offering an alternative viewpoint for understanding and deriving these established results. Next, the section examines free and harmonically bound particles, contrasting the Kelvin-wave method with Chandrasekhar's classical approach. Finally, it revisits the basic concepts introduced in Section 2, demonstrating the akin nature of the temporal-spatial evolution of vorticity in the two-dimensional flow of a viscous fluid to the dynamics of a harmonically bound particle. This finding is intriguing and unexpected, forging a connection between seemingly unrelated physical phenomena.

Section 7 considers non-Gaussian processes. It starts with a general formula for non-Gaussian dynamics, accommodating degenerate and nondegenerate processes. Then, it expands this formula to killed processes. Several interesting examples are studied. These examples include a Kolmogorov process driven by anomalous diffusion, Feller processes with constant and time-dependent coefficients, and degenerate and nondegenerate augmented Feller processes. A novel method for investigating finite-time explosions of t.p.d.fs for augmented Feller processes is developed as a helpful by-product of the analysis. In addition, arithmetic Brownian motions with path-dependent volatility and degenerate and nondegenerate arithmetic Brownian motions with stochastic volatility are analyzed in detail.

Section 8 illustrates the application of the methodology to financial engineering. To start with, it lays the foundation of financial engineering, providing a primer for the uninitiated. Then, the section introduces the geometric Brownian motion, a staple in financial modeling, and discusses the modifications necessary to reflect the complexities of financial markets better. Several traditional models, such as Bachelier, Black–Scholes, Heston, and Stein–Stein models, and a novel path-dependent volatility model are explored via the Kelvin-wave formalism. In addition, it is shown how to price Asian options with geometric averaging via the Kolmogorov's solution described in Section 3. Besides, volatility and variance swaps and swaptions, bonds and bond options are investigated by linking financial formulas to those used in physics for underdamped Brownian motion.

Section 9 succinctly outlines potential future expansions of the work presented in this Element and summarizes the conclusions. Finally, this Element is a revised and expanded version of Lipton (2023).

A note on notation: Given the wide-ranging scope of this Element, from hydrodynamics to molecular physics, probability theory, and financial engineering, adopting a unified notation system is impractical. Each field has its conventions carved in stone, leading to inevitable variations in notation. Notation is designed for consistency within and, where possible, across sections. However, readers are encouraged to remain vigilant to maintain coherence in their understanding.

2 Fluid Flows

2.1 Euler and Navier–Stokes Equations

Hydrodynamics studies how fluids (liquids and gases) move, primarily relying on fluid motion's fundamental equations: the Euler and Navier–Stokes equations, with the Euler equations applicable to inviscid (frictionless) flow and the Navier–Stokes equations describing viscous fluids. Hydrodynamics has numerous applications across various fields, including engineering, astrophysics, oceanography, and climate change, among many others.

Recall that the Euler system of partial differential equations (PDEs) describing the motion of an inviscid, incompressible fluid has the form

$$\frac{\partial \mathbf{V}}{\partial t} + (\mathbf{V}\cdot\nabla)\mathbf{V} + \nabla\left(\frac{P}{\rho}\right) = 0,$$

$$\nabla \cdot \mathbf{V} = 0; \tag{2.1}$$

where t is time, $\mathbf{x}$ is the position, $V(t,\mathbf{x})$ is the velocity vector, $P(t,\mathbf{x})$ is the pressure, ρ is the constant density, ∇ is the gradient, and $\cdot$ denotes the scalar product; see, for example, Chandrasekhar (1961). In Cartesian coordinates, the equations in (2.1) can be written as follows:

$$\frac{\partial V_i}{\partial t} + V_j\frac{\partial V_i}{\partial x_j} + \frac{\partial}{\partial x_i}\left(\frac{P}{\rho}\right) = 0,$$

$$\frac{\partial V_i}{\partial x_i} = 0. \tag{2.2}$$

Here and in what follows, Einstein's summation convention over repeated indices is used.

The motion of the incompressible viscous fluid is described by the classical Navier–Stokes equations of the form:

$$\frac{\partial \mathbf{V}}{\partial t} + (\mathbf{V}\cdot\nabla)\mathbf{V} - \nu\Delta\mathbf{V} + \nabla\left(\frac{P}{\rho}\right) = 0,$$

$$\nabla \cdot \mathbf{V} = 0; \tag{2.3}$$

where ν is the kinematic viscosity; see, for example, Chandrasekhar (1961). Explicitly,

$$\frac{\partial V_i}{\partial t} + V_j \frac{\partial V_i}{\partial x_j} - \nu \frac{\partial^2 V_i}{\partial x_j \partial x_j} + \frac{\partial}{\partial x_i}\left(\frac{P}{\rho}\right) = 0,$$

$$\frac{\partial V_i}{\partial x_i} = 0. \tag{2.4}$$

The diffusive term $-\nu\Delta\mathbf{V}$ in (2.4) describes frictions ignored in (2.3). Due to their greater generality, the Navier–Stokes equations are fundamental to understanding important phenomena, such as the transition from laminar to turbulent flow.

2.2 Linear Flows

This section studies exact solutions of the Euler and Navier–Stokes equations known as linear flows. These solutions are valuable for several reasons: (a) exact solutions provide precise, analytical descriptions of fluid flow patterns under specific conditions; (b) they serve as benchmarks for understanding fundamental hydrodynamics phenomena like wave propagation; (c) they provide a bridge which is crucial for more complex studies by simplifying the inherently complex and nonlinear nature of hydrodynamics, and making it possible to understand the behavior of more general fluid flows. Linear solutions of the Euler and Navier–Stokes equations help to study fluid flow stability. This understanding is crucial in predicting and controlling flow behavior in various engineering applications, from aerospace to hydraulic engineering. By starting with linear solutions, one can incrementally introduce nonlinear effects, allowing for a systematic study of nonlinear phenomena in hydrodynamics. This approach can uncover the mechanisms behind complex flows, including turbulence and chaotic flow behaviors. Exact linear solutions of the Euler equations provide a clear, analytical framework for exploring the behavior of fluids and validating more complicated models.

It is easy to show that the equations in (2.1) have a family of solutions $(\mathbf{V}(t,\mathbf{x}), P(t,\mathbf{x}))$, linearly depending on spatial coordinates:

$$\mathbf{V}(t,\mathbf{x}) = \mathfrak{L}(t)\,\mathbf{x}, \quad \frac{P(t,\mathbf{x})}{\rho} = \frac{P_0}{\rho} + \frac{1}{2}\mathfrak{M}(t)\,\mathbf{x}\cdot\mathbf{x}, \tag{2.5}$$

where the 3×3 matrices $\mathfrak{L}(t)$, $\mathfrak{M}(t)$, are such that

$$\frac{d\mathfrak{L}(t)}{dt} + \mathfrak{L}^2(t) + \mathfrak{M}(t) = 0,$$
$$\mathrm{Tr}(\mathfrak{L}(t)) = 0, \quad \mathfrak{M}(t) = \mathfrak{M}^*(t). \tag{2.6}$$

It is clear that linear flows, given by (2.5), are unaffected by viscosity, hence they satisfy (2.14).

Flows (2.5) have stagnation points at the origin. Typical examples are planar flows of the form

$$V_1 = \frac{1}{2}(sx_1 - wx_2), \quad V_2 = \frac{1}{2}(wx_1 - sx_2), \quad V_3 = 0,$$
$$\frac{P}{\rho} = \frac{P_0}{\rho} + \frac{1}{4}\left(w^2 - s^2\right)\left(x_1^2 + x_2^2\right). \tag{2.7}$$

These flows are elliptic when $s < w$, and hyperbolic otherwise; see, for example, Friedlander and Lipton-Lifschitz (2003).

2.3 Kelvin Waves in an Incompressible Fluid

The study of small perturbations of exact solutions of the Euler and Navier–Stokes equations is the core of the stability analysis in fluid dynamics. Examining their behavior is essential for predicting how fluid flows evolve under slight disturbances. One can determine whether a particular flow is stable or unstable by introducing small perturbations to an exact solution and observing the system's response. If these perturbations grow over time, the flow is considered unstable; if they decay or remain bounded, the flow is stable. One of this analysis's most critical applications is understanding the transition from laminar (smooth and orderly) to turbulent (chaotic and unpredictable) flows. Small perturbations can exhibit exponential growth, leading to the onset of turbulence. For more detailed investigations, direct numerical simulations of the perturbed Navier–Stokes equations can be used to study the nonlinear evolution of perturbations. This approach can capture the complete transition from initial instability to fully developed turbulence, offering insights into the complex interactions that drive flow dynamics. The study of perturbations offers theoretical insights into the fundamental nature of fluid dynamics, including the mechanisms of flow instability, transition, and turbulence structure. It helps in developing reduced-order models and theories that explain complex fluid phenomena. Here, Kelvin waves are used as the primary tool for studying small perturbations of linear flows. In the rest of this Element, Kelvin waves are used for other purposes. This section is dedicated to their brief description.

It is necessary to study the behavior of perturbations of solutions given by (2.5), which are denoted by $(\mathbf{v}(t,\mathbf{x}), p(t,\mathbf{x}))$. By neglecting the quadratic term $(v \cdot \nabla)v$, one can write the system of PDEs for $(\mathbf{v},p)$ as follows:

$$\frac{\partial \mathbf{v}}{\partial t} + (\mathfrak{L}(t)\,\mathbf{x}\cdot\nabla)\mathbf{v} + \mathfrak{L}(t)\,\mathbf{v} + \nabla\left(\frac{p}{\rho}\right) = 0,$$
$$\nabla \cdot \mathbf{v} = 0. \tag{2.8}$$

It has been known for a long time that linear PDEs (2.8) have wavelike solutions of the form:

$$\left(\mathbf{v}(t,\mathbf{x}), \frac{p(t,\mathbf{x})}{\rho}\right) = (\mathbf{a}(t), a(t)) \exp\left(i\boldsymbol{\beta}(t)\cdot(\mathbf{x} - \mathbf{r}(t))\right), \tag{2.9}$$

where $(\mathbf{a}(t), a(t))$ are time-dependent amplitudes, and $\boldsymbol{\beta}(t)$ is the time-dependent wave vector; see Kelvin (1887), Orr (1907), Craik and Criminale (1986), and Friedlander and Lipton-Lifschitz (2003). In this Element, these solutions are called the Kelvin waves. It should be emphasized that the so-called affine ansatz is a special instance of Kelvin wave. This observation allows one to discover similarities among seemingly unrelated topics, which, in turn, facilitates their holistic and comprehensive study. An excerpt from Kelvin's original paper is shown in Figure 2.

As one can see from Figure 2, Kelvin considered the special case of the so-called shear linear flow of the form

$$\mathbf{V}(t,\mathbf{x}) = (V_1(x_2), 0, 0) = (l_{12}x_2, 0, 0), \tag{2.10}$$

between two plates, $x_2 = 0$ and $x_2 = L$, the first one at rest and the second one moving in parallel.

The triplet $\mathbf{r}(t)$, $\boldsymbol{\beta}(t)$, $\mathbf{a}(t)$ satisfies the following system of ODEs:

$$\frac{d\mathbf{r}(t)}{dt} - \mathfrak{L}(t)\,\mathbf{r}(t) = 0, \quad \mathbf{r}(0) = \mathbf{r}_0,$$
$$\frac{d\boldsymbol{\beta}(t)}{dt} + \mathfrak{L}^*(t)\,\boldsymbol{\beta}(t) = 0, \quad \boldsymbol{\beta}(0) = \boldsymbol{\beta}_0,$$
$$\frac{d\mathbf{a}(t)}{dt} + \mathfrak{L}(t)\,\mathbf{a}(t) - 2\frac{\mathfrak{L}(t)\,\mathbf{a}(t)\cdot\boldsymbol{\beta}(t)}{\boldsymbol{\beta}(t)\cdot\boldsymbol{\beta}(t)}\boldsymbol{\beta}(t) = 0, \ \mathbf{a}(0) = \mathbf{a}_0,$$
$$\boldsymbol{\beta}_0 \cdot \mathbf{a}_0 = 0. \tag{2.11}$$

Here and in what follows, the superscript $*$ stands for transpose. The corresponding $p(t)$ can be found via the incompressibility condition. It is easy to show that for $t \geq 0$,

$$\boldsymbol{\beta}(t)\cdot\mathbf{r}(t) = \boldsymbol{\beta}_0\cdot\mathbf{r}_0, \quad \boldsymbol{\beta}(t)\cdot\mathbf{a}(t) = 0. \tag{2.12}$$

Viscous Fluid between two Parallel Planes. 191

These equations (15) ... (19) are of course satisfied by $u=0$, $v=0$, $w=0$, $p=0$. The question of stability is, Does every possible solution of them come to this in time? It seems to me probable that it does; but I cannot, at present at all events, enter on the investigation. The case of $b=\infty$ is specially important and interesting.

31. The present communication is confined to the much simpler case in which the two bounding planes are kept moving relatively with constant velocity; including as sub-case, the two planes held at rest, and the fluid caused by gravity to move between them. But we shall first take the much simpler sub-case, in which there is relative motion of the two planes, and no gravity. This is the very simplest of all cases of the general question of the Stability or Instability of the Motion of a Viscous Fluid. It is the second of the two cases prescribed by the Examiners for the Adams Prize of 1888. I have ascertained, and I now give (§§ 32...39 below) the proof, that in this sub-case the steady motion is wholly stable, however small or however great be the viscosity; and this without limitation to two-dimensional motion of the admissible disturbances.

32. In our present sub-case, let βb be the relative velocity of the two planes; so that in (6) we may take $F=0$, $\mathfrak{F}=\beta b$; and the corresponding steady solution of (4) is

$$v = \beta y \quad . \quad . \quad . \quad . \quad . \quad . \quad . \quad . \quad (20).$$

Thus equation (19) becomes reduced to

$$\left.\begin{aligned} \frac{d\sigma}{dt} + \beta y \frac{d\sigma}{dx} &= \mu \nabla^2 \sigma, \\ \text{where} \qquad \sigma &= \nabla^2 v \end{aligned}\right\} \quad . \quad . \quad . \quad . \quad (21);$$

and (18), (15), (16), (17) become

$$2\beta \frac{dv}{dx} = -\nabla^2 p \quad . \quad . \quad . \quad . \quad . \quad (22),$$

$$\frac{du}{dt} + \beta y \frac{du}{dx} + \beta v = \mu \nabla^2 u - \frac{dp}{dx} \quad . \quad . \quad . \quad . \quad (23),$$

$$\frac{dv}{dt} + \beta y \frac{dv}{dx} = \mu \nabla^2 v - \frac{dp}{dy} \quad . \quad . \quad . \quad . \quad (24),$$

$$\frac{dw}{dt} + \beta y \frac{dw}{dx} = \mu \nabla^2 w - \frac{dp}{dz} \quad . \quad . \quad . \quad . \quad (25).$$

It may be remarked that equations (22) ... (25) imply (1), and that any four of the five determines the four quantities u, v, w, p. It will still be convenient occasionally to use (1).

Figure 2 An excerpt from Kelvin's original paper, where Kelvin waves are introduced for the first time; see Kelvin (1887). Public domain.

We proceed to find the complete solution of the problem before us, consisting of expressions for u, v, w, p satisfying (22)...(25) for all values of x, y, z, t; and the following initial and boundary conditions :—

$$\left.\begin{array}{r}\text{when } t=0:\ u, v, w \text{ to be arbitrary functions}\\ \text{of } x, y, z, \text{ subject only to (1)}\end{array}\right\} \quad . \quad (26);$$

$$\left.\begin{array}{l}u=0,\ v=0,\ w=0, \text{ for } y=0 \text{ and all values of } x, z, t\\ u=0,\ v=0,\ w=0, \text{ for } y=b \qquad ,, \qquad ,,\end{array}\right\} \quad (27).$$

33. First let us find a particular solution $\mathbf{u}, \mathbf{v}, \mathbf{w}, \mathbf{p}$, which shall satisfy the initial conditions (26), irrespectively of the boundary conditions (27), except as follows :—

$$\left.\begin{array}{l}\mathbf{v}=0, \text{ when } t=0 \text{ and } y=0\\ \mathbf{v}=0, \text{ when } t=0 \text{ and } y=b\end{array}\right\} \quad . \quad . \quad . \quad (28).$$

Next, find another particular solution, $\mathfrak{u}, \mathfrak{v}, \mathfrak{w}, \mathfrak{p}$, satisfying the following initial and boundary equations :—

$$\mathfrak{u}=0,\ \mathfrak{v}=0,\ \mathfrak{w}=0, \text{ when } t=0 \quad . \quad . \quad . \quad (29);$$

$$\left.\begin{array}{r}\mathfrak{u}+\mathbf{u}=0,\ \mathfrak{v}+\mathbf{v}=0,\ \mathfrak{w}+\mathbf{w}=0, \text{ when } y=0\\ \text{and when } y=b\end{array}\right\} \quad . \quad . \quad (30).$$

The required complete solution will then be

$$u=\mathfrak{u}+\mathbf{u}, \quad v=\mathfrak{v}+\mathbf{v}, \quad w=\mathfrak{w}+\mathbf{w} \quad . \quad . \quad . \quad (31).$$

34. To find $\mathbf{u}, \mathbf{v}, \mathbf{w}$, remark that, if μ were zero, the complete integral of (21) would be

$$\sigma = \text{arb. func. } (x-\beta yt) \text{ ;}$$

and take therefore as a trial for a type-solution with μ not zero,

$$\sigma=\mathrm{T}\epsilon^{\iota[mx+(n-m\beta t)y+qz]} \quad . \quad . \quad . \quad . \quad . \quad (32);$$

where T is a function of t, and ι denotes $\sqrt{-1}$. Substituting accordingly in (21), we find

$$\frac{d\mathrm{T}}{dt} = -\mu[m^2+(n-m\beta t)^2+q^2]\mathrm{T} \quad . \quad . \quad . \quad (33);$$

whence, by integration,

$$\mathrm{T}=\mathrm{C}\epsilon^{-\mu t\left[m^2+n^2+q^2-nm\beta t+\frac{m^2}{3}\beta^2t^2\right]} \quad . \quad . \quad . \quad (34).$$

By the second of (21), and (32), we find

$$v=-\mathrm{T}\frac{\epsilon^{\iota[mx+(n-m\beta t)y+qz]}}{m^2+(n-m\beta t)^2+q^2} \quad . \quad . \quad . \quad . \quad . \quad (35);$$

Figure 2 (continued)

Thus, the Kelvin-wave formalism results in ingenious separation of variables and allows us to solve a system of ODEs (2.11), rather than PDEs (2.8).

Typically, the equations in (2.11) are used to study the stability of the linear flow. Such a flow is unstable whenever $\|\mathbf{a}(t)\| \to \infty$ for some choices of $\boldsymbol{\beta}_0, \mathbf{a}_0$; see Bayly (1986), Lifschitz (1995), and Bayly *et al.* (1996). Moreover, it can be shown that the same instabilities occur in general three-dimensional flows, because locally they are equivalent to linear flows; see Lifschitz and Hameiri (1991a), Friedlander and Vishik (1991), Lifschitz and Hameiri (1991b), and Friedlander and Lipton-Lifschitz (2003).

Interestingly, Chandrasekhar (1961) pointed out that the superposition of the linear flow (2.5) and the Kelvin wave (2.9), namely,

$$\begin{aligned} \tilde{\mathbf{V}}(t,\mathbf{x}) &= \mathfrak{L}(t)\,\mathbf{x} + \mathbf{v}(t,\mathbf{x}), \\ \frac{\tilde{P}(t,\mathbf{x})}{\rho} &= \frac{1}{2}\mathfrak{M}(t)\,\mathbf{x}\cdot\mathbf{x} + \frac{p(t,\mathbf{x})}{\rho}, \end{aligned} \qquad (2.13)$$

satisfies the nonlinear Euler equations (2.1) since the nonlinear term $(\mathbf{v}\cdot\nabla)\mathbf{v}$ vanishes identically due to incompressibility.[3] Studying secondary instabilities of flows with elliptic streamlines, that is, instabilities of Kelvin waves is an important and intricate topic; see Fabijonas *et al.* (1997).

Viscosity does affect small perturbations of linear flows. For viscous incompressible fluids, Kelvin waves are governed by the following equations:

$$\begin{aligned} \frac{\partial\mathbf{v}}{\partial t} + (\mathfrak{L}(t)\,\mathbf{x}\cdot\nabla)\mathbf{v} + \mathfrak{L}(t)\,\mathbf{v} - \nu\Delta\mathbf{v} + \nabla\left(\frac{p}{\rho}\right) &= 0, \\ \nabla\cdot\mathbf{v} &= 0. \end{aligned} \qquad (2.14)$$

The viscous version of (2.11) has the following form; see Lifschitz (1991):

$$\begin{aligned} &\frac{d\mathbf{r}(t)}{dt} - \mathfrak{L}(t)\,\mathbf{r}(t) = 0, \quad \mathbf{r}(0) = \mathbf{r}_0, \\ &\frac{d\boldsymbol{\beta}(t)}{dt} + \mathfrak{L}^*(t)\,\boldsymbol{\beta}(t) = 0, \quad \boldsymbol{\beta}(0) = \boldsymbol{\beta}_0, \\ &\frac{d\mathbf{a}(t)}{dt} + \mathfrak{L}(t)\,\mathbf{a}(t) - 2\frac{\mathfrak{L}(t)\,\mathbf{a}(t)\cdot\boldsymbol{\beta}(t)}{\boldsymbol{\beta}(t)\cdot\boldsymbol{\beta}(t)}\boldsymbol{\beta}(t) + \nu\,|\boldsymbol{\beta}(t)|^2\,\mathbf{a}(t) = 0, \;\; \mathbf{a}(0) = \mathbf{a}_0, \\ &\boldsymbol{\beta}_0\cdot\mathbf{a}_0 = 0. \end{aligned} \qquad (2.15)$$

It is shown in Section 6.5 that in the two-dimensional case, the Navier–Stokes equations for small perturbations of linear flows are more or less identical to the Fokker–Planck equations for harmonically bound articles, which is surprising.

[3] Thus, even the greatest minds occasionally can be myopic – it took eighty years for fluid dynamists to connect the dots and observe that $(\tilde{\mathbf{v}}, \tilde{p}/\rho)$ solve the nonlinear Euler equations.

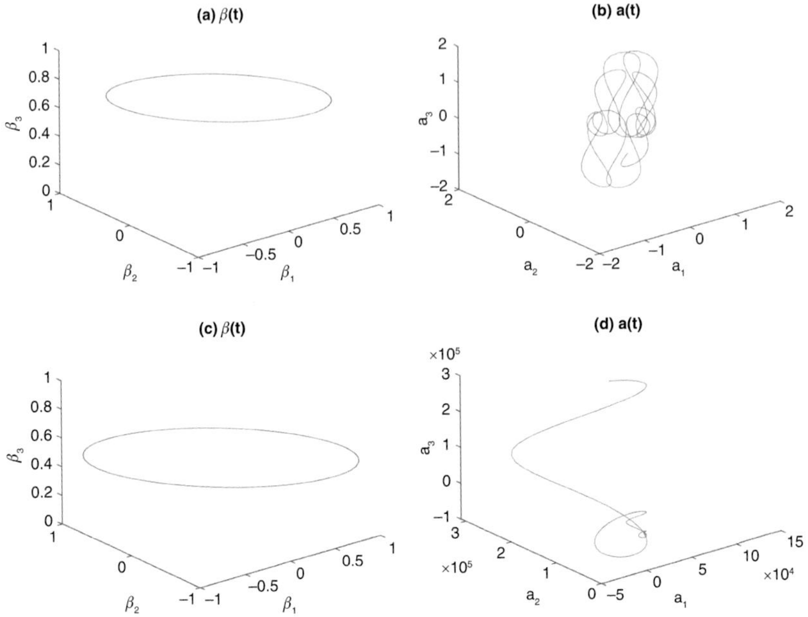

Figure 3 Kelvin waves corresponding to two different orientations of the initial wave vector $\beta(0)$ and $\mathbf{a}(0)$. (a), (b) $\beta(0) = (\sin(\pi/4), 0, \cos(\pi/4))$, $\mathbf{a}(0) = (0, \sin(\pi/4), 0)$; (c), (d) $\beta(0) = (\sin(\pi/3), 0, \cos(\pi/3))$, $\mathbf{a}(0) = (0, \sin(\pi/3), 0)$. Other parameters are as follows: $T = 100$, $\omega = 1$, $s = 0.5$. In the first case, $\mathbf{a}(t)$ stays bounded, while $\mathbf{a}(t)$ explodes in the second case. This explosion means that the underlying elliptic flow is unstable. Author's graphics.

The evolution of a typical Kelvin wave parameters triplet $\mathbf{r}(t)$, $\boldsymbol{\beta}(t)$, $\mathbf{a}(t)$ is illustrated in Figure 3. The impact of viscosity is illustrated in Figure 4. These figures show that depending on the initial orientation of the wave vector $\boldsymbol{\beta}(t)$, the amplitude $\mathbf{a}(t)$ can be either bounded or unbounded. For elliptic flows, unbounded amplitudes are always present for specific orientations, so all of them are unstable; see Bayly (1986), Bayly *et al.* (1996), Friedlander and Lipton-Lifschitz (2003), and references therein.

3 Kolmogorov Stochastic Process

3.1 Background

The Kolmogorov equation studies the evolution of a particle in the phase space. The particle's position and velocity evolve in time due to the interplay between the deterministic drift and stochastic force affecting only its velocity. Since only the particle's velocity is affected by the random force, the PDE describing

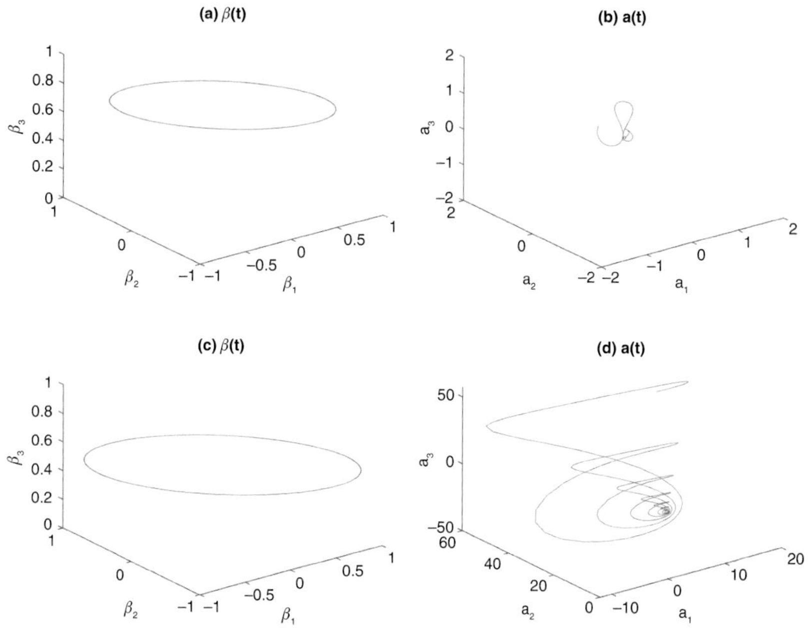

Figure 4 Kelvin waves in the viscous fluid with viscosity $\nu = 0.07$. Other parameters and initial conditions are the same as in Figure 3. Viscosity dampens the instability but, generally, does not suppress it entirely. Author's graphics.

the evolution of the t.p.d.f. in the phase space is degenerate. The Kolmogorov equation is a particular case of the Klein–Kramers equation studied in Section 4.

The significance of the Kolmogorov equation lies in its ability to model the intricate balance between deterministic behavior and stochastic dynamics, providing a basic framework for studying the evolution of systems in phase space. It has important applications in various fields, including physics for understanding particle dynamics, finance for modeling asset prices, and beyond. It demonstrates the profound interplay between stochastic processes and differential equations.

The Kolmogorov equation is hypoelliptic; as such, it serves as a prototype for a broad class of hypoelliptic PDEs. Although it does not meet the exact criteria for ellipticity (due to the second-order derivatives not being present in all directions of the phase space), the solutions to the equation are still smooth, which is particularly important in the context of stochastic processes, where hypoellipticity ensures that the probability density function remains smooth and well-behaved, facilitating the analysis of the system's dynamics over time.

3.2 Summary of Kolmogorov's Paper

In a remarkable (and remarkably concise) note, Kolmogorov considers a system of particles in n-dimensional space with coordinates $q_1, \ldots, q_n$, and velocities $\dot{q}_1, \ldots, \dot{q}_n$, assuming the probability density function

$$g\left(t, q_1, \ldots, q_n, \dot{q}_1, \ldots, \dot{q}_n, t', q'_1, \ldots, q'_n, \dot{q}'_1, \ldots, \dot{q}'_n\right)$$

exists for some time $t' > t$, and reveals (without any explanation) an analytical expression for g in the one-dimensional case; see Kolmogoroff (1934).[4] This note is the third in a series of papers, the previous two being Kolmogoroff (1931, 1933).

Kolmogorov makes the following natural assumptions:

$$\mathbf{E}\left|\Delta q_i - \dot{q}_i \Delta t\right| = o(\Delta t), \tag{3.1}$$

$$\mathbf{E}(\Delta q_i)^2 = o(\Delta t), \tag{3.2}$$

where $\Delta t = t' - t$. Equations (3.1) and (3.2) imply

$$\mathbf{E}(\Delta q_i) = \dot{q}_i \Delta t + o(\Delta t), \tag{3.3}$$

$$\mathbf{E}\left(\Delta q_i \Delta q_j\right) \leq \sqrt{\mathbf{E}(\Delta q_i)^2\, \mathbf{E}\left(\Delta q_j\right)^2} = o(\Delta t). \tag{3.4}$$

Furthermore, under very general assumptions, the following relationships hold:

$$\mathbf{E}(\Delta \dot{q}_i) = f_i(t, q, \dot{q})\, \Delta t + o(\Delta t), \tag{3.5}$$

$$\mathbf{E}(\Delta \dot{q}_i)^2 = k_{ii}(t, q, \dot{q})\, \Delta t + o(\Delta t), \tag{3.6}$$

$$\mathbf{E}\left(\Delta \dot{q}_i \Delta \dot{q}_j\right) = k_{ij}(t, q, \dot{q})\, \Delta t + o(\Delta t), \tag{3.7}$$

where f and k are continuous functions. Equations (3.2), and (3.6) imply

$$\mathbf{E}\left(\Delta \dot{q}_i \Delta \dot{q}_j\right) \leq \sqrt{\mathbf{E}(\Delta \dot{q}_i)^2\, \mathbf{E}\left(\Delta \dot{q}_j\right)^2} = o(\Delta t). \tag{3.8}$$

Under some natural physical assumptions, it follows that g satisfies the following differential equation of the Fokker–Planck type:

$$\frac{\partial g}{\partial t'} = -\sum \dot{q}'_i \frac{\partial g}{\partial q'_i} - \sum \frac{\partial}{\partial \dot{q}'_i}\left\{f_i(t, q, \dot{q})\, g\right\} + \sum\sum \frac{\partial^2}{\partial \dot{q}'_i \partial \dot{q}'_j}\left\{k(t, q, \dot{q})\, g\right\}. \tag{3.9}$$

In the one-dimensional case, one has

$$\frac{\partial g}{\partial t'} = -\dot{q}' \frac{\partial g}{\partial q'} - \frac{\partial}{\partial \dot{q}'}\left\{f(t, q, \dot{q})\, g\right\} + \frac{\partial^2}{\partial \dot{q}'^2}\left\{k(t, q, \dot{q})\, g\right\}. \tag{3.10}$$

These equations are known as ultra-parabolic Fokker–Plank–Kolmogorov equations due to their degeneracy.

[4] Kolmogorov published his seminal papers in German where his name appears under the transliteration of Kolmogoroff, the spelling used in the original articles has been retained.

When f and k are constants, (3.10) becomes

$$\frac{\partial g}{\partial t'} = -\dot{q}'\frac{\partial g}{\partial q'} - f\frac{\partial g}{\partial \dot{q}'} + k\frac{\partial^2 g}{\partial \dot{q}'^2}. \tag{3.11}$$

The corresponding fundamental solution of has the following form:

$$g = \frac{2\sqrt{3}}{\pi k^2 (t'-t)^2} \exp\left\{ -\frac{(\dot{q}' - \dot{q} - f(t'-t))^2}{4k(t'-t)} - \frac{3\left(q' - q - \frac{\dot{q}'+\dot{q}}{2}(t'-t)\right)^2}{k^3 (t'-t)^3} \right\}. \tag{3.12}$$

One can see that $\Delta\dot{q}$ is of the order $(\Delta t)^{1/2}$. At the same time

$$\Delta q = \dot{q}\Delta t + O(\Delta t)^{3/2}. \tag{3.13}$$

One can prove that a similar relation holds for the general (3.9).

Kolmogorov's original paper is shown in Figure 5.

Kolmogorov equations fascinated mathematicians for a long time and generated a great deal of research; see, for example, Weber (1951), Hörmander (1967), Kuptsov (1972), Lanconelli *et al.* (2002), Pascucci (2005), Ivasishen and Medynsky (2010), and Duong & Tran (2018), among others.

It is worth mentioning that physicists derived Equations (3.9) and (3.10) at least a decade earlier than Kolmogorov; see Section 4.

3.3 Challenge and Response

Despite its undoubted brilliance, Kolmogorov's original paper has several issues.

First, Equations (3.9) and (3.10) *are not* the Fokker–Planck equations associated with the process described by Equations (3.5)–(3.7), since they lack the prefactor $1/2$ in front of the diffusion terms. The corrected multivariate equation has the form

$$\begin{aligned}\frac{\partial g}{\partial t'} &= -\sum \dot{q}_i'\frac{\partial}{\partial q_i'}g - \sum \frac{\partial}{\partial \dot{q}_i'}\{f_i(t,q,\dot{q})\,g\} \\ &+ \frac{1}{2}\sum\sum \frac{\partial^2}{\partial \dot{q}_i'\partial \dot{q}_j'}\{\{k(t,q,\dot{q})\,g\}\},\end{aligned} \tag{3.14}$$

while the corresponding one-dimensional equation has the form

$$\frac{\partial g}{\partial t'} = -\dot{q}'\frac{\partial}{\partial q'}g - \frac{\partial}{\partial \dot{q}'}\{f(t,q,\dot{q})\,g\} + \frac{1}{2}\frac{\partial^2}{\partial \dot{q}'^2}\{\{k(t,q,\dot{q})\,g\}\}. \tag{3.15}$$

Alternatively, Equations (3.6) and (3.7) can be altered as follows:

$$\mathbf{E}(\Delta\dot{q}_i)^2 = 2k_{ii}(t,q,\dot{q})\,\Delta t + o(\Delta t), \tag{3.16}$$

Annals of Mathematics
Vol. 35, No. 1, January, 1934

ZUFÄLLIGE BEWEGUNGEN

(Zur Theorie der Brownschen Bewegung)

Von A. Kolmogoroff

(Received September 9, 1933)

In zwei früheren Arbeiten[1] (im folgenden als I und II zitiert) habe ich eine allgemeine Theorie der stetigen zufälligen Prozesse entwickelt. Es wurde dort unter sehr allgemeinen Voraussetzungen bewiesen, dass, wenn der Zustand eines physikalischen Systems in jedem gegebenen Zeitmoment mit Hilfe von n Parametern $x_1, x_2, \cdots, x_n$ vollständig bestimmt ist und diese Parameter sich mit der Zeit t stetig ändern,[2] so genügen die entsprechenden Verteilungsfunktionen der Fokker-Planckschen Differentialgleichung. Im allgemeinen Fall eines solchen zufälligen Prozesses sind die Zuwächse Δx_i der Parameter x_i von der Grössenordnung $(\Delta t)^{\frac{1}{2}}$. Folglich wächst im allgemeinen das Verhältnis $\Delta x_i : \Delta t$ mit $\Delta t \to 0$ über jede endliche Grenze, so dass man von keiner bestimmten Geschwindigkeit der Änderung von x_i sprechen kann. Wir wollen jetzt zeigen, wie man die allgemeine Theorie auf den Fall der *zufälligen Bewegungen* anwenden kann, wenn man voraussetzt, dass nicht nur die Koordinaten des Systems sondern auch ihre Ableitungen nach der Zeit sich stetig ändern.

Es seien $q_1, q_2, \cdots, q_n$ die Koordinaten eines Systems mit n Freiheitsgraden. Wir setzen voraus, es existiere, wenn q und $\dot{q}$ in einem Zeitmoment t bestimmt sind, eine bestimmte Wahrscheinlichkeitsdichte

$$G(t, q_1, \cdots, q_n, \dot{q}_1, \cdots, \dot{q}_n, t', q'_1, \cdots, q'_n, \dot{q}'_1, \cdots, \dot{q}'_n)$$

für die möglichen Werte q' und $\dot{q}'$ der Koordinaten des Systems und ihrer Zeitableitungen in jedem Zeitmoment $t' > t$. Es wird noch vorausgesetzt, dass G von dem Verhalten des Systems vor dem Momente t unabhängig ist.

Es ist natürlich vorauszusetzen, dass

$$E|\Delta q_i - \dot{q}_i \Delta t| = o(\Delta t), \tag{1}$$

$$E(\Delta q_i)^2 = o(\Delta t) \tag{2}$$

ist,[3] wobei $\Delta t = t' - t$ ist und E die mathematische Erwartung bezeichnet. Aus (1) und (2) folgt

$$E(\Delta q_i) = \dot{q}_i \Delta t + o(\Delta t), \tag{3}$$

[1] I. Über die analytischen Methoden in der Wahrscheinlichkeitsrechnung, Math. Ann 104 (1931), pp. 415–458. II. Zur Theorie der stetigen zufälligen Prozesse, Math. Ann. 108 (1933), pp. 149–160.

[2] Wegen der genaueren Bedeutung der Stetigkeitsbedingung bei zufälligen Prozessen vgl. I, §13.

[3] Da Δq_i von der Grössenordnung Δt sein muss.

116

Figure 5 Kolmogorov's original paper, presented here for the inquisitive reader to enjoy; see Kolmogoroff (1934). Reproduced by kind permission of the Editors of Annals of Mathematics.

$$\mathbf{E}\left(\Delta \dot{q}_i \Delta \dot{q}_j\right) = 2k_{ij}\left(t, q, \dot{q}\right)\Delta t + o\left(\Delta t\right). \tag{3.17}$$

In the following discussion, the Fokker–Planck equation is updated.

Second, g given by (3.12) does not solve (3.10). It also does not satisfy the (implicit) initial condition

$$g\left(t, q, \dot{q}, t, q', \dot{q}'\right) = \delta\left(q' - q\right)\delta\left(\dot{q}' - \dot{q}\right), \tag{3.18}$$

$$E(\Delta q_i \Delta q_j) \leq \sqrt{E(\Delta q_i)^2\, E(\Delta q_j)^2} = o(\Delta t). \tag{4}$$

In II ist unter einigen sehr allgemeinen Voraussetzungen bewiesen, dass ausser (2–4) noch die folgenden Relationen gelten:

$$E(\Delta \dot{q}_i) = f_i(t, q, \dot{q})\Delta t + o(\Delta t), \tag{5}$$

$$E(\Delta \dot{q}_i)^2 = k_{ii}(t, q, \dot{q})\Delta t + o(\Delta t), \tag{6}$$

$$E(\Delta \dot{q}_i \Delta \dot{q}_j) = k_{ij}(t, q, \dot{q})\Delta t + o(\Delta t), \tag{7}$$

wobei f und k stetige Funktionen sind. In manchen physikalischen Fragen sind die Voraussetzungen (5–7) auch direkt nachweisbar. Aus (2) und (6) folgt

$$E(\Delta q_i \Delta \dot{q}_j) \leq \sqrt{E(\Delta q_i)^2\, E(\Delta \dot{q}_j)^2} = o(\Delta t). \tag{8}$$

Bei einigen physikalisch ganz natürlichen Nebenvoraussetzungen folgt aus (2–8), dass G die Fundamentallösung der folgenden Differentialgleichung vom Focker-Planckschen Typus ist:[4]

$$\frac{\partial g}{\partial t'} = -\Sigma\, \dot{q}'_i \frac{\partial}{\partial q'_i} g - \Sigma \frac{\partial}{\partial \dot{q}'_i}\{f_i(t', q', \dot{q}')g\} + \Sigma\Sigma \frac{\partial^2}{\partial \dot{q}'_i\, \partial \dot{q}'_j}\{k(t', q', \dot{q}')g\}. \tag{9}$$

Im Falle $n = 1$ hat man also die Gleichung

$$\frac{\partial g}{\partial t'} = -\dot{q}' \frac{\partial}{\partial q'} g - \frac{\partial}{\partial \dot{q}'}\{f(t', q', \dot{q}')g\} + \frac{\partial^2}{\partial \dot{q}'^2}\{k(t', q', \dot{q}')g\}. \tag{10}$$

Wenn f und k konstant sind, so findet man als die fundamentale Lösung von (10) den Ausdruck

$$g = \frac{2\sqrt{3}}{\pi k^2 (t' - t)^2} \exp\left\{ -\frac{[\dot{q}' - \dot{q} - f(t' - t)]^2}{4k\,(t' - t)} - \frac{3\left[q' - q - \frac{\dot{q}' + \dot{q}}{2}(t' - t)\right]^2}{k^3\,(t' - t)^3} \right\}. \tag{11}$$

Man sieht also, dass hier $\Delta \dot{q}$ von der Grössenordnung $(\Delta t)^{1/2}$ wie bei allgemeinen zufälligen Prozessen ist. Für Δq erhält[5] man aber

$$\Delta q = \dot{q}\Delta t + O(\Delta t)^{3/2}. \tag{12}$$

Man könnte beweisen, dass die letzte Tatsache auch im Falle der allgemeinen Gleichung (9) gilt.

MOSKAU, MATHEMATISCHES INSTITUT DER UNIVERSITÄT.

[4] Wegen der Beweise vgl. II.

[5] Man hat das so zu verstehen, dass die Wahrscheinlichkeit der Ungleichung $|\Delta q - \dot{q}\Delta t| \geq K(\Delta t)$ bei einer genügend grossen Konstante K kleiner als ein beliebiges festes $\epsilon > 0$ ist und zwar gleichmässig in Δt.

Figure 5 (continued)

where $\delta(.)$ is the Dirac δ-function. The fact that expression (3.12) does not solve (3.10) can be verified by substitution. However, it is easier to verify this statement via dimensional analysis. The dimensions of the corresponding variables and coefficients are as follows:

$$[t] = [t'] = T, \ \ [q] = [q'] = L, \ \ [\dot{q}] = [\dot{q}'] = \frac{L}{T}, \ \ [g] = \frac{T}{L^2}, \ \ [f] = \frac{L}{T^2},$$
$$[k] = \frac{L^2}{T^3}. \tag{3.19}$$

It is easy to show that g is scale-invariant, so that

$$g\left(\lambda^2 t, \lambda^3 q, \lambda \dot{q}, \lambda^2 t', \lambda^3 q', \lambda \dot{q}'; \lambda^{-1} f, k\right) = \lambda^{-4} g\left(t, q, \dot{q}, t', q', \dot{q}'; f, k\right). \tag{3.20}$$

The original Kolmogorov formula contains two typos, making it dimensionally incorrect since the term

$$\frac{3\left(q' - q - \frac{\dot{q}'+\dot{q}}{2}\left(t'-t\right)\right)^2}{k^3\left(t'-t\right)^3}$$

in the exponent is not nondimensional, as it should be, and has dimension $T^6 L^{-1}$, while the prefactor

$$\frac{2\sqrt{3}}{\pi k^2 \left(t'-t\right)^2}$$

has dimension $T^4 L^{-1}$, instead of the right dimension, TL^{-2}.

Third, due to yet another typo, the solution given by (3.12) does not converge to the initial condition in the limit $t' \to t$. Indeed, asymptotically, one has

$$g \sim H\left(\frac{k^3\left(t'-t\right)^3}{6}, q' - q\right) H\left(2k\left(t'-t\right), \dot{q}' - \dot{q}\right) \to 4\delta\left(q'-q\right)\delta\left(\dot{q}'-\dot{q}\right), \tag{3.21}$$

where $H(\mu, \nu)$ is the standard heat kernel:

$$H(\mu, \nu) = \frac{\exp\left(-\frac{\nu^2}{2\mu}\right)}{\sqrt{2\pi\mu}}. \tag{3.22}$$

However, not all is lost. Dimensional analysis shows that the correct solution $g\left(t, q, \dot{q}, t', q', \dot{q}'; f, k\right)$ of (3.10) has the following form:

$$g = \frac{\sqrt{3}}{2\pi k\left(t'-t\right)^2} \exp\left\{-\frac{\left(\dot{q}' - \dot{q} - f\left(t'-t\right)\right)^2}{4k\left(t'-t\right)} - \frac{3\left(q' - q - \frac{\dot{q}'+\dot{q}}{2}\left(t'-t\right)\right)^2}{k\left(t'-t\right)^3}\right\}, \tag{3.23}$$

which is not far from Kolmogorov's formula. Similarly, the correct solution of (3.15) has the following form:

$$g = \frac{\sqrt{3}}{\pi k (t'-t)^2} \exp\left\{ -\frac{(\dot{q}' - \dot{q} - f(t'-t))^2}{2k(t'-t)} - \frac{6\left(q' - q - \frac{\dot{q}'+\dot{q}}{2}(t'-t)\right)^2}{k(t'-t)^3} \right\}. \tag{3.24}$$

3.4 Direct Verification

In order to avoid confusion, from now on, the notation is changed to make the formulas easier to read. Specifically, it is assumed that $\bar{x}$ represents the position of a particle at time $\bar{t}$ and x its position at time t, while $\bar{y}$ represents its velocity at time $\bar{t}$, and y its velocity at time t, so that

$$(t, q, \dot{q}) \rightarrow (t, x, y), \quad (t', q', \dot{q}') \rightarrow (\bar{t}, \bar{x}, \bar{y}). \tag{3.25}$$

One of our objectives is deriving the (corrected) Kolmogorov formula from first principles using Kelvin waves. Subsequently, it is shown how to use it in the financial mathematics context. The governing SDE can be written as

$$\begin{aligned} d\hat{x}_t &= \hat{y}_t dt, \quad \hat{x}_t = x, \\ d\hat{y}_t &= b dt + \sigma d\hat{W}_t, \quad \hat{y}_t = y. \end{aligned} \tag{3.26}$$

The corresponding Fokker–Planck–Kolmogorov problem for the t.p.d.f. $\varpi(t, x, y, \bar{t}, \bar{x}, \bar{y})$ has the form:

$$\begin{aligned} &\varpi_{\bar{t}}(t, x, y, \bar{t}, \bar{x}, \bar{y}) - \frac{1}{2}\sigma^2 \varpi_{\bar{y}\bar{y}}(t, x, y, \bar{t}, \bar{x}, \bar{y}) \\ &\quad + \bar{y}\varpi_{\bar{x}}(t, x, y, \bar{t}, \bar{x}, \bar{y}) + b\varpi_{\bar{y}}(t, x, y, \bar{t}, \bar{x}, \bar{y}) = 0, \end{aligned} \tag{3.27}$$

$$\varpi(t, x, y, t, \bar{x}, \bar{y}) = \delta(\bar{x} - x)\,\delta(\bar{y} - y).$$

The solution of (3.27) is as follows:

$$\varpi(t, x, y, \bar{t}, \bar{x}, \bar{y}) = \frac{\sqrt{3}}{\pi\sigma^2 T^2} \exp\left(-\Phi(t, x, y, \bar{t}, \bar{x}, \bar{y})\right), \tag{3.28}$$

where

$$\Phi(t, x, y, \bar{t}, \bar{x}, \bar{y}) = \frac{(\bar{y} - y - bT)^2}{2\sigma^2 T} + \frac{6\left(\bar{x} - x - \frac{(\bar{y}+y)T}{2}\right)^2}{\sigma^2 T^3} = \frac{A^2}{2} + 6B^2, \tag{3.29}$$

and

$$A = \frac{(\bar{y} - y - bT)}{\sqrt{\sigma^2 T}}, \quad [A] = 1, \quad B = \frac{\left(\bar{x} - x - \frac{(\bar{y}+y)T}{2}\right)}{\sqrt{\sigma^2 T^3}}, \quad [B] = 1. \tag{3.30}$$

Here and in what follows, the following shorthand notation is used:

$$T = \bar{t} - t. \tag{3.31}$$

Let us check that ϖ satisfies the Fokker–Planck equation and the initial conditions. A simple calculation yields:

$$\begin{aligned}
&\Phi_{\bar{t}} = -\left(\frac{A^2}{2T} + \frac{bA}{\sqrt{\sigma^2 T}} + \frac{18B^2}{T} + \frac{6(\bar{y}+y)B}{\sqrt{\sigma^2 T^3}}\right),\\
&\Phi_{\bar{x}} = \frac{12B}{\sqrt{\sigma^2 T^3}}, \quad \Phi_{\bar{y}} = \frac{A-6B}{\sqrt{\sigma^2 T}}, \quad \Phi_{\bar{y}\bar{y}} = \frac{4}{\sigma^2 T},
\end{aligned} \tag{3.32}$$

$$\frac{\varpi_{\bar{t}}}{\varpi} = -\frac{2}{T} - \Phi_{\bar{t}}, \quad \frac{\varpi_{\bar{x}}}{\varpi} = -\Phi_{\bar{x}}, \quad \frac{\varpi_{\bar{y}}}{\varpi} = -\Phi_{\bar{y}}, \quad \frac{\varpi_{\bar{y}\bar{y}}}{\varpi} = -\Phi_{\bar{y}\bar{y}} + \Phi_{\bar{x}}^2, \tag{3.33}$$

so that

$$\begin{aligned}
&\varpi_{\bar{t}}^K - \frac{1}{2}\sigma^2 \varpi_{\bar{y}\bar{y}}^K + \bar{y}\varpi_{\bar{x}}^K + b\varpi_{\bar{y}}^K\\
&= \varpi^K\left(-\frac{2}{T} - \Phi_{\bar{t}} + \frac{1}{2}\sigma^2\left(\Phi_{\bar{y}\bar{y}} - \Phi_{\bar{y}}^2\right) - \bar{y}\Phi_{\bar{x}} - b\Phi_{\bar{y}}\right)\\
&= \varpi^K\left(-\frac{2}{T} + \frac{A^2}{2T} + \frac{bA}{\sqrt{\sigma^2 T}} + \frac{18B^2}{T} + \frac{6(\bar{y}+y)B}{\sqrt{\sigma^2 T^3}}\right.\\
&\quad \left. + \frac{2}{T} - \frac{(A-6B)^2}{2T} - \frac{12\bar{y}B}{\sqrt{\sigma^2 T^3}} - \frac{b(A-6B)}{\sqrt{\sigma^2 T}}\right) = 0.
\end{aligned} \tag{3.34}$$

When $T \to 0$, one has the following asymptotic expression:

$$\varpi^K\left(t,x,y,\bar{t},\bar{x},\bar{y}\right) \sim H\left(\frac{\sigma^2 T^3}{12}, \bar{x} - x\right) H\left(\sigma^2 T, \bar{y} - y\right) \to \delta(\bar{x} - x)\,\delta(\bar{y} - y). \tag{3.35}$$

3.5 Solution via Kelvin Waves

Now, Kolmogorov's formula is derived by using Kelvin waves (or an affine ansatz), which requires solving the problem of the following form:

$$\begin{aligned}
&\mathcal{K}_{\bar{t}}\left(t,x,y,\bar{t},\bar{x},\bar{y},k,l\right) - \frac{1}{2}\sigma^2 \mathcal{K}_{\bar{y}\bar{y}}\left(t,x,y,\bar{t},\bar{x},\bar{y},k,l\right)\\
&+ \bar{y}\mathcal{K}_{\bar{x}}\left(t,x,y,\bar{t},\bar{x},\bar{y},k,l\right) + b\mathcal{K}_{\bar{y}}\left(t,x,y,\bar{t},\bar{x},\bar{y},k,l\right) = 0,\\
&\mathcal{K}\left(t,\bar{x},\bar{y},t,x,y,k,l\right) = \exp\left(ik(\bar{x} - x) + il(\bar{y} - y)\right).
\end{aligned} \tag{3.36}$$

Here

$$[k] = \frac{1}{L}, \quad [l] = \frac{T}{L}, \quad [\mathcal{K}] = 1. \tag{3.37}$$

By using the well-known results concerning the inverse Fourier transform of the δ-function, one gets the following expression for the t.p.d.f. $\varpi\left(t,x,y,\bar{t},\bar{x},\bar{y}\right)$:

$$\varpi\left(t,x,y,\bar{t},\bar{x},\bar{y}\right) = \frac{1}{(2\pi)^2}\int_{-\infty}^{\infty}\int_{-\infty}^{\infty}\mathcal{K}\left(t,x,y,\bar{t},\bar{x},\bar{y},k,l\right)dkdl. \tag{3.38}$$

To calculate $\mathcal{K}$, one can use the affine ansatz and represent it in the following form:

$$\mathcal{K}\left(t,x,y,\bar{t},\bar{x},\bar{y},k,l\right) = \exp\left(\Psi\left(t,x,y,\bar{t},\bar{x},\bar{y},k,l\right)\right), \tag{3.39}$$

where

$$\Psi\left(t,x,y,\bar{t},\bar{x},\bar{y},k,l\right) = \alpha\left(t,\bar{t}\right) + ik\left(\bar{x}-x\right) + i\gamma\left(t,\bar{t}\right)\bar{y} - ily. \tag{3.40}$$

and

$$\begin{gathered}\frac{\mathcal{K}_{\bar{t}}}{\mathcal{K}} = \Psi_{\bar{t}} = \left(\alpha_{\bar{t}}\left(t,\bar{t}\right) + i\gamma_{\bar{t}}\left(t,\bar{t}\right)\bar{y}\right), \quad \frac{\mathcal{K}_{\bar{x}}}{\mathcal{K}} = \Psi_{\bar{x}} = ik,\\ \frac{\mathcal{K}_{\bar{y}}}{\mathcal{K}} = \Psi_{\bar{y}} = i\gamma\left(t,\bar{t}\right), \quad \frac{\mathcal{K}_{\bar{y}\bar{y}}}{\mathcal{K}} = \Psi_{\bar{y}}^2 = -\gamma^2\left(t,\bar{t}\right).\end{gathered} \tag{3.41}$$

Accordingly,

$$\begin{gathered}\alpha_{\bar{t}}\left(t,\bar{t}\right) + \frac{1}{2}\sigma^2\gamma^2\left(t,\bar{t}\right) + i\gamma_{\bar{t}}\left(t,\bar{t}\right)\bar{y} + ik\bar{y} + ib\gamma\left(t,\bar{t}\right) = 0,\\ \alpha\left(t,t\right) = 0, \quad \gamma\left(t,t\right) = l,\end{gathered} \tag{3.42}$$

so that

$$\begin{gathered}\alpha_{\bar{t}}\left(t,\bar{t}\right) + \frac{1}{2}\sigma^2\gamma^2\left(t,\bar{t}\right) + ib\gamma\left(t,\bar{t}\right) = 0, \quad \alpha\left(t,t\right) = 0,\\ \gamma_{\bar{t}}\left(t,\bar{t}\right) + k = 0, \quad \gamma\left(t,t\right) = l.\end{gathered} \tag{3.43}$$

Straightforward calculation shows that:

$$\begin{gathered}\gamma\left(t,\bar{t}\right) = -kT + l,\\ \alpha\left(t,\bar{t}\right) = -\frac{1}{2}\sigma^2\left(\frac{k^2T^3}{3} - klT^2 + l^2T\right) - ib\left(-\frac{kT^2}{2} + lT\right).\end{gathered} \tag{3.44}$$

Equations (3.38), (3.39), (3.40) and (3.44) yield

$$\begin{aligned}&\varpi\left(t,x,y,\bar{t},\bar{x},\bar{y}\right)\\ &= \frac{1}{(2\pi)^2}\int_{-\infty}^{\infty}\int_{-\infty}^{\infty}\exp\left(-\frac{1}{2}\sigma^2\left(\frac{k^2T^3}{3} - klT^2 + l^2T\right)\right.\\ &\quad\left. + ik\left(\bar{x} - x - \bar{y}T + \frac{bT^2}{2}\right) + il\left(\bar{y} - y - bT\right)\right)dkdl.\end{aligned} \tag{3.45}$$

It is clear that $\varpi\left(t,x,y,\bar{t},\bar{x},\bar{y}\right)$ can be viewed as the characteristic function of the Gaussian density in the (k,l) space, evaluated at the point $\left(\bar{x}-x-\bar{y}T+\frac{bT^2}{2},\bar{y}-y-bT\right)$:

$$\begin{aligned}&\varpi\left(t,x,y,\bar{t},\bar{x},\bar{y}\right)\\&\quad=\frac{(\det(\mathfrak{C}))^{1/2}}{2\pi}\int_{-\infty}^{\infty}\int_{-\infty}^{\infty}G(T,k,l)\\&\quad\times\exp\left(ik\left(\bar{x}-x-\bar{y}T+\frac{bT^2}{2}\right)+il\left(\bar{y}-y-bT\right)\right)dkdl,\end{aligned}\tag{3.46}$$

where

$$G(T,k,l)=\frac{1}{2\pi\left(\det(\mathfrak{C})\right)^{1/2}}\exp\left(-\frac{1}{2}\begin{pmatrix}k\\l\end{pmatrix}\cdot\mathfrak{C}^{-1}(T)\begin{pmatrix}k\\l\end{pmatrix}\right),\tag{3.47}$$

and

$$\begin{aligned}&\mathfrak{C}(T)=\begin{pmatrix}\frac{12}{\sigma^2T^3}&\frac{6}{\sigma^2T^2}\\\frac{6}{\sigma^2T^2}&\frac{4}{\sigma^2T}\end{pmatrix},\\&\det(\mathfrak{C}(T))=\frac{12}{\sigma^4T^4}.\end{aligned}\tag{3.48}$$

As before, $\cdot$ denotes the scalar product. Accordingly,

$$\varpi\left(t,x,y,\bar{t},\bar{x},\bar{y}\right)=\frac{\sqrt{3}}{\pi\sigma^2T^2}\exp\left(-\Omega\left(t,x,y,\bar{t},\bar{x},\bar{y}\right)\right),\tag{3.49}$$

where

$$\begin{aligned}&\Omega\left(t,x,y,\bar{t},\bar{x},\bar{y}\right)=\\&=\frac{1}{2}\begin{pmatrix}\bar{x}-x-\bar{y}T+\frac{bT^2}{2}\\\bar{y}-y-bT\end{pmatrix}\cdot\mathfrak{C}\begin{pmatrix}\bar{x}-x-\bar{y}T+\frac{bT^2}{2}\\\bar{y}-y-bT\end{pmatrix}\\&=\frac{6\left(\bar{x}-x-\bar{y}T+\frac{bT^2}{2}\right)^2}{\sigma^2T^3}+\frac{6\left(\bar{x}-x-\bar{y}T+\frac{bT^2}{2}\right)\left(\bar{y}-y-bT\right)}{\sigma^2T^2}\\&+\frac{2\left(\bar{y}-y-bT\right)^2}{\sigma^2T}\\&=\frac{A^2}{2}+6B^2=\Phi\left(\bar{t},\bar{x},\bar{y},x,y\right),\end{aligned}\tag{3.50}$$

as expected. This calculation completes the derivation of the corrected Kolmogorov formula.

Note that the t.p.d.f. ϖ is a bivariate Gaussian distribution. Completing the square, one can write

$$\begin{aligned}\Phi &= \frac{(\bar{y}-y-bT)^2}{2\sigma^2 T} + \frac{6\left(\bar{x}-x-\frac{(\bar{y}+y)T}{2}\right)^2}{\sigma^2 T^3} \\ &= \frac{6}{\sigma^2 T^3}(\bar{x}-p)^2 - \frac{6}{\sigma^2 T^2}(\bar{x}-p)(\bar{y}-q) + \frac{2}{\sigma^2 T}(\bar{y}-q)^2,\end{aligned} \tag{3.51}$$

and represent ϖ the form:

$$\varpi\left(t,x,y,\bar{t},\bar{x},\bar{y}\right) = \frac{\exp\left(-\frac{1}{2(1-\rho^2)}\left(\frac{(\bar{x}-p)^2}{\sigma_x^2} - \frac{2\rho(\bar{x}-p)(\bar{y}-q)}{\sigma_x\sigma_y} + \frac{(\bar{y}-q)^2}{\sigma_y^2}\right)\right)}{2\pi\sigma_x\sigma_y\sqrt{1-\rho^2}}, \tag{3.52}$$

where

$$\begin{aligned}&\sigma_x = \sqrt{\frac{\sigma^2 T^3}{3}}, \quad \sigma_y = \sqrt{\sigma^2 T}, \quad \rho = \frac{\sqrt{3}}{2}, \\ &p = x + yT + \frac{bT^2}{2}, \quad q = y + bT.\end{aligned} \tag{3.53}$$

Equation (3.28) can be derived by using the Hankel transform. Since

$$\sigma^{-2}\mathfrak{C}^{-1}(T) = \begin{pmatrix} \frac{T^3}{3} & -\frac{T^2}{2} \\ -\frac{T^2}{2} & T \end{pmatrix} = \begin{pmatrix} \frac{T^{3/2}}{2} & -\frac{T^{1/2}}{2} \\ -\frac{T^{3/2}}{2\sqrt{3}} & \frac{\sqrt{3}T^{1/2}}{2} \end{pmatrix}^* \begin{pmatrix} \frac{T^{3/2}}{2} & -\frac{T^{1/2}}{2} \\ -\frac{T^{3/2}}{2\sqrt{3}} & \frac{\sqrt{3}T^{1/2}}{2} \end{pmatrix}, \tag{3.54}$$

one can introduce

$$\begin{aligned}&\begin{pmatrix} \bar{k} \\ \bar{l} \end{pmatrix} = \begin{pmatrix} \frac{T^{3/2}}{2} & -\frac{T^{1/2}}{2} \\ -\frac{T^{3/2}}{2\sqrt{3}} & \frac{\sqrt{3}T^{1/2}}{2} \end{pmatrix}\begin{pmatrix} k \\ l \end{pmatrix}, \\ &\begin{pmatrix} k \\ l \end{pmatrix} = \begin{pmatrix} 3T^{-3/2} & \sqrt{3}T^{-3/2} \\ T^{-1/2} & \sqrt{3}T^{-1/2} \end{pmatrix}\begin{pmatrix} \bar{k} \\ \bar{l} \end{pmatrix},\end{aligned} \tag{3.55}$$

and rewrite (3.46) as follows:

$$\begin{aligned}\varpi\left(t,x,y,\bar{t},\bar{x},\bar{y}\right) &= \frac{\sqrt{3}}{2\pi^2 T^2}\int_{-\infty}^{\infty}\int_{-\infty}^{\infty}\exp\left(-\frac{1}{2}\sigma^2\left(\bar{k}^2+\bar{l}^2\right)\right. \\ &\left. + i\begin{pmatrix} \bar{k} \\ \bar{l} \end{pmatrix}\cdot\begin{pmatrix} 3T^{-3/2} & T^{-1/2} \\ \sqrt{3}T^{-3/2} & \sqrt{3}T^{-1/2} \end{pmatrix}\begin{pmatrix} \bar{x}-x-\bar{y}T+\frac{bT^2}{2} \\ \bar{y}-y-bT \end{pmatrix}\right)d\bar{k}d\bar{l} \\ &= \frac{\sqrt{3}}{2\pi^2 T^2}\int_{-\infty}^{\infty}\int_{-\infty}^{\infty}\exp\left(-\frac{1}{2}\sigma^2\left(\bar{k}^2+\bar{l}^2\right)\right.\end{aligned}$$

$$+ i\bar{k}\frac{3\left(\bar{x} - x - \bar{y}T + \frac{bT^2}{2}\right) + (\bar{y} - y - bT)\,T}{T^{3/2}}$$

$$\left. + i\bar{l}\frac{\sqrt{3}\left(\bar{x} - x - \bar{y}T + \frac{bT^2}{2}\right) + \sqrt{3}\,(\bar{y} - y - bT)\,T}{T^{3/2}}\right) d\bar{k}d\bar{l}. \tag{3.56}$$

Thus, $\varpi\left(t, x, y, \bar{t}, \bar{x}, \bar{y}\right)$ is the Fourier transform of a *radially symmetric* function of $\left(\bar{k}, \bar{l}\right)^*$. Accordingly, it can be calculated via the Hankel transform of the function $\exp\left(-\sigma^2\bar{r}^2/2\right)$:

$$\varpi\left(t, x, y, \bar{t}, \bar{x}, \bar{y}\right) = \frac{\sqrt{3}}{\pi T^2}\mathcal{H}_0\left[e^{-\frac{\sigma^2\bar{r}^2}{2}}\right](\bar{s}) = \frac{\sqrt{3}}{\pi\sigma^2 T^2}e^{-\frac{\bar{s}^2}{2\sigma^2}}, \tag{3.57}$$

where

$$\bar{r}^2 = \bar{k}^2 + \bar{l}^2,$$

$$\bar{s}^2 = \frac{4\left(3\left(\bar{x} - x - \bar{y}T + \frac{bT^2}{2}\right)^2 + 3\left(\bar{x} - x - \bar{y}T + \frac{bT^2}{2}\right)(\bar{y} - y - bT)\,T + (\bar{y}-y-bT)^2\,T^2\right)}{T^3}. \tag{3.58}$$

See, for example, Piessens (2000). As expected, the corresponding expression coincides with the one given by (3.52).

3.6 Solution via Coordinate Transform

This section briefly considers the method of coordinate transformations, reducing the original Fokker–Planck equation for the Kolmogorov problem to a Fokker–Planck equation with spatially independent coefficients. To this end, the following ansatz is used:

$$\left(\tilde{x}, \tilde{y}\right) = \left(\bar{x} - \left(\bar{t} - t\right)\bar{y}, \bar{y}\right). \tag{3.59}$$

This choice is explained in more detail in Section 6. Straightforward calculation yields

$$\frac{\partial}{\partial\bar{t}} = \frac{\partial}{\partial\bar{t}} - \tilde{y}\frac{\partial}{\partial\tilde{x}}, \quad \frac{\partial}{\partial\bar{x}} = \frac{\partial}{\partial\tilde{x}}, \quad \frac{\partial}{\partial y} = -\left(\bar{t} - t\right)\frac{\partial}{\partial\tilde{x}} + \frac{\partial}{\partial\tilde{y}}, \tag{3.60}$$

so that (3.27) becomes

$$\begin{aligned}
&\left(\frac{\partial}{\partial\bar{t}} - \tilde{y}\frac{\partial}{\partial\tilde{x}}\right)\varpi\left(t, x, y, \bar{t}, \tilde{x}, \tilde{y}\right) - \frac{1}{2}\sigma^2\left(-\left(\bar{t} - t\right)\frac{\partial}{\partial\tilde{x}} + \frac{\partial}{\partial\tilde{y}}\right)^2\varpi\left(t, x, y, \bar{t}, \tilde{x}, \tilde{y}\right)\\
&\quad + \tilde{y}\varpi_{\tilde{x}}\left(t, x, y, \bar{t}, \tilde{x}, \tilde{y}\right) + b\left(-\left(\bar{t} - t\right)\frac{\partial}{\partial\tilde{x}} + \frac{\partial}{\partial\tilde{y}}\right)\varpi\left(t, x, y, \bar{t}, \tilde{x}, \tilde{y}\right) = 0,\\
&\varpi\left(t, x, y, t, \tilde{x}, \tilde{y}\right) = \delta\left(\tilde{x} - x\right)\delta\left(\tilde{y} - y\right).
\end{aligned} \tag{3.61}$$

Further calculations show that coefficients of the preceding equation are spatially independent:

$$\frac{\partial}{\partial \bar{t}}\varpi\left(t,x,y,\bar{t},\tilde{x},\tilde{y}\right)-\frac{1}{2}\sigma^{2}\left(-\left(\bar{t}-t\right)\frac{\partial}{\partial \tilde{x}}+\frac{\partial}{\partial \tilde{y}}\right)^{2}\varpi\left(t,x,y,\bar{t},\tilde{x},\tilde{y}\right)$$
$$+\,b\left(-\left(\bar{t}-t\right)\frac{\partial}{\partial \tilde{x}}+\frac{\partial}{\partial \tilde{y}}\right)\varpi\left(t,x,y,\bar{t},\tilde{x},\tilde{y}\right)=0, \quad (3.62)$$
$$\varpi\left(t,x,y,t,\tilde{x},\tilde{y}\right)=\delta\left(\tilde{x}-x\right)\delta\left(\tilde{y}-y\right).$$

Accordingly, one can use the classical Fourier transform and represent the solution of (3.62) in the form

$$\varpi\left(t,x,y,\bar{t},\tilde{x},\tilde{y}\right)$$
$$=\frac{1}{(2\pi)^{2}}\int_{-\infty}^{\infty}\int_{-\infty}^{\infty}\exp\left(-\frac{1}{2}\sigma^{2}\left(\frac{k^{2}T^{3}}{3}-klT^{2}+l^{2}T\right)\right. \quad (3.63)$$
$$\left.+\,ik\left(\tilde{x}-x+\frac{bT^{2}}{2}\right)+il\left(\tilde{y}-y-bT\right)\right)dkdl,$$

similar to (3.45). Thus, ϖ has the form given by (3.52) with $(\bar{x},\bar{y})$ replaced by $(\tilde{x},\tilde{y})$. The exact form is recovered once $(\tilde{x},\tilde{y})$ are expressed in terms of $(\bar{x},\bar{y})$ by virtue of (3.59).

3.7 A Representative Example

A typical solution of the Kolmogorov equation is illustrated in Figure 6. This figure clearly shows that there is a good agreement between a Monte Carlo simulation of the stochastic process $(\hat{x}_t,\hat{y}_t)$ given by the equations in (3.26) and the corrected Kolmogorov formula (3.24).

4 Klein–Kramers Stochastic Process

4.1 Background

The Klein–Kramers equation plays a vital role in statistical physics by offering a detailed mathematical framework for studying the dynamics of particles in a viscous, random medium. Specifically, it describes the evolution of the t.p.d.f. of a particle's momentum and position in the phase plane, accounting for deterministic forces arising from potential and stochastic thermal forces arising from random collisions with the medium's molecules. This equation is particularly important for studying nonequilibrium systems, which cannot be analyzed via traditional equilibrium statistical mechanics tools. By incorporating frictional forces, which tend to dampen the motion of particles, potential forces, which push them deterministically, and random thermal forces, which inject randomness into the system, the Klein–Kramers equation bridges the gap between

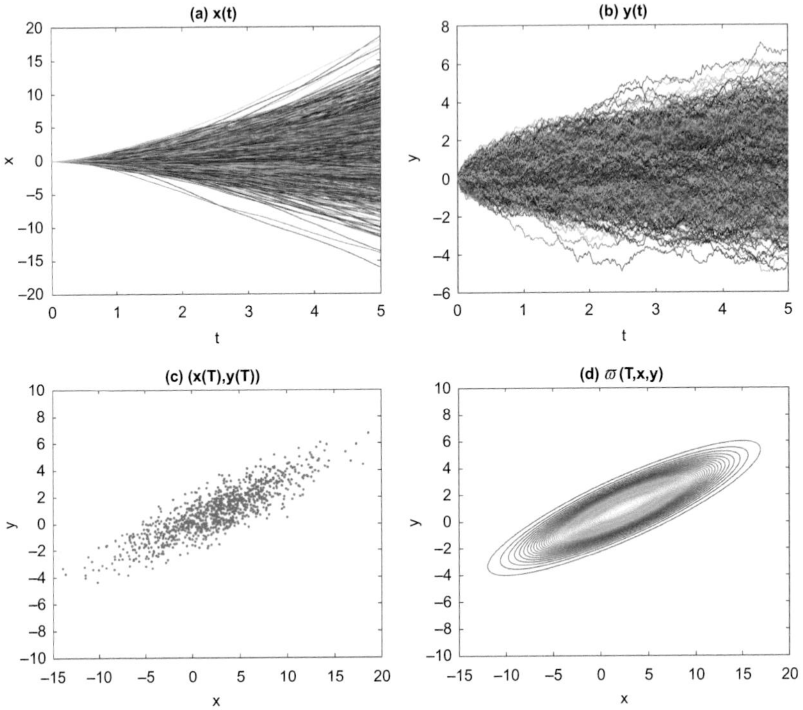

Figure 6 A thousand trajectories of a typical Kolmogorov process. Parameters are as follows: $T = 5$, $dt = 0.01$, $f = 0.2$, $\sigma = 0.8$. (a) $x(t)$, (b) $y(t)$, (c) $(\bar{x}(T), \bar{y}(T))$, (d) contour lines of $\varpi(0, 0, 0, T, \tilde{x}, \tilde{y})$. Author's graphics.

microscopic laws of motion and the macroscopic observable phenomena, such as diffusion, thermal conductivity, and viscosity. Moreover, the Klein–Kramers equation serves as a foundation for exploring more complex phenomena in nonequilibrium statistical mechanics, including the study of transition state theory in macrokinetics of chemical reactions, the behavior of particles in external fields, and the exploration of noise-induced transitions and stochastic resonance in physical and biological systems. It also arises in financial engineering, for instance, in pricing volatility and variance swaps.

4.2 Langevin Equation

Start with the Langevin equation for particles moving in a potential field and impacted by random forces; see Langevin (1908). This section uses the standard notation, rather that the original notation used in Chandresekhar (1943). Hopefully, the diligent reader will not be easily confused. The stochastic Langevin equation describes the evolution of systems under the influence of deterministic forces and random fluctuations. Because of its versatility, it is widely used in physics and other disciplines to model the dynamics of particles subjected to systematic forces derived from potential energy and random forces representing thermal fluctuations. This equation describes a particle experiencing frictional resistance proportional to its velocity (a deterministic component) and random kicks from the surrounding molecules (a stochastic component capturing the essence of Brownian motion). The Langevin equation thus provides a robust framework for studying the behavior of systems subject to noise, enabling insights into phenomena such as diffusion, thermal equilibrium, and the statistical properties of microscopic systems.

Consider an underdamped Brownian particle. In contrast to the standard Brownian motion, which is overdamped, it is assumed that the frictions are finite, so that one must treat the particle's velocity as an independent degree of freedom. Hence, the particle's state is described by a pair $(\mathbf{x}, \mathbf{y})$, where $\mathbf{x}$ and $\mathbf{y}$ are its position and velocity, respectively. Consider a d-dimensional space, with $d = 1$ and $d = 3$ of particular interest, and write the corresponding Langevin equations in the following form:

$$\begin{aligned} \frac{d\hat{\mathbf{x}}_t}{dt} &= \hat{\mathbf{y}}_t, \quad \hat{\mathbf{x}}_t = \mathbf{x}, \\ \frac{d\hat{\mathbf{y}}_t}{dt} &= -\kappa\hat{\mathbf{y}}_t - \frac{\nabla V(\hat{\mathbf{x}}_t)}{m} + \sqrt{\frac{2\kappa k_B T}{m}} \frac{d\hat{\mathbf{W}}_t}{dt}, \quad \hat{\mathbf{y}}_t = \mathbf{y}, \end{aligned} \tag{4.1}$$

where $\hat{\mathbf{W}}_t$ is a standard d-dimensional Wiener process. Here m is the particle mass, κ is the friction coefficient, k_B is the Boltzmann constant, T is the temperature, $V(\mathbf{x})$ is the external potential, and $d\hat{\mathbf{W}}_t/dt$ is a d-dimensional Gaussian white noise. Below, the ratio $\kappa k_B T/m$ is denoted as a.

Of course, one can rewrite the equations of (4.1) as a system of stochastic differential equations (SDEs):

$$\begin{aligned} d\hat{\mathbf{x}}_t &= \hat{\mathbf{y}}_t dt, \quad \hat{\mathbf{x}}_t = \mathbf{x}, \\ d\hat{\mathbf{y}}_t &= -\kappa\hat{\mathbf{y}}_t dt - \frac{\nabla V(\hat{\mathbf{x}}_t)}{m} dt + \sqrt{2a}\, d\hat{\mathbf{W}}_t, \quad \hat{\mathbf{y}}_t = \mathbf{y}. \end{aligned} \tag{4.2}$$

For a 1-dimensional particle, (4.2) becomes:

$$\begin{aligned} d\hat{x}_t &= \hat{y}_t dt, \quad \hat{x}_t = x, \\ d\hat{y}_t &= -\kappa\hat{y}_t dt - \frac{V_x(\hat{x}_t)}{m} dt + \sqrt{2a}\, d\hat{W}_t, \quad \hat{y}_t = y. \end{aligned} \tag{4.3}$$

It is clear that the Kolmogorov equation (3.11) is a special case of (4.3) with $\kappa = 0$, $V(x) = mfx$, $k = a$.

4.3 Klein–Kramers Equation

Fokker, Planck, and their numerous followers derived and studied the forward parabolic equation for the t.p.d.f. $\varpi\left(t, \mathbf{x}, \mathbf{y}, \bar{t}, \bar{\mathbf{x}}, \bar{\mathbf{y}}\right)$ associated with a stochastic process. For the stochastic process governed by SDEs (4.2), the corresponding equation, called the Klein–Kramers equation, has the following form:

$$\begin{gathered}\varpi_{\bar{t}} - a\varpi_{\bar{\mathbf{y}}\bar{\mathbf{y}}} + \bar{\mathbf{y}}\varpi_{\bar{\mathbf{x}}} - \left(\left(\kappa\bar{\mathbf{y}} + \frac{\nabla V(\bar{\mathbf{x}})}{m}\right)\varpi\right)_{\bar{\mathbf{y}}} = 0, \\ \varpi\left(t, \mathbf{x}, \mathbf{y}, t, \bar{\mathbf{x}}, \bar{\mathbf{y}}\right) = \delta\left(\bar{\mathbf{x}} - \mathbf{x}\right)\delta\left(\bar{\mathbf{y}} - \mathbf{y}\right).\end{gathered} \tag{4.4}$$

The backward parabolic Kolmogorov equation can be written as follows:

$$\begin{gathered}\varpi_t + a\varpi_{\mathbf{y}\mathbf{y}} + \mathbf{y}\varpi_{\mathbf{x}} - \left(\kappa\mathbf{y} + \frac{\nabla V(\mathbf{x})}{m}\right)\varpi_{\mathbf{y}} = 0, \\ \varpi\left(\bar{t}, \mathbf{x}, \mathbf{y}, \bar{t}, \bar{\mathbf{x}}, \bar{\mathbf{y}}\right) = \delta\left(\bar{\mathbf{x}} - \mathbf{x}\right)\delta\left(\bar{\mathbf{y}} - \mathbf{y}\right).\end{gathered} \tag{4.5}$$

Details are given in Fokker (1914), Planck (1917), Klein (1921), Chapman (1928), Kolmogoroff (1931, 1933, 1934), Kramers (1940), Chandresekhar (1943), Risken (1989), and Hänggi *et al.* (1990), as well as a multitude of subsequent sources. For fascinating historical details, see Ebeling *et al.* (2008). The Klein–Kramers equation (occasionally called Klein–Kramers–Chandrasekhar equation) describes the dynamics of a particle's probability distribution in phase space (position and momentum) for systems subjected to friction and random forces, typically at the mesoscopic scale. The Klein–Kramers equation provides a comprehensive framework for modeling and understanding complex systems far from equilibrium, linking microscopic physics with macroscopic observables. Accordingly, it is used in various fields, such as materials science, chemistry, and astrophysics, to predict the evolution of systems over time, accounting for both deterministic dynamics and the effects of randomness.

4.4 Chandrasekhar's Solutions

In a well-known survey article, Chandresekhar (1943) described elegant solutions of (4.4) for a free particle and a harmonically bound particle, which he derived by using ingenious changes of coordinates. For a free particle, Chandresekhar (1943) writes the corresponding Klein–Kramers equation as follows:

$$\begin{gathered}\varpi_{\bar{t}} - a\varpi_{\bar{y}\bar{y}} + \bar{y}\varpi_{\bar{x}} - \kappa\bar{y}\varpi_{\bar{y}} - \kappa\varpi = 0, \\ \varpi\left(t, x, y, t, \bar{x}, \bar{y}\right) = \delta\left(\bar{x} - x\right)\delta\left(\bar{y} - y\right).\end{gathered} \tag{4.6}$$

By using ingenious coordinate transforms, he shows that

$$\varpi = \frac{1}{2\pi \left(FG - H^2\right)^{1/2}} \exp\left(-\frac{\left(FR^2 - 2HRS + GS^2\right)}{2\left(FG - H^2\right)}\right), \tag{4.7}$$

where

$$\begin{aligned} R &= \bar{y} - e^{-\kappa T} y, \\ S &= (\bar{x} - x) - \frac{\left(1 - e^{-\kappa T}\right)}{\kappa} y, \\ F &= \frac{a}{\kappa^3}\left(-3 + 4e^{-\kappa T} - e^{-2\kappa T} + 2\kappa T\right), \\ G &= \frac{a}{\kappa}\left(1 - e^{-2\kappa T}\right), \\ H &= \frac{a}{\kappa^2}\left(1 - e^{-\kappa T}\right)^2. \end{aligned} \tag{4.8}$$

Here the original Chandrasekhar's notation is slightly changed to make the exposition more internally consistent.

Since it is assumed that stochastic drivers are uncorrelated, the t.p.d.f. $\varpi^{(3)}$ can be presented as a product of three 1-dimensional t.p.d.f. $\varpi^{(1)}$:

$$\begin{aligned} \varpi^{(3)} &= \varpi_1^{(1)} \varpi_2^{(1)} \varpi_3^{(1)} \\ &= \frac{1}{8\pi^3 \left(FG - H^2\right)^{3/2}} \exp\left(-\frac{\left(F|\mathbf{R}|^2 - 2H\mathbf{R} \cdot \mathbf{S} + G|\mathbf{S}|^2\right)}{2\left(FG - H^2\right)}\right), \end{aligned} \tag{4.9}$$

where $|\mathbf{R}|^2 = \left(\bar{y}_1 - e^{-\kappa T} y_1\right)^2 + \left(\bar{y}_2 - e^{-\kappa T} y_2\right)^2 + \left(\bar{y}_3 - e^{-\kappa T} y_3\right)^2$, and so on.

Chandrasekhar generalized (4.7) to the case of harmonically bound particles. We shall revisit Chandrasekhar's formulas for free and bound particles later. While Chandresekhar (1943) stopped at (4.7), for practical applications, it is more useful to represent the exponent as an explicit quadratic form of $\bar{x}$ and $\bar{y}$, which is done in Section 6.5.

5 Transition Probability Densities for Stochastic Processes

5.1 Motivation

The problems considered in Sections 3 and 4 are used in what follows to develop a general theory. For that, one needs to know some foundational information about stochastic processes discussed in this section. Stochastic processes play a crucial role across various scientific disciplines, which is fundamental for modeling systems influenced by randomness and uncertainty. These processes are pivotal in fields ranging from physics and chemistry to biology, economics, and financial engineering. They help to understand phenomena where outcomes are not deterministic but probabilistic, capturing the dynamics of complex systems over time. The analysis of stochastic processes enables scientists and engineers to predict behavior, assess risks, and make informed decisions based on the likelihood of future events.

The backward Kolmogorov and forward Fokker–Planck equations offer a mathematical description of how systems evolve under the influence of stochastic factors. This capability to model the t.p.d.fs of diverse processes underlines the equations' fundamental importance in scientific research and practical applications across disciplines.

The Kolmogorov and Fokker–Planck equations are adjoint partial differential equations that describe how the probability density of a system's state evolves in time. The Kolmogorov equation focuses on calculating the expected value at a given time of random outcomes, which become known sometime in the future. Conversely, the Fokker–Planck equation is concerned with the evolution of the conditional probability density function of a process's state at a future time, given its current state.

The Kolmogorov and Fokker–Planck equations are applied in physics and chemistry to study the random motion of particles in fluids, the statistical behavior of thermodynamic systems, and the kinetics of chemical reactions. In biology, these equations model population dynamics, genetic variation, and the spread of diseases, among other processes, providing insights into how randomness affects biological phenomena. In financial engineering, they are used to model the evolution of asset prices, interest rates, and other economic indicators, underpinning the valuation of derivatives and the management of financial risks.

5.2 Backward and Forward Equations

Start with a jump-diffusion process driven by the SDE of the form

$$d\hat{z}_t = b\left(t, \hat{z}_t\right) dt + \sigma\left(t, \hat{z}_t\right) d\hat{W}_t + \upsilon d\hat{\Pi}_t\left(t, \hat{z}_t\right), \quad \hat{z}_t = z, \tag{5.1}$$

with smooth coefficients b, σ. This process is driven by the standard Wiener process $\hat{W}_t$ and the Poisson process $\hat{\Pi}_t(t,z)$ with intensity $\lambda(t,z)$ such that

$$\mathrm{E}\left\{d\Pi_t(t,z) | \hat{z}_t = z\right\} = \lambda(t,z)\, dt, \tag{5.2}$$

while υ is drawn from a distribution with density $\phi(\upsilon, t, z)$, which (in general) is (t,z)-dependent.

More generally, it is possible to consider the so-called general compound or marked Poisson processes, such that $\upsilon = \upsilon(t,z,q)$, where υ is monotonic in z, and q is a random mark variable drawn from a distribution with density $\phi(q,t,z)$, which (in general) is (t,z)-dependent. However, since this Element is interested in a particular class of stochastic processes, solvable via Kelvin waves ansatz this generalization is not particularly useful.

It is well-known that for suitable test functions $\tilde{u}(z)$ the expectation

$$u(t,z) = E\{\tilde{u}(\hat{z}_{\bar{t}}) | \hat{z}_t = z\} \tag{5.3}$$

solves the following integro-differential backward Kolmogorov problem:

$$\begin{aligned} & u_t(t,z) + a(t,z) u_{zz}(t,z) + b(t,z) u_z(t,z) \\ & \quad + \lambda(t,z) \int_{-\infty}^{\infty} u(t,z+\upsilon) \phi(\upsilon,t,z) d\upsilon - \lambda(t,z) u(t,z) = 0, \\ & u(\bar{t},z) = \tilde{u}(z), \end{aligned} \tag{5.4}$$

where

$$a(t,z) = \frac{1}{2}\sigma^2(t,z). \tag{5.5}$$

In particular, the t.p.d.f. $\varpi(t,z,\bar{t},\bar{z})$ such that

$$\Pr\text{ob}\{\bar{z} < \hat{z}_{\bar{t}} < \bar{z} + d\bar{z} | \hat{z}_t = z\} = \varpi(t,z,\bar{t},\bar{z}) d\bar{z}, \tag{5.6}$$

solves the following backward Kolmogorov problem:

$$\begin{aligned} & \varpi_t(t,z) + a(t,z) \varpi_{zz}(t,z) + b(t,z) \varpi_z(t,z) - \\ & \quad + \lambda(t,z) \int_{-\infty}^{\infty} \varpi(t,z+\upsilon) \phi(\upsilon,t,z) d\upsilon - \lambda(t,z) \varpi(t,z) = 0, \\ & \varpi(\bar{t},z,\bar{t},\bar{z}) = \delta(z-\bar{z}). \end{aligned} \tag{5.7}$$

It is possible to derive a forward problem for $\varpi(t,z,\bar{t},\bar{z})$, which ϖ satisfies as a function of $(\bar{t},\bar{z})$, which is called Fokker–Planck or forward Kolmogorov problem. This problem has the following form:

$$\begin{aligned} & \varpi_{\bar{t}}(\bar{t},\bar{z}) - \left(a(\bar{t},\bar{z}) \varpi(\bar{t},\bar{z})\right)_{\bar{z}\bar{z}} + \left(b(\bar{t},\bar{z}) \varpi(\bar{t},\bar{z})\right)_{\bar{z}} \\ & \quad - \int_{-\infty}^{\infty} \lambda(\bar{t},\bar{z}-\upsilon) \varpi(\bar{t},\bar{z}-\upsilon) \phi(\bar{t},\bar{z}-\upsilon,\upsilon) d\upsilon + \lambda(\bar{t},\bar{z}) \varpi(\bar{t},\bar{z}) = 0, \\ & \varpi(t,z,t,\bar{z}) = \delta(\bar{z}-z). \end{aligned} \tag{5.8}$$

One can generalize backward Kolmogorov and forward Fokker–Planck equation to the multidimensional case. The underlying n_z-dimensional process $\hat{\mathbf{z}}_t = [\hat{z}_{i,t}]$, $i = 1, \ldots, n_z$, has the form

$$d\hat{\mathbf{z}}_t = \mathbf{b}(t,\hat{\mathbf{z}}_t)\,dt + \boldsymbol{\Sigma}(t,\hat{\mathbf{z}}_t)\,d\hat{\mathbf{W}}_t + \upsilon\, d\hat{\boldsymbol{\Pi}}_t(t,\mathbf{z}_t), \tag{5.9}$$

where $\hat{W}_t = \left[\hat{W}_{j,t}\right]$ is an n_W-dimensional Wiener process, $j = 1,\ldots,n_W$, and $\hat{\boldsymbol{\Pi}} = \left[\hat{\Pi}_{k,t}\right]$ is an n_Π-dimensional state-dependent Poisson process, $k = 1,\ldots,n_\Pi$ with intensity $\boldsymbol{\lambda}$. The corresponding state-dependent coefficients are as follows:

$$\begin{aligned}
\mathbf{b}(t,\mathbf{z}) &= \left[b_i(t,\mathbf{z})\right], \quad i = 1,\ldots,n_z, \\
\boldsymbol{\Sigma}(t,\mathbf{z}) &= \left[\Sigma_{ij}(t,\mathbf{z})\right], \quad i = 1,\ldots,n_z, \quad j = 1,\ldots,n_W, \\
\boldsymbol{\lambda}(t,\mathbf{z}) &= \left[\lambda_i(t,\mathbf{z})\right], \quad i = 1,\ldots,n_\Pi, \\
\upsilon &= \left[\upsilon_{ik}\right], \quad i = 1,\ldots,n_z, \quad k = 1,\ldots,n_\Pi,
\end{aligned} \tag{5.10}$$

while υ_k are drawn from distributions with densities $\phi_k(\upsilon,t,\mathbf{z})$, which (in general) are $(t,\mathbf{z})$-dependent. Explicitly, the equations in (5.9) can be written as follows:

$$d\hat{z}_{i,t} = b_i(t,\hat{\mathbf{z}}_t)\,dt + \boldsymbol{\Sigma}_{ij}(t,\hat{\mathbf{z}}_t)\,d\hat{W}_{j,t} + \upsilon_{ik}\,d\hat{\Pi}_k(t,\hat{\mathbf{z}}_t). \tag{5.11}$$

The backward and forward equations for the t.p.d.f. ϖ can be written as follows:

$$\begin{aligned}
&\varpi_t(t,\mathbf{z}) + a_{ij}(t,\mathbf{z})\,\varpi_{z_i z_j}(t,\mathbf{z}) + b_i(t,\mathbf{z})\,\varpi_{z_i}(t,\mathbf{z}) \\
&\quad + \lambda_k(t,\mathbf{z}) \int_{-\infty}^{\infty} \varpi(t,\mathbf{z}+\boldsymbol{\upsilon}_k)\,\phi_k(\boldsymbol{\upsilon}_k,t,z)\,d\boldsymbol{\upsilon}_k - \Lambda(t,\mathbf{z})\,\varpi(t,\mathbf{z}) = 0,
\end{aligned} \tag{5.12}$$

$$\begin{aligned}
&\varpi\left(\bar{t},\mathbf{z},\bar{t},\bar{\mathbf{z}}\right) = \delta(\mathbf{z}-\bar{\mathbf{z}}), \\
&\mathfrak{A}(t,\mathbf{z}) = \left(a_{ii'}(t,\mathbf{z})\right) = \frac{1}{2}\boldsymbol{\Sigma}(t,z)\,\boldsymbol{\Sigma}^*(t,\mathbf{z}) = \frac{1}{2}\sigma_{ij}(t,\mathbf{z})\,\sigma_{i'j}(t,\mathbf{z}), \\
&\Lambda(t,\mathbf{z}) = \sum_{k=1}^{n_\Pi} \lambda_k(t,\mathbf{z}).
\end{aligned} \tag{5.13}$$

For the generic terminal condition $\tilde{u}(\mathbf{z})$, the corresponding backward problem has the following form:

$$\begin{aligned}
&u_t(t,\mathbf{z}) + a_{ij}(t,\mathbf{z})\,u_{z_i z_j}(t,\mathbf{z}) + b_i(t,z)\,u_{z_i}(t,\mathbf{z}) \\
&\quad + \lambda_k(t,\mathbf{z}) \int_{-\infty}^{\infty} u(t,\mathbf{z}+\boldsymbol{\upsilon}_k)\,\phi_k(\boldsymbol{\upsilon}_k,t,\mathbf{z})\,d\boldsymbol{\upsilon}_k - \Lambda(t,\mathbf{z})\,u(t,\mathbf{z}) = 0,
\end{aligned} \tag{5.14}$$

$$u\left(\bar{t},\mathbf{z}\right) = \tilde{u}(\mathbf{z}),$$

The forward equations for the t.p.d.f. ϖ can be written as follows:

$$\begin{aligned}
&\varpi_{\bar{t}}\left(\bar{t},\bar{\mathbf{z}}\right) - \left(a_{ij}\left(\bar{t},\bar{\mathbf{z}}\right)\varpi\left(\bar{t},\bar{\mathbf{z}}\right)\right)_{\bar{z}_i\bar{z}_j} + \left(b_i\left(\bar{t},\bar{\mathbf{z}}\right)\varpi\left(\bar{t},\bar{\mathbf{z}}\right)\right)_{\bar{z}_i} \\
&\quad - \int_{-\infty}^{\infty} \lambda_k\left(\bar{t},\bar{\mathbf{z}}-\boldsymbol{\upsilon}_k\right)\varpi\left(\bar{t},\bar{\mathbf{z}}-\boldsymbol{\upsilon}_k\right)\phi_k\left(\boldsymbol{\upsilon}_k,\bar{t},\bar{\mathbf{z}}-\boldsymbol{\upsilon}_k\right)d\boldsymbol{\upsilon}_k + \Lambda\left(\bar{t},\bar{\mathbf{z}}\right)\varpi\left(\bar{t},\bar{\mathbf{z}}\right) = 0,
\end{aligned}$$

$$\varpi(t,\mathbf{z},t,\bar{\mathbf{z}}) = \delta(\bar{\mathbf{z}} - \mathbf{z}). \tag{5.15}$$

Further details can be found in Bharucha-Reid (1960), Feller (1971), Gihman and Skorohod (1972), Arnold (1974), and Hanson (2007), among others.

Although, depending on the actual problem at hand, it might be preferable to work with either the backward or the forward problem, experience suggests that in the context of mathematical finance the backward problem is easier to deal with, not least because they are meaningful for the generic terminal value $\tilde{u}(\bar{z})$.

Since the preceding definitions are very general, it is necessary to be more specific in defining the class of problems which can be solved by using Kelvin waves. Consider processes such that

$$\begin{aligned}
&\mathfrak{A}(t,\mathbf{z}) = \mathfrak{A}^0(t) + z_i\mathfrak{A}^i(t), \quad \mathbf{b}(t,\mathbf{z}) = \mathbf{b}^0(t) + z_i\mathbf{b}^i(t),\\
&\boldsymbol{\lambda}(t,\mathbf{z}) = \boldsymbol{\lambda}^0(t) + z_i\boldsymbol{\lambda}^i(t), \quad \phi(\upsilon,t,\mathbf{z}) = \phi(\upsilon,t),
\end{aligned} \tag{5.16}$$

so that the corresponding backward Kolmogorov problem has the form

$$\begin{aligned}
&u_t(t,\mathbf{z}) + \left(a_{ij}^0(t) + z_l a_{ij}^l(t)\right) u_{z_i z_j}(t,\mathbf{z}) + \left(b_i^0(t) + z_l b_i^l(t)\right) u_{z_i}(t,\mathbf{z})\\
&\quad + \left(\lambda_k^0(t) + z_l\lambda_k^l(t)\right)\int_{-\infty}^{\infty} u(t,\mathbf{z}+\upsilon_k)\,\phi_k(\upsilon_k,t)\,d\upsilon_k\\
&\quad - \left(\Lambda^0(t) + z_l\Lambda^l(t)\right) u(t,\mathbf{z}) = 0,\\
&u\left(\bar{t},\mathbf{z}\right) = \tilde{u}(\mathbf{z}).
\end{aligned} \tag{5.17}$$

Symbolically, (5.17) can be written as follows:

$$\begin{aligned}
&u_t(t,\mathbf{z}) + \mathcal{L}^{(0)}[u](t,\mathbf{z}) + \sum_{l=1}^{n_z} z_l\mathcal{L}^{(l)}[u](t,\mathbf{z}) = 0,\\
&u\left(\bar{t},\mathbf{z}\right) = \tilde{u}(\mathbf{z}),
\end{aligned} \tag{5.18}$$

where $\mathcal{L}^{(0)}$, $\mathcal{L}^{(l)}$ are spatially homogeneous operators, with coefficients depending only on time (at most):

$$\begin{aligned}
&\mathcal{L}^{(0)}[u](t,\mathbf{z}) = a_{ij}^0(t)\,u_{z_i z_j}(t,\mathbf{z}) + b_i^0(t)\,u_{z_i}(t,\mathbf{z})\\
&\quad + \lambda_k^0(t)\int_{-\infty}^{\infty} u(t,\mathbf{z}+\upsilon_k)\,\phi_k(\upsilon_k,t)\,d\upsilon_k - \Lambda^0(t)\,u(t,\mathbf{z}),\\
&\mathcal{L}^{(l)}[u](t,\mathbf{z}) = a_{ij}^l(t)\,u_{z_i z_j}(t,\mathbf{z}) + b_i^l(t)\,u_{z_i}(t,\mathbf{z})\\
&\quad + \lambda_k^l(t)\int_{-\infty}^{\infty} u(t,\mathbf{z}+\upsilon_k)\,\phi_k(\upsilon_k,t)\,d\upsilon_k - \Lambda^l(t)\,u(t,\mathbf{z}).
\end{aligned} \tag{5.19}$$

For the t.p.d.f. ϖ, one has

$$\varpi_t(t,\mathbf{z}) + \mathcal{L}^{(0)}\varpi(t,\mathbf{z}) + \sum_{l=1}^{n_z} z_l \mathcal{L}^{(l)}[u]\,u(t,\mathbf{z}) = 0,$$
$$\varpi\left(\bar{t},\mathbf{z},\bar{t},\bar{\mathbf{z}}\right) = \delta(\mathbf{z}-\bar{\mathbf{z}}). \tag{5.20}$$

Moreover, to cover interesting and important cases, such as anomalous diffusions and the like, generalize (5.18) and consider pseudo-differential operators $\mathcal{L}^{(\bar{l})}$, $\bar{l} = 0,\ldots,n_z$. Recall that a translationally invariant pseudo-differential operator $\mathcal{L}$ is defined as follows:

$$\mathcal{L}[u](\mathbf{z}) = \frac{1}{(2\pi)^{n_z}}\int_{-\infty}^{\infty}\int_{-\infty}^{\infty} \mathrm{L}(\mathbf{m})\,u(\mathbf{z}')\,e^{i\mathbf{m}(\mathbf{z}-\mathbf{z}')}d\mathbf{z}'d\mathbf{m}, \tag{5.21}$$

where $\mathrm{L}(\mathbf{m})$ is called the symbol of a pseudo-differential operator; see, for example, Cordes (1995) and Wong (2014). It is clear that all diffusion operators belong to this category, and so do jump-diffusion operators. The symbol of the operator $\mathcal{L}^{(\bar{l})}(t)$

$$\mathrm{L}^{(\bar{l})}(t,\mathbf{m}) = -a_{ij}^{(\bar{l})}(t)\,m_i m_j + i b_i^{(\bar{l})}(t)\,m_i + \lambda_k^{(\bar{l})}(t)\,\psi_k(t,\mathbf{m}) - \Lambda^{(\bar{l})}(t), \tag{5.22}$$

where $\psi_k(\mathbf{m})$ is the characteristic function of $\phi_k(\upsilon)$:

$$\psi_k(t,\mathbf{m}) = \int_{-\infty}^{\infty} e^{i\mathbf{m}\upsilon_k}\phi_k(t,\upsilon_k)\,d\upsilon_k. \tag{5.23}$$

While frequently studied in the pure and applied mathematical context, in the financial engineering context pseudo-differential operators are seldom discussed; see, however, Jacob and Schilling (2001).

By definition, Fourier and Kelvin modes are eigenfunctions of the operators $\mathcal{L}^{(0)}$, $\mathcal{L}^{(l)}$. Accordingly, when all $\mathcal{L}^{(l)} = 0$, one can solve the corresponding backward problem via the standard Fourier modes $\mathcal{F}$ given by (1.1):

$$u(t,\mathbf{z}) = \frac{1}{(2\pi)^{n_z}}\int_{-\infty}^{\infty}\int_{-\infty}^{\infty} \tilde{u}(\mathbf{z}')\,e^{\alpha(t,\bar{t},\mathbf{m})+i\mathbf{m}(\mathbf{z}-\mathbf{z}')}d\mathbf{z}'d\mathbf{m}, \tag{5.24}$$

where

$$\alpha_t\left(t,\bar{t},\mathbf{m}\right) + \mathrm{L}^{(0)}(t,\mathbf{m}) = 0, \quad \alpha\left(\bar{t},\bar{t},\mathbf{m}\right) = 0, \tag{5.25}$$

so that

$$\alpha\left(t,\bar{t},\mathbf{m}\right) = \int_t^{\bar{t}} \mathrm{L}^{(0)}(s,\mathbf{m})\,ds. \tag{5.26}$$

However, in general, one needs to use Kelvin modes $\mathcal{K}$, given by (1.2):

$$u(t,\mathbf{z}) = \frac{1}{(2\pi)^{n_z}} \int_{-\infty}^{\infty} \int_{-\infty}^{\infty} \tilde{u}(\mathbf{z}') \, e^{\alpha(t,\bar{t},\mathbf{m})+i\delta(t,\bar{t},\mathbf{m})\mathbf{z}-i\mathbf{m}\mathbf{z}'} d\mathbf{z}' d\mathbf{m}, \tag{5.27}$$

where

$$\begin{aligned} &\alpha_t\left(t,\bar{t},\mathbf{m}\right) + \mathrm{L}^{(0)}\left(t,\boldsymbol{\delta}\left(t,\bar{t},\mathbf{m}\right)\right) = 0, \quad \alpha\left(\bar{t},\bar{t},\mathbf{m}\right) = 0, \\ &\delta_{l,t}\left(t,\bar{t},\mathbf{m}\right) + \mathrm{L}^{(l)}\left(t,\boldsymbol{\delta}\left(t,\bar{t},\mathbf{m}\right)\right) = 0, \quad \boldsymbol{\delta}\left(\bar{t},\bar{t},\mathbf{m}\right) = \mathbf{m}. \end{aligned} \tag{5.28}$$

Of course, finding explicit solutions of ODEs (5.28) is possible only in exceptional cases, some of which are discussed below. However, it is *always* possible to solve them numerically, which is much easier than trying to solve the corresponding PDEs directly.

As mentioned earlier, three archetypal stochastic processes are arithmetic Wiener processes (or Brownian motions), Ornstein-Uhlenbeck (OU) and Feller processes; see Uhlenbeck and Ornstein (1930), Chandresekhar (1943), and Feller (1951, 1952). These processes are described by the following SDEs:

$$d\hat{y}_t = \chi dt + \varepsilon d\hat{W}_t, \quad \hat{y}_t = y, \tag{5.29}$$

$$d\hat{y}_t = (\chi - \kappa\hat{y}_t)\, dt + \varepsilon d\hat{W}_t, \quad \hat{y}_t = y, \tag{5.30}$$

$$d\hat{y}_t = (\chi - \kappa\hat{y}_t)\, dt + \varepsilon\sqrt{\hat{y}_t} d\hat{W}_t, \quad \hat{y}_t = y, \tag{5.31}$$

respectively. It is clear that the corresponding $\mathcal{L}^{(0)}, \mathcal{L}^{(1)}$ are:

$$\mathcal{L}^{(0)}[u] = \frac{1}{2}\varepsilon^2 u_{yy} + \chi u_y, \quad \mathcal{L}^{(1)}[u] = 0, \tag{5.32}$$

$$\mathcal{L}^{(0)}[u] = \frac{1}{2}\varepsilon^2 u_{yy} + \chi u_y, \quad \mathcal{L}^{(1)}[u] = -\kappa u_y, \tag{5.33}$$

$$\mathcal{L}^{(0)}[u] = \chi u_y, \quad \mathcal{L}^{(1)}[u] = \frac{1}{2}\varepsilon^2 u_{yy} - \kappa u_y. \tag{5.34}$$

There are important differences among these processes. For an arithmetic Brownian motion, the operator $\mathcal{L}^{(0)}$ is a second-order differential operator, while $\mathcal{L}^{(1)}$ is zero, and the process is defined on the whole axis. For an OU process the operator $\mathcal{L}^{(0)}$ is a second-order differential operator, while $\mathcal{L}^{(1)}$ is a first-order operator; accordingly, this process is defined on the entire axis. In contrast, for a Feller process $\mathcal{L}^{(0)}$ is a first-order differential operator, while $\mathcal{L}^{(1)}$ is a second-order operator; hence, the process is only defined on a positive semiaxis.[5]

[5] A Feller process might or might not be able to reach zero, which depends on the magnitude of the ratio $2\chi/\varepsilon^2$.

5.3 Augmentation Procedure

While covering a lot of useful applications, OU and Feller processes are not sufficient to study all the practically important problems. Hence, one needs to enrich them via the so-called augmentation procedure; see Lipton (2001). The underlying idea is straightforward. Given a stochastic process, say, an arithmetic Brownian motion, or an OU process, one can expand it by introducing additional stochastic variables depending on the original process. For example, an augmented Brownian motion (5.29) becomes a one-dimensional Kolmogorov process:

$$d\hat{x}_t = \hat{y}_t dt, \quad \hat{x}_t = x, \tag{5.35}$$
$$d\hat{y}_t = \chi dt + \varepsilon d\hat{W}_t, \quad \hat{y}_t = y.$$

Similarly, one can augment OU and Feller processes as follows:

$$d\hat{x}_t = \hat{y}_t dt, \quad x_t = x, \tag{5.36}$$
$$d\hat{y}_t = (\chi - \kappa \hat{y}_t)\, dt + \varepsilon d\hat{W}_t, \quad y_t = y,$$
$$d\hat{x}_t = \hat{y}_t dt, \quad x_t = x, \tag{5.37}$$
$$d\hat{y}_t = (\chi - \kappa \hat{y}_t)\, dt + \varepsilon \sqrt{\hat{y}_t} d\hat{W}_t, \quad y_t = y,$$

respectively. Of course, many other possibilities are practically important. In what follows, the Element analyzes several practically relevant and mathematically interesting augmented stochastic processes.

5.4 Reduction Procedure

Stochastic processes, which are not inherently affine, can often be transformed into an affine form through appropriate modifications. While some transformations are readily apparent, others demand significant effort and inspiration to identify, as highlighted by Carr *et al.* (2002) and referenced works.

Consider the geometric Brownian motion, the cornerstone of mathematical finance and other disciplines. The associated stochastic process is not affine and is described by

$$d\hat{X}_t = \mu(t) \hat{X}_t dt + \nu(t) \hat{X}_t d\hat{W}_t, \quad \hat{X}_t = X. \tag{5.38}$$

Applying a logarithmic transformation,

$$\hat{X}_t \to \hat{x}_t = \ln\left(\hat{X}_t\right), \tag{5.39}$$

converts it into an arithmetic Brownian motion, which is affine:

$$d\hat{x}_t = \left(\mu(t) - \frac{1}{2}\nu^2(t)\right) dt + \nu(t)\, d\hat{W}_t, \quad \hat{x}_t = x = \ln(X). \tag{5.40}$$

This example illustrates that, with some ingenuity, even nonaffine processes like the geometric Brownian motion can be adapted for use with the existing analytical frameworks.

Another helpful example is transforming the Rayleigh process into the Feller process. Recall that the Rayleigh process describes a stochastic process on the positive semiaxis. We write this process as follows:

$$d\hat{\sigma}_t = \left(\frac{A}{\hat{\sigma}_t} - B\hat{\sigma}_t\right) dt + Cd\hat{W}_t, \quad \hat{\sigma}_t = \sigma, \tag{5.41}$$

where $A, B, C > 0$. Define $\hat{v}_t = \hat{\sigma}_t^2$; then, according to Ito's lemma, the dynamics of the process $\hat{v}_t$ have the following form:

$$d\hat{v}_t = \left(2A + C^2 - 2B\hat{v}_t\right) dt + 2C\sqrt{\hat{v}_t}d\hat{W}_t, \quad \hat{v}_t = v = \sigma^2. \tag{5.42}$$

In financial applications considered in Section 8, the pair σ, v represents the volatility and variance of a price process.

6 Gaussian Stochastic Processes

6.1 Regular Gaussian Processes

Consider the governing system of SDEs, which might or might not be degenerate, and write the governing system of SDEs as follows:

$$d\hat{\mathbf{z}}_t = (\mathbf{b} + \mathfrak{B}\hat{\mathbf{z}}_t)\, dt + \boldsymbol{\Sigma} d\hat{\mathbf{W}}_t, \quad \hat{\mathbf{z}}_t = \mathbf{z}, \tag{6.1}$$

where $\hat{\mathbf{z}}_t, \mathbf{b}$ are $(M \times 1)$ vectors, and $\mathfrak{B}$ and $\boldsymbol{\Sigma}$ are $(M \times M)$ matrices. Below, it is assumed that the corresponding coefficients are time-dependent.

The Fokker–Plank equation has the following form:

$$\begin{aligned} &\varpi_{\bar{t}}\left(t, \mathbf{z}, \bar{t}, \bar{\mathbf{z}}\right) - \sum\sum \mathfrak{A}\varpi_{\bar{\mathbf{z}}\bar{\mathbf{z}}}\left(t, \mathbf{z}, \bar{t}, \bar{\mathbf{z}}\right) \\ &\quad + (\mathbf{b} + \mathfrak{B}\bar{\mathbf{z}}) \cdot \varpi_{\bar{\mathbf{z}}}\left(t, \mathbf{z}, \bar{t}, \bar{\mathbf{z}}\right) + b\varpi\left(t, \mathbf{z}, \bar{t}, \bar{\mathbf{z}}\right) = 0, \\ &\varpi\left(t, \mathbf{z}, t, \bar{\mathbf{z}}\right) = \delta\left(\bar{\mathbf{z}} - \mathbf{z}\right), \end{aligned} \tag{6.2}$$

where, in agreement with the general (5.13), $\mathfrak{A}$ is proportional to the covariance matrix,

$$\mathfrak{A} = (a_{mm'}) = \frac{1}{2}\boldsymbol{\Sigma}\boldsymbol{\Sigma}^* = \frac{1}{2}\sigma_{mk}\sigma_{m'k}, \quad b = \mathrm{Tr}\,(\mathfrak{B}) = b_{mm}. \tag{6.3}$$

Recall that Einstein's summation rule is used throughout the Element. Explicitly,

$$\begin{aligned} &\partial_{\bar{t}}\varpi - a_{mm'}\partial_{\bar{z}_m}\partial_{\bar{z}_{m'}}\varpi + (b_m + b_{mm'}\bar{z}_{m'})\,\partial_{\bar{z}_m}\varpi + b\varpi = 0, \\ &\varpi\left(t, \mathbf{z}, t, \bar{\mathbf{z}}\right) = \delta\left(\bar{\mathbf{z}} - \mathbf{z}\right). \end{aligned} \tag{6.4}$$

The general Kolmogorov-type SDE, solvable via the Kelvin (or affine) ansatz, can be written in the following form:

$$d\hat{\mathbf{x}}_t = \left(\mathbf{b}^{(x)} + \mathfrak{B}^{(xx)}\hat{\mathbf{x}}_t + \mathfrak{B}^{(xy)}\hat{\mathbf{y}}_t\right) dt, \quad \hat{\mathbf{x}}_t = \mathbf{x}, \tag{6.5}$$

$$d\hat{\mathbf{y}}_t = \left(\mathbf{b}^{(y)} + \mathfrak{B}^{(yx)}\hat{\mathbf{x}}_t + \mathfrak{B}^{(yy)}\hat{\mathbf{y}}_t\right) dt + \mathbf{\Sigma}^{(yy)} d\hat{\mathbf{W}}_t^{(y)}, \quad \mathbf{y}_t = \mathbf{y},$$

where $\hat{\mathbf{x}}_t$ and $\mathbf{b}^{(x)}$ are $(K \times 1)$ column vectors, $\hat{\mathbf{y}}_t$ and $\mathbf{b}^{(y)}$ are $(L \times 1)$ column vectors, $\mathfrak{B}^{(xx)}$, $\mathfrak{B}^{(xy)}$, $\mathfrak{B}^{(yx)}$, $\mathfrak{B}^{(yy)}$, and $\mathbf{\Sigma}^{(yy)}$ are $(K \times K)$, $(K \times L)$, $(L \times K)$, $(L \times L)$, and $(L \times L)$ matrices, respectively. In what follows, it is assumed that the corresponding coefficients are time-dependent. As usual, $\hat{W}_t$ is a standard L-dimensional Brownian motion.

More compactly, one can write the system of SDEs as follows:

$$d\hat{\mathbf{z}}_t = \left(\mathbf{b}^{(z)} + \mathfrak{B}^{(zz)}\hat{\mathbf{z}}_t\right) dt + \begin{pmatrix} 0 \\ \mathbf{\Sigma}^{(yy)} d\hat{\mathbf{W}}_t^{(y)} \end{pmatrix}, \quad \hat{\mathbf{z}}_t = \begin{pmatrix} \mathbf{x} \\ \mathbf{y} \end{pmatrix}, \tag{6.6}$$

where

$$\hat{\mathbf{z}}_t = \begin{pmatrix} \hat{\mathbf{x}}_t \\ \hat{\mathbf{y}}_t \end{pmatrix}, \quad \mathbf{b}^{(z)} = \begin{pmatrix} \mathbf{b}^{(x)} \\ \mathbf{b}^{(y)} \end{pmatrix}, \quad \mathfrak{B}^{(zz)} = \begin{pmatrix} \mathfrak{B}^{(xx)} & \mathfrak{B}^{(xy)} \\ \mathfrak{B}^{(yx)} & \mathfrak{B}^{(yy)} \end{pmatrix}, \tag{6.7}$$

so that $\hat{\mathbf{z}}_t$ and $\mathbf{b}^{(z)}$ are $(M \times 1)$ column vectors, and $\mathfrak{B}^{(zz)}$ is a $(M \times M)$ matrix, with $M = K + L$. In addition, define a scalar $b^{(z)} = \mathrm{Tr}\left(\mathfrak{B}^{(zz)}\right) = \mathrm{Tr}\left(\mathfrak{B}^{(xx)}\right) + \mathrm{Tr}\left(\mathfrak{B}^{(yx)}\right)$.

The corresponding Fokker–Plank problem has the following form:

$$\begin{aligned} &\varpi_{\bar{t}}\left(t, \mathbf{z}, \bar{t}, \bar{\mathbf{z}}\right) - \sum\sum \mathfrak{A}\varpi_{\mathbf{yy}}\left(t, \mathbf{z}, \bar{t}, \bar{\mathbf{z}}\right) \\ &\quad + \left(\mathbf{b}^{(z)} + \mathfrak{B}^{(z)}\bar{\mathbf{z}}\right) \cdot \varpi_{\bar{\mathbf{z}}}\left(t, \mathbf{z}, \bar{t}, \bar{\mathbf{z}}\right) + b^{(z)}\varpi\left(t, \mathbf{z}, \bar{t}, \bar{\mathbf{z}}\right) = 0, \\ &\varpi\left(t, \mathbf{z}, t, \bar{\mathbf{z}}\right) = \delta\left(\mathbf{x} - \mathbf{x}\right)\delta\left(\mathbf{y} - \mathbf{y}\right), \end{aligned} \tag{6.8}$$

where $\mathfrak{A}$ has the following form:

$$\mathfrak{A} = \left(a_{ll'}\right) = \frac{1}{2}\sigma_{\bar{l}\bar{l}}\sigma_{l'\bar{l}} = \frac{1}{2}\mathbf{\Sigma}^{(yy)}\mathbf{\Sigma}^{(yy)*}. \tag{6.9}$$

Explicitly,

$$\partial_{\bar{t}}\varpi - a_{ll'}\partial_{\bar{z}_{K+l}}\partial_{\bar{z}_{K+l'}}\varpi + \left(b_m^{(z)} + b_{mm'}^{(zz)}\bar{z}_{m'}\right)\partial_{\bar{z}_m}\varpi + b^{(z)}\varpi = 0, \tag{6.10}$$

6.1.1 Solution via Kelvin Waves

By using the Kelvin-inspired ansatz, one can represent ϖ in the following form:

$$\begin{aligned}
\varpi\left(t,\mathbf{z},\bar{t},\bar{\mathbf{z}}\right) &= \frac{1}{(2\pi)^M}\int_{-\infty}^{\infty}\cdots\int_{-\infty}^{\infty}\mathcal{K}\left(t,\mathbf{z},\bar{t},\bar{\mathbf{z}},\mathbf{m}\right)d\mathbf{m},\\
\mathcal{K}\left(t,\mathbf{z},\bar{t},\bar{\mathbf{z}},\mathbf{m}\right) &= \exp\left(\Psi\left(t,\mathbf{z},\bar{t},\bar{\mathbf{z}},\mathbf{m}\right)\right),\\
\Psi\left(t,\mathbf{z},\bar{t},\bar{\mathbf{z}},\mathbf{m}\right) &= \alpha\left(t,\bar{t}\right) + i\boldsymbol{\delta}\left(t,\bar{t}\right)\cdot\bar{\mathbf{z}} - i\mathbf{m}\cdot\mathbf{z},
\end{aligned} \tag{6.11}$$

where $\mathbf{m}$ is an $(M\times 1)$ column vector, $\boldsymbol{\delta}$ is an $(M\times 1)$ column vector, and

$$\alpha(t,t) = 0, \quad \boldsymbol{\delta}(t,t) = \mathbf{m}. \tag{6.12}$$

Accordingly:

$$\begin{aligned}
&\frac{\mathcal{K}_{\bar{t}}}{\mathcal{K}} = \Psi_{\bar{t}} = \left(\alpha_{\bar{t}}\left(t,\bar{t}\right) + i\boldsymbol{\delta}_{\bar{t}}\left(t,\bar{t}\right)\cdot\bar{\mathbf{z}}\right),\\
&\frac{\mathcal{K}_{\bar{\mathbf{z}}}}{\mathcal{K}} = \Psi_{\bar{\mathbf{z}}} = i\boldsymbol{\delta}\left(t,\bar{t}\right), \quad \frac{\mathcal{K}_{\bar{\mathbf{z}}\bar{\mathbf{z}}}}{\mathcal{K}} = \Psi_{\bar{\mathbf{z}}}^2 = -\boldsymbol{\delta}\left(t,\bar{t}\right)\boldsymbol{\delta}^*\left(t,\bar{t}\right).
\end{aligned} \tag{6.13}$$

The coupled equations for α, $\boldsymbol{\delta}$ have the following form:

$$\alpha_{\bar{t}}\left(t,\bar{t}\right) + i\boldsymbol{\delta}_{\bar{t}}\left(t,\bar{t}\right)\cdot\bar{\mathbf{z}} + \boldsymbol{\delta}\left(t,\bar{t}\right)\cdot\mathfrak{A}\boldsymbol{\delta}\left(t,\bar{t}\right) + i\boldsymbol{\delta}\left(t,\bar{t}\right)\cdot\left(\mathbf{b}+\mathfrak{B}\bar{\mathbf{z}}\right) + b = 0, \tag{6.14}$$

so that

$$\alpha_{\bar{t}}\left(t,\bar{t}\right) + \boldsymbol{\delta}\left(t,\bar{t}\right)\cdot\mathfrak{A}\boldsymbol{\delta}\left(t,\bar{t}\right) + i\boldsymbol{\delta}\left(t,\bar{t}\right)\cdot\mathbf{b} + b = 0, \quad \alpha(t,t) = 0, \tag{6.15}$$

$$\boldsymbol{\delta}_{\bar{t}}\left(t,\bar{t}\right) + \mathfrak{B}^*\boldsymbol{\delta}\left(t,\bar{t}\right) = 0, \quad \boldsymbol{\delta}(t,t) = \mathbf{m}. \tag{6.16}$$

Let $\mathfrak{L}\left(t,\bar{t}\right)$ be the fundamental solution of the homogeneous system of ODEs (6.16), namely, the matrix such that

$$\partial_{\bar{t}}\mathfrak{L}\left(t,\bar{t}\right) + \mathfrak{B}^*\left(\bar{t}\right)\mathfrak{L}\left(t,\bar{t}\right) = 0, \quad \mathfrak{L}(t,t) = \mathfrak{I}. \tag{6.17}$$

The solution of (6.16) has the following form:

$$\boldsymbol{\delta}\left(t,\bar{t}\right) = \mathfrak{L}\left(t,\bar{t}\right)\mathbf{m}. \tag{6.18}$$

Thus,

$$\alpha\left(t,\bar{t}\right) = -\frac{1}{2}\mathbf{m}\cdot\mathfrak{C}^{-1}\left(t,\bar{t}\right)\mathbf{m} - i\mathbf{m}\cdot\mathbf{d}\left(t,\bar{t}\right) - \varsigma\left(t,\bar{t}\right), \tag{6.19}$$

where $\mathfrak{C}^{-1}$ is an $M\times M$ positive-definite matrix of the following form:

$$\mathfrak{C}^{-1}\left(t,\bar{t}\right) = 2\int_t^{\bar{t}}\mathfrak{L}^*(t,s)\,\mathfrak{A}(s)\,\mathfrak{L}(t,s)\,ds, \tag{6.20}$$

while $\mathbf{d}$ is an $(M\times 1)$ column vector,

$$\mathbf{d}\left(t,\bar{t}\right) = \int_t^{\bar{t}}\mathfrak{L}^*(t,s)\,\mathbf{b}(s)\,ds, \tag{6.21}$$

and ς is a scalar,

$$\varsigma\left(t,\bar{t}\right) = \int_t^{\bar{t}} b\left(s\right) ds. \tag{6.22}$$

Accordingly,

$$\Psi\left(t,\bar{t},\bar{\mathbf{z}},\mathbf{m}\right) = -\frac{1}{2}\mathbf{m}\cdot\mathfrak{C}^{-1}\left(t,\bar{t}\right)\mathbf{m} + i\mathbf{m}\cdot\left(\mathfrak{L}^{*}\left(t,\bar{t}\right)\bar{\mathbf{z}}-\mathbf{d}\left(t,\bar{t}\right)-\mathbf{z}\right) - \varsigma\left(t,\bar{t}\right). \tag{6.23}$$

Thus,

$$\begin{aligned}\varpi\left(t,\mathbf{z},\bar{t},\bar{\mathbf{z}}\right) &= \frac{\det\left(\mathfrak{C}\left(t,\bar{t}\right)\right)^{1/2}\exp\left(-\varsigma\left(t,\bar{t}\right)\right)}{\left(2\pi\right)^{M/2}} \\ &\times\int_{-\infty}^{\infty}\cdots\int_{-\infty}^{\infty} G\left(t,\bar{t},\mathbf{m}\right)\exp\left(i\mathbf{m}\cdot\left(\mathfrak{L}^{*}\left(t,\bar{t}\right)\bar{\mathbf{z}}-\mathbf{d}\left(t,\bar{t}\right)-\mathbf{z}\right)\right)d\mathbf{m},\end{aligned} \tag{6.24}$$

where $G\left(t,\bar{t},\mathbf{m}\right)$ is the density of a multivariate Gaussian distribution in the **m**-space. It is clear that $\varpi\left(t,\mathbf{z},\bar{t},\bar{\mathbf{z}}\right)$ is proportional to the characteristic function of G evaluated at the point $\left(\mathfrak{L}^{*}\left(t,\bar{t}\right)\bar{\mathbf{z}}-\mathbf{d}\left(t,\bar{t}\right)-\mathbf{z}\right)$, so that

$$\begin{aligned}\varpi\left(t,\mathbf{z},\bar{t},\bar{\mathbf{z}}\right) &= \frac{\det\left(\mathfrak{C}\left(t,\bar{t}\right)\right)^{1/2}\exp\left(-\varsigma\left(t,\bar{t}\right)\right)}{\left(2\pi\right)^{M/2}} \\ &\times\exp\left(-\frac{1}{2}\left(\mathfrak{L}^{*}\left(t,\bar{t}\right)\bar{\mathbf{z}}-\mathbf{d}\left(t,\bar{t}\right)-\mathbf{z}\right)\cdot\mathfrak{C}\left(t,\bar{t}\right)\left(\mathfrak{L}^{*}\left(t,\bar{t}\right)\bar{\mathbf{z}}-\mathbf{d}\left(t,\bar{t}\right)-\mathbf{z}\right)\right).\end{aligned} \tag{6.25}$$

Thus, ϖ can be represented in the form:

$$\varpi\left(t,\mathbf{z},\bar{t},\bar{\mathbf{z}}\right) = \mathrm{N}\left(\mathbf{r}\left(t,\bar{t}\right),\mathfrak{H}\left(t,\bar{t}\right)\right), \tag{6.26}$$

where

$$\begin{aligned}\mathfrak{H}\left(t,\bar{t}\right) &= \left(\mathfrak{L}^{*}\left(t,\bar{t}\right)\right)^{-1}\mathfrak{C}^{-1}\left(t,\bar{t}\right)\mathfrak{L}^{-1}\left(t,\bar{t}\right), \\ \mathbf{r}\left(t,\bar{t}\right) &= \left(\mathfrak{L}^{*}\left(t,\bar{t}\right)\right)^{-1}\left(\mathbf{d}\left(t,\bar{t}\right)+\mathbf{z}\right).\end{aligned} \tag{6.27}$$

These results are applicable to the general Kolmogorov-type SDE solvable via the Kelvin (or affine) ansatz, which have the form (6.5). By using the same Kelvin ansatz as before, one can represent ϖ in the form (6.11):

$$\begin{aligned}\varpi\left(t,\mathbf{z},\bar{t},\bar{\mathbf{z}}\right) &= \frac{1}{\left(2\pi\right)^{M}}\int_{-\infty}^{\infty}\cdots\int_{-\infty}^{\infty}\mathcal{K}\left(t,\mathbf{z},\bar{t},\bar{\mathbf{z}},\mathbf{m}\right)d\mathbf{m}, \\ \mathcal{K}\left(t,\mathbf{z},\bar{t},\bar{\mathbf{z}},\mathbf{m}\right) &= \exp\left(\Psi\left(t,\mathbf{z},\bar{t},\bar{\mathbf{z}},\mathbf{m}\right)\right), \\ \Psi\left(t,\mathbf{z},\bar{t},\bar{\mathbf{z}},\mathbf{m}\right) &= \alpha\left(t,\bar{t}\right)+i\delta\left(t,\bar{t}\right)\cdot\bar{\mathbf{z}}-i\mathbf{m}\cdot\mathbf{z},\end{aligned} \tag{6.28}$$

where $\mathbf{m}$ is an $(M \times 1)$ column vector, $\mathbf{m} = (\mathbf{k}, \mathbf{l})^*$, $\mathbf{k}$ is a $(K \times 1)$ column vector, $\mathbf{l}$ is an $(L \times 1)$ column vector, $\boldsymbol{\delta}$ is an $(M \times 1)$ column vector, $\boldsymbol{\delta} = (\boldsymbol{\beta}, \gamma)^*$, $\boldsymbol{\beta}$ is a $(K \times 1)$ column vector, γ is an $(L \times 1)$ column vector, and

$$\alpha(t,t) = 0, \quad \boldsymbol{\delta}(t,t) = (\boldsymbol{\beta}(t,t), \gamma(t,t))^* = \mathbf{m} = (\mathbf{k}, \mathbf{l})^*. \tag{6.29}$$

As before:

$$\begin{aligned} &\frac{\mathcal{K}_t}{\mathcal{K}} = \Psi_t = \left(\alpha_{\bar{t}}(t,\bar{t}) + i\boldsymbol{\delta}_{\bar{t}}(t,\bar{t}) \cdot \bar{\mathbf{z}}\right), \quad \frac{\mathcal{K}_{\mathbf{x}}}{\mathcal{K}} = \Psi_{\mathbf{x}} = i\boldsymbol{\beta}(t,\bar{t}), \\ &\frac{\mathcal{K}_{\mathbf{y}}}{\mathcal{K}} = \Psi_{\mathbf{y}} = i\gamma(t,\bar{t}), \quad \frac{\mathcal{K}_{\mathbf{yy}}}{\mathcal{K}} = \Psi_{\mathbf{y}}^2 = -\gamma(t,\bar{t})\gamma^*(t,\bar{t}). \end{aligned} \tag{6.30}$$

The equations for $\alpha, \boldsymbol{\delta}$ have the following form:

$$\alpha_{\bar{t}}(t,\bar{t}) + i\boldsymbol{\delta}_{\bar{t}}(t,\bar{t}) \cdot \bar{\mathbf{z}} + \gamma(t,\bar{t}) \cdot \mathfrak{A}\gamma(t,\bar{t}) + i\boldsymbol{\delta}(t,\bar{t}) \cdot \left(\mathbf{b}^{(z)} + \mathfrak{B}^{(zz)}\bar{\mathbf{z}}\right) + b^{(z)} = 0. \tag{6.31}$$

Accordingly,

$$\alpha_{\bar{t}}(t,\bar{t}) + \gamma(t,\bar{t}) \cdot \mathfrak{A}\gamma(t,\bar{t}) + i\boldsymbol{\delta}(t,\bar{t}) \cdot \mathbf{b}^{(z)} + b^{(z)} = 0, \quad \alpha(t,t) = 0, \tag{6.32}$$

$$\boldsymbol{\delta}_{\bar{t}}(t,\bar{t}) + \mathfrak{B}^{(zz)*}\boldsymbol{\delta}(t,\bar{t}) = 0, \quad \boldsymbol{\delta}(t,t) = \mathbf{m} = (\mathbf{k}, \mathbf{l})^*. \tag{6.33}$$

Let $\mathfrak{L}(t,\bar{t})$ be the fundamental solution of the homogeneous system of ODEs (6.33), namely, the matrix such that

$$\partial_{\bar{t}}\mathfrak{L}(t,\bar{t}) + \mathfrak{B}^{(zz)*}(\bar{t})\,\mathfrak{L}(t,\bar{t}) = 0, \quad \mathfrak{L}(t,t) = \mathfrak{I}, \tag{6.34}$$

where $\mathfrak{I}$ is the identity matrix. The well-known Liouville's formula yields

$$\det\left(\mathfrak{L}(t,\bar{t})\right) = \exp\left(-\int_t^{\bar{t}} b^{(z)}(s)\,ds\right). \tag{6.35}$$

The solution of (6.32) is

$$\boldsymbol{\delta}(t,\bar{t}) = \mathfrak{L}(t,\bar{t})\,\mathbf{m}. \tag{6.36}$$

It is convenient to write $\mathfrak{L}(t,\bar{t})$ in the block form:

$$\mathfrak{L}(t,\bar{t}) = \begin{pmatrix} \mathfrak{L}^{(xx)}(t,\bar{t}) & \mathfrak{L}^{(xy)}(t,\bar{t}) \\ \mathfrak{L}^{(yx)}(t,\bar{t}) & \mathfrak{L}^{(yy)}(t,\bar{t}) \end{pmatrix}. \tag{6.37}$$

It follows from (6.33) that

$$\alpha(t,\bar{t}) = -\frac{1}{2}\mathbf{m} \cdot \mathfrak{C}^{-1}(t,\bar{t})\,\mathbf{m} - i\mathbf{m} \cdot \mathbf{d}^{(z)}(t,\bar{t}) - \varsigma(t,\bar{t}), \tag{6.38}$$

where $\mathfrak{C}^{-1}$ is an $M \times M$ positive-definite matrix split into four blocks of the form:

$$\mathfrak{C}^{-1}\left(t,\bar{t}\right) = 2\begin{pmatrix} \int_t^{\bar{t}} \mathfrak{L}^{(yx)*}(t,s)\,\mathfrak{A}(s)\,\mathfrak{L}^{(yx)}(t,s)\,ds & \int_t^{\bar{t}} \mathfrak{L}^{(yx)*}(t,s)\,\mathfrak{A}(s)\,\mathfrak{L}^{(yy)}(t,s)\,ds \\ \int_t^{\bar{t}} \mathfrak{L}^{(yy)*}(t,s)\,\mathfrak{A}(s)\,\mathfrak{L}^{(yx)}(t,s)\,ds & \int_t^{\bar{t}} \mathfrak{L}^{(yy)*}(t,s)\,\mathfrak{A}(s)\,\mathfrak{L}^{(yy)}(t,s)\,ds \end{pmatrix}, \tag{6.39}$$

while $\mathbf{d}^{(z)} = \left(\mathbf{d}^{(x)}, \mathbf{d}^{(y)}\right)^*$, $\mathbf{d}^{(x)}$ and $\mathbf{d}^{(y)}$ are $(M \times 1)$ and $(N \times 1)$ column vectors, and ς is a scalar:

$$\mathbf{d}^{(z)}\left(t,\bar{t}\right) = \int_t^{\bar{t}} \mathfrak{L}^*(t,s)\,\mathbf{b}^{(z)}(s)\,ds, \tag{6.40}$$

$$\varsigma\left(t,\bar{t}\right) = \int_t^{\bar{t}} b^{(z)}(s)\,ds. \tag{6.41}$$

Accordingly,

$$\begin{aligned}\Psi\left(t,\mathbf{z},\bar{t},\bar{\mathbf{z}},\mathbf{m}\right) &= -\frac{1}{2}\mathbf{m}\cdot\mathfrak{C}^{-1}\left(t,\bar{t}\right)\mathbf{m} + i\mathfrak{L}\left(t,\bar{t}\right)\mathbf{m}\cdot\bar{\mathbf{z}} - i\mathbf{m}\cdot\left(\mathbf{d}^{(z)}\left(t,\bar{t}\right)+\mathbf{z}\right) - \varsigma\left(t,\bar{t}\right) \\ &= -\frac{1}{2}\mathbf{m}\cdot\mathfrak{C}^{-1}\left(t,\bar{t}\right)\mathbf{m} + i\mathbf{m}\cdot\left(\mathfrak{L}^*\left(t,\bar{t}\right)\bar{\mathbf{z}} - \mathbf{d}^{(z)}\left(t,\bar{t}\right) - \mathbf{z}\right) - \varsigma\left(t,\bar{t}\right).\end{aligned} \tag{6.42}$$

Thus,

$$\begin{aligned}\varpi\left(t,\mathbf{z},\bar{t},\bar{\mathbf{z}}\right) &= \frac{\det\left(\mathfrak{C}\right)^{1/2}\exp\left(-\varsigma\left(t,\bar{t}\right)\right)}{(2\pi)^{M/2}}\int_{-\infty}^{\infty}\cdots\int_{-\infty}^{\infty} G\left(t,\bar{t},\mathbf{m}\right) \\ &\quad\times\exp\left(i\mathbf{m}\cdot\left(\mathfrak{L}^*\left(t,\bar{t}\right)\bar{\mathbf{z}} - \mathbf{d}^{(z)}\left(t,\bar{t}\right) - \mathbf{z}\right)\right)d\mathbf{m},\end{aligned} \tag{6.43}$$

where $G\left(t,\bar{t},\mathbf{m}\right)$ is the density of a multivariate Gaussian distribution in the $\mathbf{m}$-space. It is clear that $\varpi\left(t,\mathbf{z},\bar{t},\bar{\mathbf{z}}\right)$ is proportional to the characteristic function of G evaluated at the point $\left(\mathfrak{L}^*\left(t,\bar{t}\right)\bar{\mathbf{z}} - \mathbf{d}^{(z)}\left(t,\bar{t}\right) - \mathbf{z}\right)$, so that

$$\begin{aligned}\varpi\left(t,\mathbf{z},\bar{t},\bar{\mathbf{z}}\right) &= \frac{\det\left(\mathfrak{C}\right)^{1/2}\exp\left(-\varsigma\left(t,\bar{t}\right)\right)}{(2\pi)^{M/2}} \\ &\quad\times\exp\left(-\frac{1}{2}\left(\mathfrak{L}^*\left(t,\bar{t}\right)\bar{\mathbf{z}} - \mathbf{d}^{(z)}\left(t,\bar{t}\right) - \mathbf{z}\right)\cdot\mathfrak{C}\left(\mathfrak{L}^*\left(t,\bar{t}\right)\bar{\mathbf{z}} - \mathbf{d}^{(z)}\left(t,\bar{t}\right) - \mathbf{z}\right)\right).\end{aligned} \tag{6.44}$$

By using (6.35), one can rewrite (6.44) in the standard Gaussian form:

$$\varpi\left(t,\mathbf{z},\bar{t},\bar{\mathbf{z}}\right) = \mathrm{N}\left(\mathbf{r}\left(t,\bar{t}\right),\mathfrak{H}\left(t,\bar{t}\right)\right), \tag{6.45}$$

where the covariance matrix $\mathfrak{H}$ and the mean $\mathbf{r}$ are as follows:

$$\mathfrak{H}\left(t,\bar{t}\right)=\left(\mathfrak{L}^{*}\left(t,\bar{t}\right)\right)^{-1}\mathfrak{C}^{-1}\left(t,\bar{t}\right)\mathfrak{L}^{-1}\left(t,\bar{t}\right),$$
$$\mathbf{r}\left(t,\bar{t}\right)=\left(\mathfrak{L}^{*}\left(t,\bar{t}\right)\right)^{-1}\left(\mathbf{d}^{(z)}\left(t,\bar{t}\right)+\mathbf{z}\right). \tag{6.46}$$

6.1.2 Solution via Coordinate Transform

Consider the Fokker–Planck problem (6.4). Introduce new variables:

$$\left(\bar{t},\bar{\mathbf{z}}\right)\to\left(\bar{t},\tilde{\mathbf{z}}\right)=\left(\bar{t},\mathfrak{R}\left(\bar{t}\right)\bar{\mathbf{z}}\right),\quad \tilde{z}_m=r_{mm'}\left(\bar{t}\right)\bar{z}_{m'},\quad r_{mm'}(0)=\delta_{mm'}. \tag{6.47}$$

Then

$$\partial_{\bar{t}}=\partial_{\bar{t}}+\partial_{\bar{t}}r_{mm'}\bar{z}_{m'}\partial_{\tilde{z}_m},\quad \partial_{\bar{z}_m}=r_{m'm}\partial_{\tilde{z}_{m'}}. \tag{6.48}$$

The transformed Fokker–Planck problem becomes

$$\partial_{\bar{t}}\tilde{\varpi}-a_{mm'}r_{nm}r_{n'm'}\partial_{\tilde{z}_n}\partial_{\tilde{z}_{n'}}\tilde{\varpi}+\left(\left(b_{mm'}\bar{z}_{m'}+b_m\right)r_{nm}+\partial_{\bar{t}}r_{nm'}\bar{z}_{m'}\right)\partial_{\tilde{z}_n}\tilde{\varpi}$$
$$+b\tilde{\varpi}=0,$$
$$\tilde{\varpi}\left(t,\mathbf{z},t,\tilde{\mathbf{z}}\right)=\delta\left(\tilde{\mathbf{z}}-\mathbf{z}\right). \tag{6.49}$$

To simplify the drift term, it is required that

$$\partial_{\bar{t}}r_{mm'}\left(t,\bar{t}\right)+b_{nm'}\left(t,\bar{t}\right)r_{mn}\left(t,\bar{t}\right)=0,\quad r_{mm'}(t,t)=\delta_{nm'}. \tag{6.50}$$

In matrix notation:

$$\partial_{\bar{t}}\mathfrak{R}\left(t,\bar{t}\right)+\mathfrak{R}\left(t,\bar{t}\right)\mathfrak{B}(t)=0,\quad \mathfrak{R}(t,t)=\mathfrak{I}. \tag{6.51}$$

Thus, $\mathfrak{R}=\mathfrak{L}^{*}$, $r_{mm'}=l_{m'm}$, where $\mathfrak{L}$ is given by (6.34). It is easy to see that $\tilde{\varpi}$ satisfies the Fokker–Planck problem of the following form:

$$\partial_{\bar{t}}\tilde{\varpi}-\tilde{a}_{nn'}\left(t,\bar{t}\right)\partial_{\tilde{z}_n}\partial_{\tilde{z}_{n'}}\tilde{\varpi}+\tilde{b}_n\left(t,\bar{t}\right)\partial_{\tilde{z}_n}\tilde{\varpi}+b\left(t,\bar{t}\right)\tilde{\varpi}=0,$$
$$\tilde{\varpi}\left(t,\mathbf{z},t,\tilde{\mathbf{z}}\right)=\delta\left(\tilde{\mathbf{z}}-\mathbf{z}\right), \tag{6.52}$$

with

$$\tilde{a}_{nn'}\left(t,\bar{t}\right)=l_{mn}\left(t,\bar{t}\right)a_{mm'}\left(t,\bar{t}\right)l_{m'n'}\left(t,\bar{t}\right),$$
$$\tilde{b}_n\left(\bar{t}\right)=l_{m'n}\left(t,\bar{t}\right)b_{m'}\left(\bar{t}\right). \tag{6.53}$$

In matrix notation:

$$\widetilde{\mathfrak{A}}=\mathfrak{L}^{*}\left(t,\bar{t}\right)\mathfrak{A}\left(t,\bar{t}\right)\mathfrak{L}\left(t,\bar{t}\right),\quad \widetilde{\mathbf{b}}=\mathfrak{L}^{*}\left(t,\bar{t}\right)\mathbf{b}. \tag{6.54}$$

Accordingly,

$$\tilde{\varpi}\left(t,\mathbf{z},\bar{t},\tilde{\mathbf{z}}\right)=\exp\left(-\int_{t}^{\bar{t}}b\left(s\right)ds\right)\mathrm{N}\left(\tilde{z}|\,\mathbf{z}+\int_{t}^{\bar{t}}\tilde{b}_{n}\left(s\right)ds,\int_{t}^{\bar{t}}\widetilde{\mathfrak{C}}\left(s\right)ds\right).\tag{6.55}$$

Reverting back to the original variables, $\left(\bar{t},\tilde{\mathbf{z}}\right)\rightarrow\left(\bar{t},\bar{\mathbf{z}}\right)$, one recovers (6.45), as expected.

6.2 Killed Gaussian Processes

Consider a process governed by a system of SDEs (6.1), which is killed with intensity $\bar{c}$ linearly depending on $\bar{\mathbf{z}}$, namely,

$$\bar{c}=c+\mathbf{c}\cdot\bar{\mathbf{z}},\tag{6.56}$$

where c is a scalar, and $\mathbf{c}^{(z)}$ is an $(M\times 1)$ column vector. Thus, $\bar{c}$ is the intensity at which the process goes into a "killed" state at some random time. The Fokker–Planck equation for a killed process has the following form:

$$\begin{aligned}&\varpi_{\bar{t}}\left(t,\mathbf{z},\bar{t},\bar{\mathbf{z}}\right)-\sum\sum\mathfrak{A}\varpi_{\bar{\mathbf{z}}\bar{\mathbf{z}}}\left(t,\mathbf{z},\bar{t},\bar{\mathbf{z}}\right)\\&\quad+\left(\mathbf{b}+\mathfrak{B}\bar{\mathbf{z}}\right)\cdot\varpi_{\bar{\mathbf{z}}}\left(t,\mathbf{z},\bar{t},\bar{\mathbf{z}}\right)+\left(b+c+\mathbf{c}\cdot\bar{\mathbf{z}}\right)\varpi\left(t,\mathbf{z},\bar{t},\bar{\mathbf{z}}\right)=0,\\&\varpi\left(t,\bar{\mathbf{z}},t,\mathbf{z}\right)=\delta\left(\bar{\mathbf{z}}-\mathbf{z}\right).\end{aligned}\tag{6.57}$$

Explicitly,

$$\begin{aligned}&\varpi_{\bar{t}}-a_{mm'}\varpi_{\bar{z}_m\bar{z}_{m'}}+\left(b_m+b_{mm'}\bar{z}_{m'}\right)\varpi_{\bar{z}_m}+\left(b+c+c_m\bar{z}_m\right)\varpi=0,\\&\varpi\left(t,\bar{\mathbf{z}},t,\mathbf{z}\right)=\delta\left(\bar{\mathbf{z}}-\mathbf{z}\right).\end{aligned}\tag{6.58}$$

This problem can be solved by the same technique as before.

6.2.1 Solution via Kelvin Waves

The familiar Kelvin ansatz yields

$$\alpha_{\bar{t}}\left(t,\bar{t}\right)+\boldsymbol{\delta}\left(t,\bar{t}\right)\cdot\mathfrak{A}\boldsymbol{\delta}\left(t,\bar{t}\right)+i\boldsymbol{\delta}\left(t,\bar{t}\right)\cdot\mathbf{b}+b+c=0,\quad\alpha\left(t,t\right)=0,\tag{6.59}$$

$$\boldsymbol{\delta}_{\bar{t}}\left(t,\bar{t}\right)+\mathfrak{B}^{*}\boldsymbol{\delta}\left(t,\bar{t}\right)-i\mathbf{c}=0,\quad\boldsymbol{\delta}\left(t,t\right)=\mathbf{m}.\tag{6.60}$$

Let $\mathfrak{L}\left(t,\bar{t}\right)$ be the fundamental solution of the homogeneous system of ODEs (6.60), namely, the matrix such that

$$\partial_{\bar{t}}\mathfrak{L}\left(t,\bar{t}\right)+\mathfrak{B}^{*}\left(\bar{t}\right)\mathfrak{L}\left(t,\bar{t}\right)=0,\quad\mathfrak{L}\left(t,t\right)=\mathfrak{I},\tag{6.61}$$

The solution of (6.60) has the following form:

$$\delta\left(t,\bar{t}\right) = \mathfrak{L}\left(t,\bar{t}\right)\mathbf{m} + i\mathfrak{L}\left(t,\bar{t}\right)\int_t^{\bar{t}} \mathfrak{L}^{-1}\left(t,s\right)\mathbf{c}\left(s\right)ds \equiv \mathfrak{L}\left(t,\bar{t}\right)\left(\mathbf{m} + i\mathbf{e}\left(t,\bar{t}\right)\right),$$

$$\mathbf{e}\left(t,\bar{t}\right) = \int_t^{\bar{t}} \mathfrak{L}^{-1}\left(t,s\right)\mathbf{c}\left(s\right)ds. \tag{6.62}$$

Thus,

$$\alpha = -\frac{1}{2}\mathbf{m}\cdot\mathfrak{C}^{-1}\mathbf{m} - i\mathbf{m}\cdot\mathbf{d} - \varsigma, \tag{6.63}$$

where $\mathfrak{C}^{-1}$ is an $M \times M$ positive-definite matrix of the form:

$$\mathfrak{C}^{-1}\left(t,\bar{t}\right) = 2\int_t^{\bar{t}} \mathfrak{L}^{*}\left(t,s\right)\mathfrak{A}\left(s\right)\mathfrak{L}\left(t,s\right)ds, \tag{6.64}$$

while $\mathbf{d}$ is an $(M \times 1)$ column vector,

$$\mathbf{d}\left(t,\bar{t}\right) = \int_t^{\bar{t}} \mathfrak{L}^{*}\left(t,s\right)\left(\mathbf{b}\left(s\right) + \mathfrak{A}\left(s\right)\mathfrak{L}\left(t,s\right)\mathbf{e}\left(s\right)\right)ds, \tag{6.65}$$

and $\varsigma = \varsigma_0 + \varsigma_1$ is a scalar,

$$\varsigma_0\left(t,\bar{t}\right) = \int_t^{\bar{t}} b\left(s\right)ds,$$

$$\varsigma_1\left(t,\bar{t}\right) = \int_t^{\bar{t}}\left(c\left(s\right) - \frac{1}{2}\mathbf{e}\left(t,s\right)\cdot\mathfrak{L}^{*}\left(t,s\right)\mathfrak{A}\left(s\right)\mathfrak{L}\left(t,s\right)\mathbf{e}\left(s\right)\right.$$
$$\left. - \mathbf{e}\left(t,s\right)\cdot\mathfrak{L}^{*}\left(t,s\right)\mathbf{b}\left(s\right)\right)ds. \tag{6.66}$$

Accordingly,

$$\Psi\left(t,\bar{t},\bar{\mathbf{z}},\mathbf{m}\right) = -\frac{1}{2}\mathbf{m}\cdot\mathfrak{C}^{-1}\left(t,\bar{t}\right)\mathbf{m} + i\mathbf{m}\cdot\left(\mathfrak{L}^{*}\left(t,\bar{t}\right)\bar{\mathbf{z}} - \mathbf{d}\left(t,\bar{t}\right) - \mathbf{z}\right)$$
$$- \mathfrak{L}\left(t,\bar{t}\right)\mathbf{e}\left(t,\bar{t}\right)\cdot\bar{\mathbf{z}} - \varsigma\left(t,\bar{t}\right). \tag{6.67}$$

Thus,

$$\varpi\left(t,\mathbf{z},\bar{t},\bar{\mathbf{z}}\right) = \frac{\det\left(\mathfrak{C}\left(t,\bar{t}\right)\right)^{1/2}\exp\left(-\mathfrak{L}\left(t,\bar{t}\right)\mathbf{e}\left(t,\bar{t}\right)\cdot\bar{\mathbf{z}} - \varsigma_0\left(t,\bar{t}\right) - \varsigma_1\left(t,\bar{t}\right)\right)}{\left(2\pi\right)^{M/2}}$$
$$\times\int_{-\infty}^{\infty}\cdots\int_{-\infty}^{\infty} G\left(t,\bar{t},\mathbf{m}\right)\exp\left(i\mathbf{m}\cdot\left(\mathfrak{L}^{*}\left(t,\bar{t}\right)\bar{\mathbf{z}} - \mathbf{d}\left(t,\bar{t}\right) - \mathbf{z}\right)\right)d\mathbf{m}, \tag{6.68}$$

where $G\left(t,\bar{t},\mathbf{m}\right)$ is the density of a multivariate Gaussian distribution in the $\mathbf{m}$-space. It is clear that $\varpi\left(t,\mathbf{z},\bar{t},\bar{\mathbf{z}}\right)$ is proportional to the characteristic function of G evaluated at the point $\left(\mathfrak{L}^{*}\left(t,\bar{t}\right)\bar{\mathbf{z}} - \mathbf{d}\left(t,\bar{t}\right) - \mathbf{z}\right)$, so that

$$\varpi\left(t,\mathbf{z},\bar{t},\bar{\mathbf{z}}\right)=\frac{\det\left(\mathfrak{C}\left(t,\bar{t}\right)\right)^{1/2}\exp\left(-\mathfrak{L}\left(t,\bar{t}\right)\mathbf{e}\left(t,\bar{t}\right)\cdot\bar{\mathbf{z}}-\varsigma_0\left(t,\bar{t}\right)-\varsigma_1\left(t,\bar{t}\right)\right)}{(2\pi)^{M/2}} \tag{6.69}$$

$$\times\exp\left(-\frac{1}{2}\left(\mathfrak{L}^*\left(t,\bar{t}\right)\bar{\mathbf{z}}-\mathbf{d}\left(t,\bar{t}\right)-\mathbf{z}\right)\cdot\mathfrak{C}\left(t,\bar{t}\right)\left(\mathfrak{L}^*\left(t,\bar{t}\right)\bar{\mathbf{z}}-\mathbf{d}\left(t,\bar{t}\right)-\mathbf{z}\right)\right).$$

It is often convenient to rewrite (6.69) as follows:

$$\varpi\left(t,\mathbf{z},\bar{t},\bar{\mathbf{z}}\right)=Q\left(t,\bar{t},\bar{\mathbf{z}}\right)\mathrm{N}\left(\mathbf{q}\left(t,\bar{t}\right),\mathfrak{H}\left(t,\bar{t}\right)\right), \tag{6.70}$$

where

$$\begin{aligned}\mathfrak{H}\left(t,\bar{t}\right)&=\left(\mathfrak{L}^*\left(t,\bar{t}\right)\right)^{-1}\mathfrak{C}^{-1}\left(t,\bar{t}\right)\mathfrak{L}^{-1}\left(t,\bar{t}\right),\\ \mathbf{q}\left(t,\bar{t}\right)&=\left(\mathfrak{L}^*\left(t,\bar{t}\right)\right)^{-1}\left(\mathbf{d}\left(t,\bar{t}\right)+\mathbf{z}\right),\\ Q\left(t,\bar{t},\bar{\mathbf{z}}\right)&=\exp\left(-\mathfrak{L}\left(t,\bar{t}\right)\mathbf{e}\left(t,\bar{t}\right)\cdot\bar{\mathbf{z}}-\varsigma_1\left(t,\bar{t}\right)\right).\end{aligned} \tag{6.71}$$

As could be expected, the probability ϖ is no longer conserved due to a prefactor Q, reflecting the fact that the process is killed with intensity $\bar{c}$.

It is worth noting that Q depends on $\bar{\mathbf{z}}$ but does not depend on $\mathbf{z}$. Completing the square, one can represent ϖ in the form:

$$\varpi\left(t,\mathbf{z},\bar{t},\bar{\mathbf{z}}\right)=R\left(t,\mathbf{z},\bar{t}\right)\mathrm{N}\left(\mathbf{r}\left(t,\bar{t}\right),\mathfrak{H}\left(t,\bar{t}\right)\right), \tag{6.72}$$

where

$$\begin{aligned}\mathbf{r}\left(t,\bar{t}\right)&=\left(\mathfrak{L}^*\left(t,\bar{t}\right)\right)^{-1}\left(\mathbf{d}\left(t,\bar{t}\right)+\mathbf{z}-\mathfrak{C}^{-1}\left(t,\bar{t}\right)\mathbf{e}\left(t,\bar{t}\right)\right)\\ &=\mathbf{q}\left(t,\bar{t}\right)-\mathfrak{H}\left(t,\bar{t}\right)\mathfrak{L}\left(t,\bar{t}\right)\mathbf{e}\left(t,\bar{t}\right),\\ R\left(t,\mathbf{z},\bar{t}\right)&=\exp\left(-\mathbf{e}\left(t,\bar{t}\right)\cdot\left(\mathbf{d}\left(t,\bar{t}\right)+\mathbf{z}\right)+\frac{1}{2}\mathbf{e}\left(t,\bar{t}\right)\cdot\mathfrak{C}^{-1}\left(t,\bar{t}\right)\mathbf{e}\left(t,\bar{t}\right)-\varsigma_1\left(t,\bar{t}\right)\right).\end{aligned} \tag{6.73}$$

It is clear that R depends on $\mathbf{z}$ but does not depend on $\bar{\mathbf{z}}$. Accordingly, (6.72) is easier to use than (6.70) when future expectations are calculated.

The same formulas can be derived via the method of coordinate transforms. Details are left to the interested reader.

6.3 Example: Kolmogorov Process

Extend the Kolmogorov formula to the case when b and σ are functions of time, $b(t)$ and $\sigma(t)$. The corresponding SDE has the following form:

$$\begin{aligned}d\hat{x}_t&=\hat{y}_t dt, \quad \hat{x}_t=x,\\ d\hat{y}_t&=b(t)\,dt+\sigma(t)\,d\hat{W}_t, \quad \hat{y}_t=y.\end{aligned} \tag{6.74}$$

Accordingly, (6.34) can be written as follows:

$$\mathfrak{L}'\left(t,\bar{t}\right)+\begin{pmatrix}0&0\\1&0\end{pmatrix}\mathfrak{L}\left(t,\bar{t}\right)=0,\quad \mathfrak{L}\left(t,t\right)=\begin{pmatrix}1&0\\0&1\end{pmatrix}, \tag{6.75}$$

so that

$$\mathfrak{L}\left(t,\bar{t}\right)=\begin{pmatrix}1&0\\-T&1\end{pmatrix},\quad \mathfrak{L}^{-1}\left(t,\bar{t}\right)=\begin{pmatrix}1&0\\T&1\end{pmatrix}. \tag{6.76}$$

Once $\mathfrak{L}\left(t,\bar{t}\right)$ is known, one can compute $\mathfrak{C}^{-1}\left(t,\bar{t}\right)$, $\mathbf{d}^{(z)}\left(t,\bar{t}\right)$, $\varsigma\left(t,\bar{t}\right)$:

$$\begin{aligned}
\mathfrak{C}^{-1}\left(t,\bar{t}\right)&=\begin{pmatrix}\psi_2\left(t,\bar{t}\right)&-\psi_1\left(t,\bar{t}\right)\\-\psi_1\left(t,\bar{t}\right)&\psi_0\left(t,\bar{t}\right)\end{pmatrix},\\
\mathbf{d}^{(z)}\left(t,\bar{t}\right)&=\begin{pmatrix}d^{(x)}\left(t,\bar{t}\right)\\d^{(y)}\left(t,\bar{t}\right)\end{pmatrix}=\begin{pmatrix}-\phi_1\left(t,\bar{t}\right)\\\phi_0\left(t,\bar{t}\right)\end{pmatrix},\\
\varsigma\left(t,\bar{t}\right)&=0,
\end{aligned} \tag{6.77}$$

where

$$\phi_i\left(t,\bar{t}\right)=\int_t^{\bar{t}}(s-t)^i\,b(s)\,ds,\qquad \psi_i\left(t,\bar{t}\right)=\int_t^{\bar{t}}(s-t)^i\,\sigma^2(s)\,ds. \tag{6.78}$$

Next, the covariance matrix $\mathfrak{H}\left(t,\bar{t}\right)$, and the mean $\mathbf{r}\left(t,\bar{t}\right)$ are calculated as follows:

$$\begin{aligned}
\mathfrak{H}\left(t,\bar{t}\right)&=\left(\mathfrak{L}^*\left(t,\bar{t}\right)\right)^{-1}\mathfrak{C}^{-1}\left(t,\bar{t}\right)\mathfrak{L}^{-1}\left(t,\bar{t}\right)\\
&=\begin{pmatrix}1&T\\0&1\end{pmatrix}\begin{pmatrix}\psi_2\left(t,\bar{t}\right)&-\psi_1\left(t,\bar{t}\right)\\-\psi_1\left(t,\bar{t}\right)&\psi_0\left(t,\bar{t}\right)\end{pmatrix}\begin{pmatrix}1&0\\T&1\end{pmatrix}\\
&=\begin{pmatrix}\psi_0\left(t,\bar{t}\right)T^2-2\psi_1\left(t,\bar{t}\right)T+\psi_2\left(t,\bar{t}\right)&\psi_0\left(t,\bar{t}\right)T-\psi_1\left(t,\bar{t}\right)\\\psi_0\left(t,\bar{t}\right)T-\psi_1\left(t,\bar{t}\right)&\psi_0\left(t,\bar{t}\right)\end{pmatrix},
\end{aligned} \tag{6.79}$$

$$\mathbf{r}\left(t,\bar{t}\right)=\begin{pmatrix}-\phi_1\left(t,\bar{t}\right)+x+\left(\phi_0\left(t,\bar{t}\right)+y\right)T\\\phi_0\left(t,\bar{t}\right)+y\end{pmatrix}. \tag{6.80}$$

Accordingly, $\varpi\left(t,x,y,\bar{t},\bar{x},\bar{y}\right)$ is a bivariate Gaussian distribution of the form (6.26), with

$$\begin{aligned}
&\sigma_{\bar{x}}^2\left(t,\bar{t}\right)=\psi_0\left(t,\bar{t}\right)T^2-2\psi_1\left(t,\bar{t}\right)T+\psi_2\left(t,\bar{t}\right),\quad \sigma_{\bar{y}}^2=\psi_0\left(t,\bar{t}\right),\\
&\rho\left(t,\bar{t}\right)=\frac{\left(\psi_0\left(t,\bar{t}\right)T-\psi_1\left(t,\bar{t}\right)\right)}{\sqrt{\psi_0\left(t,\bar{t}\right)\left(\psi_0\left(t,\bar{t}\right)T^2-2\psi_1\left(t,\bar{t}\right)T+\psi_2\left(t,\bar{t}\right)\right)}},\\
&p\left(t,\bar{t}\right)=-\phi_1\left(t,\bar{t}\right)+x+\left(\phi_0\left(t,\bar{t}\right)+y\right)T,\quad q\left(t,\bar{t}\right)=\phi_0\left(t,\bar{t}\right)+y.
\end{aligned} \tag{6.81}$$

It is left to the interested reader to verify that (6.81) coincides with (3.52) when σ and b are constant. Therefore, the classical Kolmogorov solution can be extended to the case of time-dependent parameters.

6.4 Example: OU Process

6.4.1 OU Process

It is worth deriving the well-known t.p.d.f. for the OU process using Kelvin waves for benchmarking purposes. The following SDE governs the OU process:

$$d\hat{y}_t = (\chi(t) - \kappa(t)\hat{y}_t)\,dt + \varepsilon(t)\,d\hat{W}_t, \quad \bar{y}_t = y. \tag{6.82}$$

Equivalently,

$$d\hat{y}_t = \kappa(t)(\theta(t) - \hat{y}_t)\,dt + \varepsilon(t)\,d\hat{W}_t, \quad \bar{y}_t = y, \tag{6.83}$$

where $\theta(t) = \chi(t)/\kappa(t)$.

The corresponding Fokker–Planck problem has the following form:

$$\begin{aligned}
&\varpi_{\bar{t}}(t,y,\bar{t},\bar{y}) - \frac{1}{2}\varepsilon^2\varpi_{\bar{y}\bar{y}}(t,y,\bar{t},\bar{y}) + \left(\chi(\bar{t}) - \kappa(\bar{t})\bar{y}\right)\varpi_{\bar{y}}(t,y,\bar{t},\bar{y}) \\
&\quad - \kappa(\bar{t})\,\varpi(t,y,\bar{t},\bar{y}) = 0, \\
&\varpi(t,y,\bar{t},\bar{y}) = \delta(\bar{y} - y).
\end{aligned} \tag{6.84}$$

The associated function $\mathcal{K}(t,y,\bar{t},\bar{y},l)$ has the following form:

$$\mathcal{K} = \exp\left(\alpha(t,\bar{t}) + i\gamma(t,\bar{t})\bar{y} - ily\right), \tag{6.85}$$

so that

$$\begin{aligned}
&\alpha_{\bar{t}}(t,\bar{t}) + \frac{1}{2}\varepsilon^2(\bar{t})\gamma^2(t,\bar{t}) + i\chi(\bar{t})\gamma(t,\bar{t}) - \kappa(\bar{t}) = 0, \quad \alpha(t,t) = 0, \\
&\gamma_{\bar{t}}(t,\bar{t}) - \kappa(\bar{t})\gamma(t,\bar{t}) = 0, \quad \gamma(t,t) = l.
\end{aligned} \tag{6.86}$$

Thus,

$$\gamma(t,\bar{t}) = e^{\eta(t,\bar{t})}l, \tag{6.87}$$

$$\alpha(t,\bar{t}) = -\frac{1}{2}\psi_0(t,\bar{t})l^2 - \left(\int_t^{\bar{t}} e^{\eta(t,s)}\chi(s)\,ds\right)il + \eta(t,\bar{t}).$$

where

$$\eta(t,\bar{t}) = \int_t^{\bar{t}} \kappa(s)\,ds, \tag{6.88}$$

$$\psi_0\left(t,\bar{t}\right) = \int_t^{\bar{t}} e^{2\eta(t,s)}\varepsilon^2(s)\,ds. \tag{6.89}$$

Since the same quantities will appear regularly throughout the Element, it is convenient to introduce the following notation:

$$\begin{aligned}
&\mathsf{A}_\kappa\left(t,\bar{t}\right) = e^{-\eta(t,\bar{t})},\quad \mathsf{B}_\kappa\left(t,\bar{t}\right) = \int_t^{\bar{t}} e^{-\eta(t,s)}ds,\quad \bar{\mathsf{B}}_\kappa\left(t,\bar{t}\right) = \int_t^{\bar{t}} e^{-\eta(s,\bar{t})}ds,\\
&\mathsf{A}_{-\kappa}\left(t,\bar{t}\right) = e^{\eta(t,\bar{t})},\quad \mathsf{B}_{-\kappa}\left(t,\bar{t}\right) = \int_t^{\bar{t}} e^{\eta(t,s)}ds,\quad \bar{\mathsf{B}}_{-\kappa}\left(t,\bar{t}\right) = \int_t^{\bar{t}} e^{\eta(s,\bar{t})}ds,
\end{aligned} \tag{6.90}$$

In particular, for constant κ, one has

$$\begin{aligned}
&\mathsf{A}_\kappa\left(t,\bar{t}\right) = e^{-\kappa T} = \mathsf{A}_\kappa(T),\quad \mathsf{A}_{-\kappa}\left(t,\bar{t}\right) = e^{\kappa T} = \mathsf{A}_{-\kappa}(T),\\
&\mathsf{B}_\kappa\left(t,\bar{t}\right) = \bar{\mathsf{B}}_\kappa\left(t,\bar{t}\right) = \frac{1-e^{-\kappa T}}{\kappa} = \mathsf{B}_\kappa(T) = \bar{\mathsf{B}}_\kappa(T),\\
&\mathsf{B}_{-\kappa}\left(t,\bar{t}\right) = \bar{\mathsf{B}}_{-\kappa}\left(t,\bar{t}\right) = \frac{e^{\kappa T}-1}{\kappa} = \mathsf{B}_{-\kappa}(T) = \bar{\mathsf{B}}_{-\kappa}(T),
\end{aligned} \tag{6.91}$$

and

$$\mathsf{A}_0\left(t,\bar{t}\right) = 1,\quad \mathsf{B}_0\left(t,\bar{t}\right) = \bar{\mathsf{B}}_0\left(t,\bar{t}\right) = T. \tag{6.92}$$

In this notation, ψ_0 can be written as follows:

$$\psi_0\left(t,\bar{t}\right) = \int_t^{\bar{t}} \mathsf{A}_{-2\kappa}(t,s)\,\varepsilon^2(s)\,ds. \tag{6.93}$$

Thus, the following well-known expression is obtained:

$$\begin{aligned}
&\varpi\left(t,y,\bar{t},\bar{y}\right)\\
&= \frac{1}{2\pi}\int_{-\infty}^{\infty}\exp\left(-\frac{\psi_0\left(t,\bar{t}\right)l^2}{2} + \left(e^{\eta(t,\bar{t})}\bar{y} - \int_t^{\bar{t}} e^{\eta(t,s)}\chi(s)\,ds - y\right)il + \eta\left(t,\bar{t}\right)\right)dl\\
&= \frac{\mathsf{A}_{-\kappa}\left(t,\bar{t}\right)}{\sqrt{2\pi\psi_0\left(t,\bar{t}\right)}}\exp\left(-\frac{\left(\mathsf{A}_{-\kappa}\left(t,\bar{t}\right)\bar{y} - \int_t^{\bar{t}}\mathsf{A}_{-\kappa}(t,s)\,\chi(s)\,ds - y\right)^2}{2\psi_0\left(t,\bar{t}\right)}\right)\\
&= \frac{1}{\sqrt{2\pi\hat{\psi}_0\left(t,\bar{t}\right)}}\exp\left(-\frac{\left(\bar{y} - \int_t^{\bar{t}}\mathsf{A}_\kappa(t,s)\,\chi(s)\,ds - \mathsf{A}_\kappa\left(t,\bar{t}\right)y\right)^2}{2\hat{\psi}_0\left(t,\bar{t}\right)}\right),
\end{aligned} \tag{6.94}$$

where

$$\hat{\psi}_0\left(t,\bar{t}\right) = \mathsf{A}_{2\kappa}\left(t,\bar{t}\right)\psi_0\left(t,\bar{t}\right) = \int_t^{\bar{t}} \mathsf{A}_{2\kappa}\left(s,\bar{t}\right)\varepsilon^2(s)\,ds. \tag{6.95}$$

For further discussion, see the original paper by Uhlenbeck and Ornstein (1930), as well as Chandresekhar (1943), Risken (1989), and references therein.

For time-independent parameters, (6.94) has the form:

$$\varpi\left(t,y,\bar{t},\bar{y}\right) = \frac{1}{\sqrt{2\pi\Sigma^2\left(t,\bar{t}\right)}}\exp\left(-\frac{\left(\bar{y}-\theta-\mathsf{A}_\kappa\left(T\right)\left(y-\theta\right)\right)^2}{2\Sigma^2\left(t,\bar{t}\right)}\right), \tag{6.96}$$

with

$$\Sigma^2\left(t,\bar{t}\right) = \frac{\varepsilon^2\left(1-e^{-2\kappa T}\right)}{2\kappa} = \varepsilon^2\mathsf{B}_{2\kappa}\left(T\right). \tag{6.97}$$

6.4.2 Gaussian Augmented OU Process

This subsection considers an augmented one-dimensional OU process of the form:

$$\begin{aligned} d\hat{x}_t &= \hat{y}_t dt, \quad \hat{x}_t = x, \\ d\hat{y}_t &= \left(\chi\left(t\right)-\kappa\left(t\right)\hat{y}_t\right)dt + \varepsilon\left(t\right)d\hat{W}_t, \quad \hat{y}_t = y. \end{aligned} \tag{6.98}$$

To align the analysis with the existing body of work, switch from the general notation, used above, to a specific one customarily used for the OU process. Here and in what follows, the word "augmentation" means that one expands the original process by incorporating its integral or other path-dependent characteristics, such as running maximum or minimum as part of the process; see Section 5. The augmentation is a very useful tool. In particular, in financial engineering it is used for handling large classes of path-dependent options; details can be found in Lipton (2001), chapter 13.

For an OU process, (6.34) can be written as follows:

$$\mathfrak{L}_{\bar{t}}\left(t,\bar{t}\right) + \begin{pmatrix} 0 & 0 \\ 1 & -\kappa\left(\bar{t}\right) \end{pmatrix}\mathfrak{L}\left(t,\bar{t}\right) = 0, \quad \mathfrak{L}\left(t,t\right) = \begin{pmatrix} 1 & 0 \\ 0 & 1 \end{pmatrix}, \tag{6.99}$$

so that

$$\mathfrak{L}\left(t,\bar{t}\right) = \begin{pmatrix} 1 & 0 \\ -\mathsf{B}_{-\kappa}\left(t,\bar{t}\right) & \mathsf{A}_{-\kappa}\left(t,\bar{t}\right) \end{pmatrix}, \quad \mathfrak{L}^{-1}\left(t,\bar{t}\right) = \begin{pmatrix} 1 & 0 \\ \mathsf{B}_\kappa\left(t,\bar{t}\right) & \mathsf{A}_\kappa\left(t,\bar{t}\right) \end{pmatrix}. \tag{6.100}$$

Now, one can compute $\mathfrak{C}^{-1}\left(t,\bar{t}\right)$, $\mathbf{d}^{(z)}\left(t,\bar{t}\right)$, and $\varsigma\left(t,\bar{t}\right)$:

$$\mathfrak{C}^{-1}\left(t,\bar{t}\right) = \begin{pmatrix} \psi_2\left(t,\bar{t}\right) & -\psi_1\left(t,\bar{t}\right) \\ -\psi_1\left(t,\bar{t}\right) & \psi_0\left(t,\bar{t}\right) \end{pmatrix}, \tag{6.101}$$

where

$$\psi_0\left(t,\bar{t}\right) = \int_t^{\bar{t}} \mathsf{A}_{-\kappa}^2\left(t,s\right)\varepsilon^2\left(s\right)ds,$$

$$\psi_1\left(t,\bar{t}\right) = -\int_t^{\bar{t}} \bar{\mathsf{B}}_{-\kappa}\left(t,s\right)\mathsf{A}_{-\kappa}\left(t,s\right)\varepsilon^2\left(s\right)ds, \tag{6.102}$$

$$\psi_2\left(t,\bar{t}\right) = \int_t^{\bar{t}} \bar{\mathsf{B}}_{-\kappa}^2\left(t,s\right)\varepsilon^2\left(s\right)ds.$$

$$\mathbf{d}^{(z)}\left(t,\bar{t}\right) = \begin{pmatrix} d^{(x)}\left(t,\bar{t}\right) \\ d^{(y)}\left(t,\bar{t}\right) \end{pmatrix} = \begin{pmatrix} -\int_t^{\bar{t}} \bar{\mathsf{B}}_{-\kappa}\left(t,s\right)\chi\left(s\right)ds \\ \int_t^{\bar{t}} \mathsf{A}_{-\kappa}\left(t,s\right)\chi\left(s\right)ds, \end{pmatrix}, \tag{6.103}$$

$$\varsigma\left(t,\bar{t}\right) = -\eta\left(t,\bar{t}\right). \tag{6.104}$$

Next, one can calculate the covariance matrix $\mathfrak{H}\left(t,\bar{t}\right)$, and mean vector $\mathbf{r}\left(t,\bar{t}\right)$ as follows:

$$\begin{aligned} \mathfrak{H}\left(t,\bar{t}\right) &= \left(\mathfrak{L}^*\left(t,\bar{t}\right)\right)^{-1}\mathfrak{C}^{-1}\left(t,\bar{t}\right)\mathfrak{L}^{-1}\left(t,\bar{t}\right) \\ &= \begin{pmatrix} 1 & \mathsf{B}_\kappa\left(t,\bar{t}\right) \\ 0 & \mathsf{A}_\kappa\left(t,\bar{t}\right) \end{pmatrix}\begin{pmatrix} \psi_2\left(t,\bar{t}\right) & -\psi_1\left(t,\bar{t}\right) \\ -\psi_1\left(t,\bar{t}\right) & \psi_0\left(t,\bar{t}\right) \end{pmatrix}\begin{pmatrix} 1 & 0 \\ \mathsf{B}_\kappa\left(t,\bar{t}\right) & \mathsf{A}_\kappa\left(t,\bar{t}\right) \end{pmatrix} \\ &= \begin{pmatrix} h_0\left(t,\bar{t}\right) & h_1\left(t,\bar{t}\right) \\ h_1\left(t,\bar{t}\right) & h_2\left(t,\bar{t}\right) \end{pmatrix}, \end{aligned} \tag{6.105}$$

$$\mathbf{r}\left(t,\bar{t}\right) = \left(\mathfrak{L}^*\left(t,\bar{t}\right)\right)^{-1}\left(\mathbf{d}^{(z)}\left(t,\bar{t}\right) + \begin{pmatrix} x \\ y \end{pmatrix}\right) = \begin{pmatrix} p\left(t,\bar{t}\right) \\ q\left(t,\bar{t}\right) \end{pmatrix}. \tag{6.106}$$

Here

$$\begin{aligned} h_0\left(t,\bar{t}\right) &= \psi_0\,\mathsf{B}_\kappa^2\left(t,\bar{t}\right) - 2\psi_1\,\mathsf{B}_\kappa\left(t,\bar{t}\right) + \psi_2, \\ h_1\left(t,\bar{t}\right) &= \left(\psi_0\,\mathsf{B}_\kappa\left(t,\bar{t}\right) - \psi_1\right)\,\mathsf{A}_\kappa\left(t,\bar{t}\right), \\ h_2\left(t,\bar{t}\right) &= \psi_0\mathsf{A}_\kappa^2\left(t,\bar{t}\right), \end{aligned} \tag{6.107}$$

$$p\left(t,\bar{t}\right) = -\int_t^{\bar{t}} \bar{\mathsf{B}}_{-\kappa}\left(t,s\right)\chi\left(s\right)ds + x + \mathsf{B}_\kappa\left(t,\bar{t}\right)\left(\int_t^{\bar{t}} \mathsf{A}_{-\kappa}\left(t,s\right)\chi\left(s\right)ds + y\right),$$

$$q\left(t,\bar{t}\right) = \mathsf{A}_\kappa\left(t,\bar{t}\right)\left(\int_t^{\bar{t}} \mathsf{A}_{-\kappa}\left(t,s\right)\chi\left(s\right)ds + y\right). \tag{6.108}$$

Thus, $\varpi\left(t,x,y,\bar{t},\bar{x},\bar{y}\right)$ is a bivariate Gaussian distribution of the form (6.26) with the covariance matrix $\mathfrak{H}$, given by (6.105) centered at the point $\mathbf{r} = (p,q)^*$ given by (6.106). Explicitly, one has

$$\sigma_x^2\left(t,\bar{t}\right) = h_0\left(t,\bar{t}\right), \quad \sigma_y^2\left(t,\bar{t}\right) = h_2\left(t,\bar{t}\right), \quad \rho\left(t,\bar{t}\right) = \frac{h_1\left(t,\bar{t}\right)}{\sqrt{h_0\left(t,\bar{t}\right)h_2\left(t,\bar{t}\right)}}. \tag{6.109}$$

When $\chi, \kappa, \theta, \varepsilon$ are constant, the preceding formulas become significantly simpler. Namely,

$$\mathfrak{L}(T) = \begin{pmatrix} 1 & 0 \\ -\mathsf{B}_{-\kappa}(T) & \mathsf{A}_{-\kappa}(T) \end{pmatrix}, \quad \mathfrak{L}^{-1}(T) = \begin{pmatrix} 1 & 0 \\ \mathsf{B}_{\kappa}(T) & \mathsf{A}_{\kappa}(T) \end{pmatrix}, \tag{6.110}$$

$$\mathfrak{C}^{-1}(T) = \begin{pmatrix} \frac{\varepsilon^2}{\kappa^2}\left(\mathsf{B}_0(T) - 2\mathsf{B}_{-\kappa}(T) + \mathsf{B}_{-2\kappa}(T)\right) & -\frac{\varepsilon^2}{2}\mathsf{B}_{-\kappa}(T) \\ -\frac{\varepsilon^2}{2}\mathsf{B}_{-\kappa}(T) & \varepsilon^2\mathsf{B}_{-2\kappa}(T) \end{pmatrix}, \tag{6.111}$$

$$\mathbf{d}^{(z)}(T) = \begin{pmatrix} (T - \mathsf{B}_{-\kappa}(T))\theta \\ \mathsf{B}_{-\kappa}(T)\chi \end{pmatrix}, \tag{6.112}$$

$$\varsigma(T) = -\kappa T, \tag{6.113}$$

$$\mathfrak{H}(T) = \begin{pmatrix} \frac{\varepsilon^2}{\kappa^2}\left(\mathsf{B}_0(T) - 2\mathsf{B}_{\kappa}(T) + \mathsf{B}_{2\kappa}(T)\right) & \frac{\varepsilon^2}{2}\mathsf{B}_{\kappa}(T) \\ \frac{\varepsilon^2}{2}\mathsf{B}_{\kappa}(T) & \varepsilon^2\mathsf{B}_{2\kappa}(T) \end{pmatrix}, \tag{6.114}$$

$$\mathbf{r}(T) = \begin{pmatrix} x + \theta T - \mathsf{B}_{\kappa}(T)(\theta - y) \\ \theta - \mathsf{A}_{\kappa}(T)(\theta - y) \end{pmatrix}. \tag{6.115}$$

Thus, when coefficients are constant, $\varpi\left(t,x,y,\bar{t},\bar{x},\bar{y}\right)$ is a bivariate Gaussian distribution of the form (6.26) with the covariance matrix $\mathfrak{H}$, given by (6.114) and the mean vector $\mathbf{r} = (p,q)^*$ given by (6.115).

Calculate the marginal distribution of $\bar{x}$, denoted by $\varpi^{(x)}\left(t,y,\bar{t},\bar{x}\right)$, which is used on several occasions in what follows. It is well known that marginal distributions of a multivariate Gaussian distribution are also Gaussian, so that

$$\varpi^{(x)}\left(t,y,\bar{t},\bar{x}\right) = \frac{1}{\sqrt{2\pi h_0\left(t,\bar{t}\right)}}\exp\left(\frac{\left(\bar{x} - p\left(t,\bar{t}\right)\right)^2}{2h_0\left(t,\bar{t}\right)}\right), \tag{6.116}$$

where h_0 is given by the equations in (6.114). At the same time, the density of marginal distribution for $\bar{y}$ has the form

$$\varpi^{(y)}\left(t,y,\bar{t},\bar{y}\right) = \frac{1}{\sqrt{2\pi h_2\left(t,\bar{t}\right)}}\exp\left(\frac{\left(\bar{y} - q\left(t,\bar{t}\right)\right)^2}{2h_2\left(t,\bar{t}\right)}\right), \tag{6.117}$$

where h_2 is given by the equations in (6.114), which is the familiar density of the OU process derived in the previous section.

6.5 Example: Diffusion of Free and Harmonically Bound Particles

The preceding results can be used to revisit the motion of free and harmonically bound particles considered in Section 3.

To describe a free particle, it is assumed that $\chi = 0$. Equation (6.114) does not change, while (6.115) can be simplified as follows:

$$\begin{pmatrix} p(T) \\ q(T) \end{pmatrix} = \begin{pmatrix} x + \mathsf{B}_\kappa(T)y \\ \mathsf{A}_\kappa(T)y \end{pmatrix}. \tag{6.118}$$

It is clear that Equations (4.7), (4.8) and (6.114), (6.118) are in agreement. A typical free particle behavior is illustrated in Figure 7.

Analysis of a harmonically bound particle requires additional efforts. In the case in question, (6.34) can be written as follows:

$$\mathfrak{L}'\left(t,\bar{t}\right) + \begin{pmatrix} 0 & -\omega^2 \\ 1 & -\kappa \end{pmatrix} \mathfrak{L}\left(t,\bar{t}\right) = 0, \quad \mathfrak{L}(t,t) = \begin{pmatrix} 1 & 0 \\ 0 & 1 \end{pmatrix}. \tag{6.119}$$

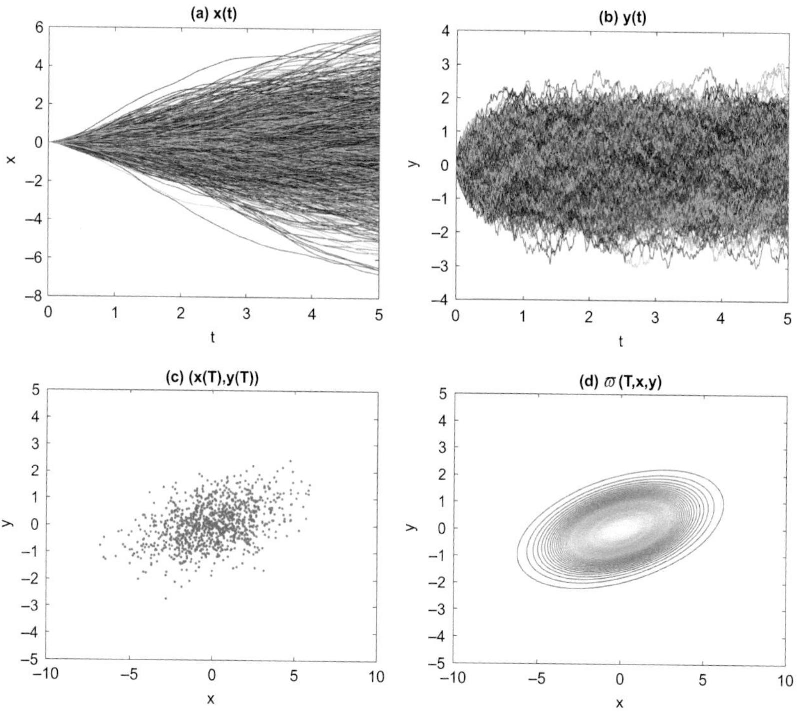

Figure 7 A thousand trajectories of a typical free particle. Parameters are as follows: $T = 5$, $dt = 0.01$, $\kappa = 0.8$, $\sigma = 1.0$. (a) $x(t)$, (b) $y(t)$, (c) $(\bar{x}(T), \bar{y}(T))$, (d) contour lines of $\varpi(0,0,0,T,\tilde{x},\tilde{y})$. Author's graphics.

The corresponding characteristic equation and its solutions are as follows:

$$\lambda^2 - \kappa\lambda + \omega^2 = 0, \tag{6.120}$$

$$\lambda_\pm = \mu \pm \zeta, \tag{6.121}$$

$$\mu = \frac{\kappa}{2}, \quad \zeta = \frac{\sqrt{\kappa^2 - 4\omega^2}}{2}.$$

Introduce

$$\mathsf{E}_0(T) = e^{\mu T} = e^{\kappa T/2}, \quad \mathsf{E}_\pm(T) = e^{\pm\zeta T}. \tag{6.122}$$

It is left to the reader to check that

$$\mathfrak{L} = \frac{\mathsf{E}_0}{\sqrt{\kappa^2 - 4\omega^2}} \begin{pmatrix} -(\lambda_-\mathsf{E}_+ - \lambda_+\mathsf{E}_-) & \omega^2(\mathsf{E}_+ - \mathsf{E}_-) \\ -(\mathsf{E}_+ - \mathsf{E}_-) & (\lambda_+\mathsf{E}_+ - \lambda_-\mathsf{E}_-) \end{pmatrix}, \tag{6.123}$$

$$\mathfrak{L}^{-1} = \frac{\mathsf{E}_0^{-1}}{\sqrt{\kappa^2 - 4\omega^2}} \begin{pmatrix} (\lambda_+\mathsf{E}_+ - \lambda_-\mathsf{E}_-) & -\omega^2(\mathsf{E}_+ - \mathsf{E}_-) \\ (\mathsf{E}_+ - \mathsf{E}_-) & -(\lambda_-\mathsf{E}_+ - \lambda_+\mathsf{E}_-) \end{pmatrix}, \tag{6.124}$$

$$\det\mathfrak{L} = \left(\det\mathfrak{L}^{-1}\right)^{-1} = \mathsf{E}_0^2 = e^{\kappa T}, \tag{6.125}$$

Accordingly,

$$\varpi\left(t, \mathbf{z}, \bar{t}, \bar{\mathbf{z}}\right) = \mathrm{N}\left(\mathbf{r}\left(t, \bar{t}\right), \mathfrak{H}\left(t, \bar{t}\right)\right), \tag{6.126}$$

with

$$\mathfrak{H} = (\mathfrak{L}^*)^{-1}\,\mathfrak{C}^{-1}\mathfrak{L}^{-1}, \tag{6.127}$$

$$\mathbf{r} = (\mathfrak{L}^*)^{-1}\,\mathbf{z}.$$

Here,

$$\mathfrak{C}^{-1} = \begin{pmatrix} \psi_2 & -\psi_1 \\ -\psi_1 & \psi_0 \end{pmatrix}, \tag{6.128}$$

where

$$\begin{aligned}
\psi_0 &= \frac{\varepsilon^2}{\left(\kappa^2 - 4\omega^2\right)} \int_t^{\bar{t}} \left(\lambda_+ e^{\lambda_+(s-t)} - \lambda_- e^{\lambda_-(s-t)}\right)^2 ds \\
&= \frac{\varepsilon^2}{2\kappa\left(\kappa^2 - 4\omega^2\right)} \left(\mathsf{E}_0^2\left(\kappa\lambda_+\mathsf{E}_+^2 - 4\omega^2 + \kappa\lambda_-\mathsf{E}_-^2\right) - \left(\kappa^2 - 4\omega^2\right)\right), \\
\psi_1 &= \frac{\varepsilon^2}{\left(\kappa^2 - 4\omega^2\right)} \int_t^{\bar{t}} \left(e^{\lambda_+(s-t)} - e^{\lambda_-(s-t)}\right)\left(\lambda_+ e^{\lambda_+(s-t)} - \lambda_- e^{\lambda_-(s-t)}\right) ds \\
&= \frac{\varepsilon^2}{2\left(\kappa^2 - 4\omega^2\right)} \mathsf{E}_0^2 \left(\mathsf{E}_+ - \mathsf{E}_-\right)^2,
\end{aligned}$$

$$\psi_2 = \frac{\varepsilon^2}{\left(\kappa^2 - 4\omega^2\right)} \int_t^{\bar{t}} \left(e^{\lambda_+(s-t)} - e^{\lambda_-(s-t)}\right)^2 ds$$
$$= \frac{\varepsilon^2}{2\kappa\omega^2\left(\kappa^2 - 4\omega^2\right)} \left(\mathsf{E}_0^2\left(\kappa\lambda_-\mathsf{E}_+^2 - 4\omega^2 + \kappa\lambda_+\mathsf{E}_-^2\right) - \left(\kappa^2 - 4\omega^2\right)\right). \tag{6.129}$$

Further,

$$\mathfrak{H} = \frac{\mathsf{E}_0^{-2}}{\left(\kappa^2 - 4\omega^2\right)} \begin{pmatrix} (\lambda_+\mathsf{E}_+ - \lambda_-\mathsf{E}_-) & (\mathsf{E}_+ - \mathsf{E}_-) \\ -\omega^2(\mathsf{E}_+ - \mathsf{E}_-) & -(\lambda_-\mathsf{E}_+ - \lambda_+\mathsf{E}_-) \end{pmatrix} \tag{6.130}$$
$$\times \begin{pmatrix} \psi_2 & -\psi_1 \\ -\psi_1 & \psi_0 \end{pmatrix} \begin{pmatrix} (\lambda_+\mathsf{E}_+ - \lambda_-\mathsf{E}_-) & -\omega^2(\mathsf{E}_+ - \mathsf{E}_-) \\ (\mathsf{E}_+ - \mathsf{E}_-) & -(\lambda_-\mathsf{E}_+ - \lambda_+\mathsf{E}_-) \end{pmatrix}.$$

Straightforward but tedious calculation yields

$$h_0 = \frac{\varepsilon^2}{2\kappa\omega^2}\left(1 - \frac{\mathsf{E}_0^{-2}\left(\omega^2(\mathsf{E}_+ - \mathsf{E}_-)^2 + (\lambda_+\mathsf{E}_+ - \lambda_-\mathsf{E}_-)^2\right)}{\left(\kappa^2 - 4\omega^2\right)}\right),$$
$$h_1 = \frac{\varepsilon^2}{2}\frac{\mathsf{E}_0^{-2}(\mathsf{E}_+ - \mathsf{E}_-)^2}{\left(\kappa^2 - 4\omega^2\right)}, \tag{6.131}$$
$$h_2 = \frac{\varepsilon^2}{2\kappa}\left(1 - \frac{\mathsf{E}_0^{-2}\left(\omega^2(\mathsf{E}_+ - \mathsf{E}_-)^2 + (\lambda_-\mathsf{E}_+ - \lambda_+\mathsf{E}_-)^2\right)}{\left(\kappa^2 - 4\omega^2\right)}\right).$$

In the limit $\omega^2 \to 0$,

$$h_0 = \frac{\varepsilon^2}{\kappa^2}(\mathsf{B}_0 - 2\mathsf{B}_\kappa + \mathsf{B}_{2\kappa}), \quad h_1 = \frac{\varepsilon^2}{2}\mathsf{B}_\kappa^2, \quad h_2 = \varepsilon^2\mathsf{B}_{2\kappa}, \tag{6.132}$$

so that Equations (6.114) and (6.132) are in agreement.

Here

$$\mathbf{r} = \begin{pmatrix} p \\ q \end{pmatrix} = \begin{pmatrix} \frac{\mathsf{E}_0^{-1}((\lambda_+\mathsf{E}_+ - \lambda_-\mathsf{E}_-)x + (\mathsf{E}_+ - \mathsf{E}_-)y)}{\sqrt{\kappa^2 - 4\omega^2}} \\ -\frac{\mathsf{E}_0^{-1}\left(\omega^2(\mathsf{E}_+ - \mathsf{E}_-)x + (\lambda_-\mathsf{E}_+ - \lambda_+\mathsf{E}_-)y\right)}{\sqrt{\kappa^2 - 4\omega^2}} \end{pmatrix}. \tag{6.133}$$

In the limit $\omega^2 \to 0$,

$$\mathbf{r} = \begin{pmatrix} p \\ q \end{pmatrix} = \begin{pmatrix} x + \mathsf{B}_\kappa(T)y \\ \mathsf{A}_\kappa(T)y \end{pmatrix}. \tag{6.134}$$

Moreover, while it is easy to show that Chandrasekhar's solution given in Chandresekhar (1943) is in agreement with the solution given by (6.126), the solution is more convenient from a practical standpoint, since it is *explicitly* written as a Gaussian density in the $(\bar{x}, \bar{y})$ space. A typical bounded particle behavior is shown in Figure 8.

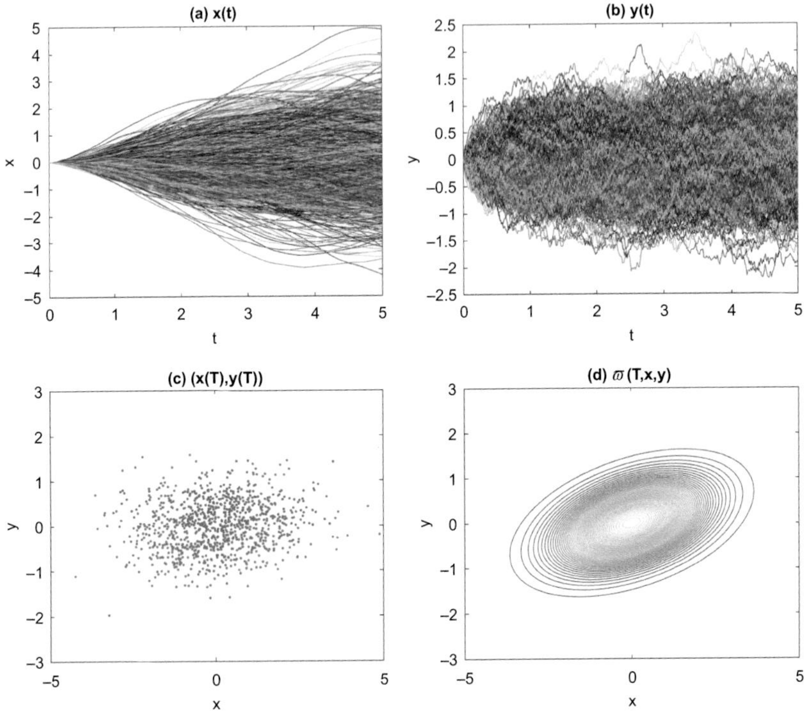

Figure 8 A thousand trajectories of a harmonically bounded particle. Parameters are as follows: $T = 5$, $dt = 0.01$, $\kappa = 0.2$, $\omega = 0.5$, $\sigma = 0.5$. (a) $x(t)$, (b) $y(t)$, (c) $(\bar{x}(T), \bar{y}(T))$, (d) contour lines of $\varpi(0,0,0,T,\bar{x},\bar{y})$. Author's graphics.

6.6 Example: Vorticity of Two-Dimensional Flows

Briefly return to the starting point and consider strictly two-dimensional flows; see Friedlander and Lipton-Lifschitz (2003). Velocity fields of such flows have the following form:

$$\mathbf{V}\left(\bar{t},\bar{x}_1,\bar{x}_2\right) = \left(V_1\left(\bar{t},\bar{x}_1,\bar{x}_2\right), V_2\left(\bar{t},\bar{x}_1,\bar{x}_2\right)\right),$$
$$\mathbf{v}\left(\bar{t},\bar{x}_1,\bar{x}_2\right) = \left(v_1\left(\bar{t},\bar{x}_1,\bar{x}_2\right), v_2\left(\bar{t},\bar{x}_1,\bar{x}_2\right)\right). \tag{6.135}$$

By virtue of incompressibility, one can introduce the so-called stream functions such that

$$V_1 = -\frac{\partial \Psi}{\partial \bar{x}_2}, \quad V_2 = \frac{\partial \Psi}{\partial \bar{x}_1}, \quad v_1 = -\frac{\partial \psi}{\partial \bar{x}_2}, \quad v_2 = \frac{\partial \psi}{\partial \bar{x}_1}, \tag{6.136}$$

and define the scalar vorticity as follows:

$$\Omega = \Delta \Psi, \quad \omega = \Delta \psi. \tag{6.137}$$

Contour lines of Ψ are called streamlines of the flow.

By using the preceding definitions, the two-dimensional Navier–Stokes equations can be written as equations for the stream and vorticity:

$$\frac{\partial \Omega}{\partial \bar{t}} - \frac{\partial \Psi}{\partial \bar{x}_2}\frac{\partial \Omega}{\partial \bar{x}_1} + \frac{\partial \Psi}{\partial \bar{x}_1}\frac{\partial \Omega}{\partial \bar{x}_2} - \nu \Delta \Omega = 0,$$
$$\Delta \Psi - \Omega = 0. \tag{6.138}$$

Time-independent quadratic stream functions $\Psi(\bar{x}_1, \bar{x}_2)$ generate exact equilibrium solutions of the equations in (6.138). Consider fields consisting of pure strain and pure rotation. The corresponding Ψ have the following form:

$$\Psi(\bar{x}_1, \bar{x}_2) = \frac{1}{4}\left(w\left(\bar{x}_1^2 + \bar{x}_2^2\right) - 2s\bar{x}_1\bar{x}_2\right), \tag{6.139}$$

where $w > s$, to ensure that streamlines are elliptic rather than hyperbolic, so that

$$V_1 = -\frac{\partial \Psi}{\partial \bar{x}_2} = \frac{1}{2}(s\bar{x}_1 - w\bar{x}_2), \quad V_2 = \frac{\partial \Psi}{\partial \bar{x}_1} = \frac{1}{2}(w\bar{x}_1 - s\bar{x}_2). \tag{6.140}$$

Recall that these flows were introduced in Section 2, Equation (2.7).

Small perturbations ψ of the time-independent quadratic stream function Ψ satisfy the following equations:

$$\frac{\partial \omega}{\partial \bar{t}} - \frac{\partial \Psi}{\partial \bar{x}_2}\frac{\partial \omega}{\partial \bar{x}_1} + \frac{\partial \Psi}{\partial \bar{x}_1}\frac{\partial \omega}{\partial \bar{x}_2} - \nu \Delta \omega = 0,$$
$$\Delta \psi - \omega = 0. \tag{6.141}$$

It is helpful to study the first equation (6.141) in isolation, by writing it explicitly as follows:

$$\frac{\partial \omega}{\partial \bar{t}} + \frac{1}{2}(s\bar{x}_1 - w\bar{x}_2)\frac{\partial \omega}{\partial \bar{x}_1} + \frac{1}{2}(w\bar{x}_1 - s\bar{x}_2)\frac{\partial \omega}{\partial \bar{x}_2} - \nu \Delta \omega = 0, \tag{6.142}$$

and supplying it with the initial condition at time t:

$$\omega(t, \bar{x}_1, \bar{x}_2) = \delta(\bar{x}_1 - x_1)\,\delta(\bar{x}_2 - x_2). \tag{6.143}$$

Once the solution of Equations (6.142) and (6.143) is found, one can find ψ by solving the corresponding Laplace equation.

Surprisingly, this equation is identical to the Fokker–Planck equation associated with the following SDEs for $\hat{\mathbf{z}}_t = (\hat{x}_{1t}, \hat{x}_{2t})$:

$$d\hat{\mathbf{z}}_t = \mathfrak{B}\hat{\mathbf{z}}_t dt + \boldsymbol{\Sigma} d\hat{\mathbf{W}}_t, \quad \hat{\mathbf{z}}_t = \begin{pmatrix} x_1 \\ x_2 \end{pmatrix}, \tag{6.144}$$

where

$$\mathfrak{B} = \frac{1}{2}\begin{pmatrix} s & -w \\ w & -s \end{pmatrix}, \quad \boldsymbol{\Sigma} = \sqrt{2\nu}\begin{pmatrix} 1 & 0 \\ 0 & 1 \end{pmatrix}. \tag{6.145}$$

Thus, one can use Section 6.1 results. Equation (6.34) becomes

$$\mathfrak{L}'\left(t,\bar{t}\right) + \frac{1}{2}\begin{pmatrix} s & w \\ -w & -s \end{pmatrix}\mathfrak{L}\left(t,\bar{t}\right) = 0, \quad \mathfrak{L}(t,t) = \begin{pmatrix} 1 & 0 \\ 0 & 1 \end{pmatrix}. \tag{6.146}$$

The corresponding characteristic equation has the following form:

$$\lambda^2 + \frac{1}{4}\left(w^2 - s^2\right) = 0. \tag{6.147}$$

Its solutions are

$$\lambda_{\pm} = \pm\zeta, \quad \zeta = \frac{i\sqrt{w^2 - s^2}}{2}. \tag{6.148}$$

Simple but tedious calculations, omitted for the sake of brevity, show that

$$\begin{aligned} \mathfrak{L} &= \begin{pmatrix} \mathsf{c}_1 - \frac{s}{2|\zeta|}\mathsf{s}_1 & -\frac{w}{2|\zeta|}\mathsf{s}_1 \\ \frac{w}{2|\zeta|}\mathsf{s}_1 & \mathsf{c}_1 + \frac{s}{2|\zeta|}\mathsf{s}_1 \end{pmatrix}, \quad \det(\mathfrak{L}) = 1 \\ \mathfrak{L}^{-1} &= \begin{pmatrix} \mathsf{c}_1 + \frac{s}{2|\zeta|}\mathsf{s}_1 & \frac{w}{2|\zeta|}\mathsf{s}_1 \\ -\frac{w}{2|\zeta|}\mathsf{s}_1 & \mathsf{c}_1 - \frac{s}{2|\zeta|}\mathsf{s}_1 \end{pmatrix}, \quad \det\left(\mathfrak{L}^{-1}\right) = 1, \end{aligned} \tag{6.149}$$

where

$$\mathsf{c}_1\left(t,\bar{t}\right) = \cos\left(|\zeta|\, T\right), \quad \mathsf{s}_1\left(t,\bar{t}\right) = \sin\left(|\zeta|\, T\right). \tag{6.150}$$

Next, (6.39) yields

$$\mathfrak{C}^{-1} = 2\nu\int_t^{\bar{t}} \mathfrak{L}^*(t,s)\,\mathfrak{L}(t,s)\,ds = \begin{pmatrix} \psi_2 & -\psi_1 \\ -\psi_1 & \psi_0 \end{pmatrix}, \tag{6.151}$$

where

$$\begin{aligned} \psi_0 &= 2\nu\int_t^{\bar{t}}\left(1 + \frac{s}{2|\zeta|}\mathsf{s}_2(t,s) + \frac{s^2}{4|\zeta|^2}\left(1 - \mathsf{c}_2(t,s)\right)\right)ds \\ &= 2\nu\left(\left(1 + \frac{s^2}{4|\zeta|^2}\right)T - \frac{s}{4|\zeta|^2}\mathsf{c}_2 - \frac{s^2}{8|\zeta|^3}\mathsf{s}_2\right), \\ \psi_1 &= -\frac{\nu s w}{2|\zeta|^2}\int_t^{\bar{t}}\left(1 - \mathsf{c}_2(t,s)\right)ds = -\frac{\nu s w}{2|\zeta|^2}\left(T - \frac{1}{2|\zeta|}\mathsf{s}_2\right), \\ \psi_2 &= 2\nu\int_t^{\bar{t}}\left(1 - \frac{s}{2|\zeta|}\mathsf{s}_2(t,s) + \frac{s^2}{4|\zeta|^2}\left(1 - \mathsf{c}_2(t,s)\right)\right)ds \\ &= 2\nu\left(\left(1 + \frac{s^2}{4|\zeta|^2}\right)T + \frac{s}{4|\zeta|^2}\mathsf{c}_2 - \frac{s^2}{8|\zeta|^3}\mathsf{s}_2\right), \end{aligned} \tag{6.152}$$

and

$$\mathsf{c}_2\left(t,\bar{t}\right) = \cos\left(2\left|\zeta\right| T\right), \quad \mathsf{s}_2\left(t,\bar{t}\right) = \sin\left(2\left|\zeta\right| T\right). \tag{6.153}$$

Finally, Equations (6.26) and (6.27) yield:

$$\omega\left(t,\mathbf{z},\bar{t},\bar{\mathbf{z}}\right) = \mathrm{N}\left(\mathbf{r}\left(t,\bar{t}\right),\mathfrak{H}\left(t,\bar{t}\right)\right). \tag{6.154}$$

The corresponding covariance matrix $\mathfrak{H}$ and mean $\mathbf{r}$ are as follows:

$$\mathfrak{H} = \begin{pmatrix} h_0 & h_1 \\ h_1 & h_2 \end{pmatrix}, \tag{6.155}$$

where

$$\begin{aligned} h_0 &= \left(\frac{w^2}{8\left|\zeta\right|^2} + \frac{\left(4\left|\zeta\right|^2 - s^2\right)}{8\left|\zeta\right|^2}\mathsf{c}_2 + \frac{s}{2\left|\zeta\right|}\mathsf{s}_2\right)\psi_2 \\ &\quad + \frac{w}{2\left|\zeta\right|}\left(\frac{s}{2\left|\zeta\right|}\left(1-\mathsf{c}_2\right) + \mathsf{s}_2\right)\psi_1 + \frac{w^2}{8\left|\zeta\right|^2}\left(1-\mathsf{c}_2\right)\psi_0, \\ h_1 &= \frac{w}{4\left|\zeta\right|}\left(\frac{s}{2\left|\zeta\right|}\left(1-\mathsf{c}_2\right) + \mathsf{s}_2\right)\psi_2 \\ &\quad - \left(1 + \frac{w^2}{4\left|\zeta\right|^2}\left(1-\mathsf{c}_2\right)\right)\psi_1 + \frac{w}{4\left|\zeta\right|}\left(\frac{s}{2\left|\zeta\right|}\left(1-\mathsf{c}_2\right) - \mathsf{s}_2\right)\psi_0, \\ h_2 &= \frac{w^2}{8\left|\zeta\right|^2}\left(1-\mathsf{c}_2\right)\psi_2 + \frac{w}{2\left|\zeta\right|}\left(\frac{s}{2\left|\zeta\right|}\left(1-\mathsf{c}_2\right) - \mathsf{s}_2\right)\psi_1 \\ &\quad + \left(\frac{w^2}{8\left|\zeta\right|^2} + \frac{\left(4\left|\zeta\right|^2 - s^2\right)}{8\left|\zeta\right|^2}\mathsf{c}_2 - \frac{s}{2\left|\zeta\right|}\mathsf{s}_2\right)\psi_0, \end{aligned} \tag{6.156}$$

and

$$\mathbf{r} = \begin{pmatrix} r_1 \\ r_2 \end{pmatrix} = \begin{pmatrix} \left(\mathsf{c}_1 + \frac{s}{2|\zeta|}\mathsf{s}_1\right)x_1 - \frac{w}{2|\zeta|}\mathsf{s}_1 x_2 \\ \frac{w}{2|\zeta|}\mathsf{s}_1 x_1 + \left(\mathsf{c}_1 - \frac{s}{2|\zeta|}\mathsf{s}_1\right)x_2 \end{pmatrix}. \tag{6.157}$$

The equations in (6.156) are symmetric, namely $h_0 \rightarrow h_2$ when $(a,b) \rightarrow (-a,-b)$ and $(\psi_0,\psi_2) \rightarrow (\psi_2,\psi_0)$. The second of the equations in (6.138), which is a static Poisson equation, allows us to find ψ, since ω is known. Its analytical solution is not easy to derive and is not presented here due to lack of space. However, the special case of purely rotational flow, $s = 0$, can be done easily; see (6.165).

It is interesting to note that

$$\Psi\left(r_1,r_2\right) = \Psi\left(x_1,x_2\right), \tag{6.158}$$

so that the location of the Gaussian distribution ω moves along streamlines of the flow defined by the stream function Ψ.

When the flow is purely rotational, so that $s = 0$, the preceding formulas considerably simplify. Specifically, one has the following:

$$\begin{aligned} &\psi_0 = 2\nu T, \ \psi_1 = 0, \quad \psi_2 = 2\nu T, \\ &h_0 = 2\nu T, \ \psi_1 = 0, \quad h_2 = 2\nu T, \\ &r_1 = \mathrm{c}_1 x_1 - \mathrm{s}_1 x_2, \quad r_2 = \mathrm{s}_1 x_1 + \mathrm{c}_1 x_2, \end{aligned} \tag{6.159}$$

so that

$$\begin{aligned} &\omega\left(t, x_1, x_2, \bar{t}, \bar{x}_1, \bar{x}_2\right) \\ &= \frac{1}{4\pi\nu T} \exp\left(-\frac{\left(\bar{x}_1 - \mathrm{c}_1 x_1 + \mathrm{s}_1 x_2\right)^2 + \left(\bar{x}_2 - \mathrm{s}_1 x_1 - \mathrm{c}_1 x_2\right)^2}{4\nu T}\right). \end{aligned} \tag{6.160}$$

The stream function ψ can be calculated directly by solving the corresponding Poisson equation.[6] To start, notice that *both* ω and ψ are rotational symmetric around the point (x_1, x_2). Thus, ω and ψ have the following form:

$$\omega = \omega(R) = \frac{1}{4\pi\nu T} \exp\left(-\frac{R^2}{2}\right), \quad \psi = \psi(R), \tag{6.161}$$

where

$$R^2 = \frac{\left(\bar{x}_1 - \mathrm{c}_1 x_1 + \mathrm{s}_1 x_2\right)^2 + \left(\bar{x}_2 - \mathrm{s}_1 x_1 - \mathrm{c}_1 x_2\right)^2}{2\nu T}. \tag{6.162}$$

Then $\psi(R)$ solves a radially symmetric Poisson equation of the following form:

$$\frac{1}{R}\left(R\psi_R(R)\right)_R = \frac{1}{2\pi} \exp\left(-\frac{R^2}{2}\right). \tag{6.163}$$

Thus,

$$R\psi_R(R) = -\frac{1}{2\pi} \exp\left(-\frac{R^2}{2}\right) + C, \tag{6.164}$$

where C is an arbitrary constant. Next,

$$\psi(R) = \frac{1}{2\pi}\left(\ln(R) + \frac{1}{2} E_1\left(\frac{R^2}{2}\right)\right), \tag{6.165}$$

where the choice of C guarantees that ψ has the right behavior when $R \to 0$ and $R \to \infty$. Here $E_1(\eta)$ is the exponential integral of the following form:

$$E_1(\eta) = \int_{\eta}^{\infty} \frac{e^{-\eta'}}{\eta'} d\eta'. \tag{6.166}$$

[6] We are grateful to Andrey Itkin for pointing this out.

7 Non-Gaussian Stochastic Processes

7.1 Regular Non-Gaussian Processes

In many situations, it is useful to consider processes governed by more general SDEs of the following form:

$$\begin{aligned} d\hat{\mathbf{z}}_t &= \left(\mathbf{b}(t) + \mathfrak{B}(t)\,\hat{\mathbf{z}}_t\right) dt \\ &\quad + \boldsymbol{\Sigma}(t)\left(\mathrm{diag}\left(\mathbf{d}^{(0)}(t) + \mathfrak{D}(t)\,\hat{\mathbf{z}}_t\right)\right)^{1/2} d\hat{\mathbf{W}}_t^{(z)}, \\ \hat{\mathbf{z}}_t &= \mathbf{z}. \end{aligned} \tag{7.1}$$

Here, in addition to the functions $\mathbf{b}(t)$, $\mathfrak{B}(t)$ introduced in the previous section, define an $(M \times 1)$ column vector $\mathbf{d}^{(0)}$, and an $(M \times M)$ matrix $\mathfrak{D}$. It is convenient to introduce auxiliary vectors $\mathbf{d}^{(i)}$ equal to the ith column of $\mathfrak{D}$.

Since the corresponding $(M \times M)$ covariance matrix $\mathfrak{A}$ has the form:

$$\mathfrak{A} = \frac{1}{2}\boldsymbol{\Sigma}\left(\mathrm{diag}\left(\mathbf{d}^{(0)}(t) + \mathfrak{D}(t)\,\mathbf{z}_t\right)\right)^{1/2}\left(\boldsymbol{\Sigma}\left(\mathrm{diag}\left(\mathbf{d}^{(0)}(t) + \mathfrak{D}(t)\,\mathbf{z}_t\right)\right)^{1/2}\right)^{*}, \tag{7.2}$$

it linearly depends on $\mathbf{z}$:

$$\mathfrak{A} = \frac{1}{2}\boldsymbol{\Sigma}\left(\mathrm{diag}\left(\mathbf{d}^{(0)} + \mathfrak{D}\mathbf{z}\right)\right)\boldsymbol{\Sigma}^{*} = \frac{1}{2}\mathfrak{A}^{(0)} + \frac{1}{2}\mathfrak{A}^{(m)} z_m, \tag{7.3}$$

where

$$\mathfrak{A}^{(0)} = \frac{1}{2}\boldsymbol{\Sigma}\mathrm{diag}\left(\mathbf{d}^{(0)}\right)\Sigma^{*}, \quad \mathfrak{A}^{(i)} = \frac{1}{2}\boldsymbol{\Sigma}\mathrm{diag}\left(\mathbf{d}^{(i)}\right)\Sigma^{*}. \tag{7.4}$$

In contrast to the Gaussian case, the equations in (7.2) have to be defined in the domain D such that

$$D = \left\{\mathbf{z} \,|\, \mathbf{d}^{(0)} + \mathfrak{D}\mathbf{z} \geq 0\right\}, \tag{7.5}$$

rather than in the whole space. In financial engineering, covariance matrices of the form (7.2) were introduced by Dai and Singleton (2000), and discussed by Duffie *et al.* (2003), Filipovic (2009), and many others.

The corresponding Fokker–Plank problem has the following form:

$$\begin{aligned} &\varpi_{\bar{t}}\left(t,\mathbf{z},\bar{t},\bar{\mathbf{z}}\right) - \sum\sum\left(\mathfrak{A}^{0} + \bar{z}_m\mathfrak{A}^{(m)}\right)\varpi_{\bar{\mathbf{z}}\bar{\mathbf{z}}}\left(t,\mathbf{z},\bar{t},\bar{\mathbf{z}}\right) \\ &\quad + \left(\hat{\mathbf{b}} + \mathfrak{B}\bar{\mathbf{z}}\right)\cdot\varpi_{\bar{\mathbf{z}}}\left(t,\mathbf{z},\bar{t},\bar{\mathbf{z}}\right) + b\varpi\left(t,\mathbf{z},\bar{t},\bar{\mathbf{z}}\right) = 0, \\ &\varpi\left(t,\mathbf{z},t,\bar{\mathbf{z}}\right) = \delta\left(\bar{\mathbf{z}} - \mathbf{z}\right), \end{aligned} \tag{7.6}$$

where

$$\begin{aligned} \hat{b}_m &= b_m - \left(2a_{mm}^{(m)} + a_{mm'}^{(m')} + a_{m'm}^{(m')}\right), \quad \text{(no summation over } m\text{)}, \\ b &= \mathrm{Tr}\left(\mathfrak{B}\right). \end{aligned} \tag{7.7}$$

Equation (6.11) expressing ϖ in terms of $\mathcal{K}$ holds. The equations for $\alpha, \boldsymbol{\delta}$ have the following form:

$$\alpha_{\bar{t}}\left(t,\bar{t}\right)+i\boldsymbol{\delta}_{\bar{t}}\left(t,\bar{t}\right)\cdot\bar{\mathbf{z}}+\boldsymbol{\delta}\left(t,\bar{t}\right)\cdot\mathfrak{A}\boldsymbol{\delta}\left(t,\bar{t}\right)+i\boldsymbol{\delta}\left(t,\bar{t}\right)\cdot\left(\hat{\mathbf{b}}+\mathfrak{B}\bar{\mathbf{z}}\right)+b=0, \tag{7.8}$$

or, more explicitly,

$$\begin{aligned}\alpha_{\bar{t}}\left(t,\bar{t}\right)+i\boldsymbol{\delta}_{\bar{t}}\left(t,\bar{t}\right)\cdot\bar{\mathbf{z}}+\boldsymbol{\delta}\left(t,\bar{t}\right)\cdot\mathfrak{A}^{(0)}\boldsymbol{\delta}\left(t,\bar{t}\right)+\boldsymbol{\delta}\left(t,\bar{t}\right)\cdot\mathfrak{A}^{(k)}\boldsymbol{\delta}\left(t,\bar{t}\right)\bar{z}_k \\ +i\boldsymbol{\delta}\left(t,\bar{t}\right)\cdot\left(\hat{\mathbf{b}}+\mathfrak{B}\bar{\mathbf{z}}\right)+b=0.\end{aligned} \tag{7.9}$$

Thus, the system of ODEs for $\alpha, \boldsymbol{\delta}$ can be written as follows:

$$\begin{aligned}&\alpha_{\bar{t}}\left(t,\bar{t}\right)+\boldsymbol{\delta}\left(t,\bar{t}\right)\cdot\mathfrak{A}^{(0)}\left(t,\bar{t}\right)\delta\left(t,\bar{t}\right)+i\boldsymbol{\delta}\left(t,\bar{t}\right)\cdot\hat{\mathbf{b}}\left(t,\bar{t}\right)+b\left(t,\bar{t}\right)=0,\quad\alpha\left(t,t\right)=0,\\&i\delta_i'\left(t,\bar{t}\right)+\boldsymbol{\delta}\left(t,\bar{t}\right)\cdot\mathfrak{A}^{(i)}\boldsymbol{\delta}\left(t,\bar{t}\right)+i\mathfrak{B}_{ij}\delta_j\left(t,\bar{t}\right)=0,\quad\delta_i\left(t,t\right)=m_i.\end{aligned} \tag{7.10}$$

In the case in question, the equation for $\boldsymbol{\delta}$ is no longer linear. Instead, $\boldsymbol{\delta}$ satisfies the so-called matrix Riccati equation. Such equations are important for several applications, such as optimal control. Solving a matrix Riccati equation is quite hard, so it is more an art than a science; some of the results in this direction are reported here. However, in the one-dimensional case, the corresponding Riccati equation can be converted into the second-order ODE, and then solved explicitly when the coefficients $\mathfrak{A}$, $\mathbf{b}$, b are time-independent.

In case of an augmented process, one must consider an SDE of the following form:

$$\begin{aligned}d\hat{\mathbf{x}}_t&=\left(\mathbf{b}^{(x)}\left(t\right)+\mathfrak{B}^{(xx)}\left(t\right)\hat{\mathbf{x}}_t+\mathfrak{B}^{(xy)}\left(t\right)\hat{\mathbf{y}}_t\right)dt,\\d\hat{\mathbf{y}}_t&=\left(\mathbf{b}^{(y)}\left(t\right)+\mathfrak{B}^{(yx)}\left(t\right)\hat{\mathbf{x}}_t+\mathfrak{B}^{(yy)}\left(t\right)\hat{\mathbf{y}}_t\right)dt\\&\quad+\boldsymbol{\Sigma}^{(yy)}\left(t\right)\left(\mathrm{diag}\left(\mathbf{d}^{(0)}\left(t\right)+\mathfrak{D}\left(t\right)\hat{\mathbf{z}}_t\right)\right)^{1/2}d\hat{\mathbf{W}}_t^{(y)},\\\hat{\mathbf{x}}_t&=\mathbf{x},\quad\hat{\mathbf{y}}_t=\mathbf{y},\end{aligned} \tag{7.11}$$

or, more compactly,

$$\begin{aligned}d\hat{\mathbf{z}}_t&=\left(\mathbf{b}\left(t\right)+\mathfrak{B}\left(t\right)\hat{\mathbf{z}}_t\right)dt+\begin{pmatrix}0\\\boldsymbol{\Sigma}^{(yy)}\left(t\right)\left(\mathrm{diag}\left(\mathbf{d}^{(0)}\left(t\right)+\mathfrak{D}\left(t\right)\hat{\mathbf{z}}_t\right)\right)^{1/2}d\hat{\mathbf{W}}_t^{(y)}\end{pmatrix},\\\hat{\mathbf{z}}_t&=\mathbf{z}=\begin{pmatrix}\mathbf{x}\\\mathbf{y}\end{pmatrix}.\end{aligned} \tag{7.12}$$

Here $\mathbf{b}^{(x)}$, $\mathbf{b}^{(y)}$, $\mathbf{b}=\left(\mathbf{b}^{(x)},\mathbf{b}^{(y)}\right)^*$, $\mathbf{d}^{(0)}$ are column vectors, and $\mathfrak{B}^{(xx)}$, $\mathfrak{B}^{(xy)}$, $\mathfrak{B}^{(yx)}$, $\mathfrak{B}^{(yy)}$, $\mathfrak{B}$, and $\mathfrak{D}$ are matrices of appropriate dimensions.

The equations for $\alpha, \delta = (\boldsymbol{\beta}, \boldsymbol{\gamma})$ have the following form:

$$\alpha_{\bar{t}}(t,\bar{t}) + i\boldsymbol{\delta}_{\bar{t}}(t,\bar{t}) \cdot \bar{\mathbf{z}} + \boldsymbol{\gamma}(t,\bar{t}) \cdot \mathfrak{A}\boldsymbol{\gamma}(t,\bar{t}) + i\boldsymbol{\delta}(t,\bar{t}) \cdot \left(\hat{\mathbf{b}} + \mathfrak{B}\bar{\mathbf{z}}\right) + b = 0, \tag{7.13}$$

or, more explicitly,

$$\begin{aligned} &\alpha_{\bar{t}}(t,\bar{t}) + i\boldsymbol{\delta}_{\bar{t}}(t,\bar{t}) \cdot \bar{\mathbf{z}} + \boldsymbol{\gamma}(t,\bar{t}) \cdot \mathfrak{A}^{(0)}\boldsymbol{\gamma}(t,\bar{t}) + \boldsymbol{\gamma}(t,\bar{t}) \cdot \mathfrak{A}^{(k)}\boldsymbol{\gamma}(t,\bar{t})\,\bar{z}_k \\ &\quad + i\boldsymbol{\delta}(t,\bar{t}) \cdot \left(\mathbf{b}^{(z)} + \mathfrak{B}^{(zz)}\bar{\mathbf{z}}\right) + b = 0. \end{aligned} \tag{7.14}$$

Thus, the system of ODEs for $\alpha, \boldsymbol{\delta}$ can be written as follows:

$$\begin{aligned} &\alpha_{\bar{t}}(t,\bar{t}) + \boldsymbol{\gamma}(t,\bar{t}) \cdot \mathfrak{A}^{(0)}(t,\bar{t})\,\boldsymbol{\gamma}(t,\bar{t}) + i\boldsymbol{\delta}(t,\bar{t}) \cdot \hat{\mathbf{b}}^{(z)}(t,\bar{t}) + b(t,\bar{t}) = 0, \\ &\quad \alpha(t,t) = 0, \\ &i\delta_{i,\bar{t}}(t,\bar{t}) + \boldsymbol{\gamma}(t,\bar{t}) \cdot \mathfrak{A}^{(i)}\boldsymbol{\gamma}(t,\bar{t}) + i\mathfrak{B}^{(zz)}_{ij}\delta_j(t,\bar{t}) = 0, \quad \delta_i(t,t) = m_i. \end{aligned} \tag{7.15}$$

7.2 Killed Non-Gaussian Processes

The non-Gaussian governing SDE has the following form:

$$d\hat{\mathbf{z}}_t = (\mathbf{b} + \mathfrak{B}\hat{\mathbf{z}}_t)\,dt + \boldsymbol{\Sigma}\left(\mathrm{diag}\left(\mathbf{d}^{(0)} + \mathfrak{D}\hat{\mathbf{z}}_t\right)\right)^{1/2} d\hat{\mathbf{W}}_t, \tag{7.16}$$

where $\hat{\mathbf{z}}_t$, $\mathbf{b}$, $\mathbf{d}^{(0)}$ are $(M \times 1)$ vectors, and $\boldsymbol{\Sigma}$, $\mathfrak{B}$, $\mathfrak{D}$ are the $(M \times M)$ matrices defined previously. As before, the correlation matrix Σ can be a full-rank (non-degenerate) matrix. Once again, it is assumed that the process is killed with intensity $\bar{c}$ linearly depending on $\mathbf{z}$, namely,

$$\bar{c} = c + \mathbf{c} \cdot \mathbf{z}, \tag{7.17}$$

where c is a scalar, and $\mathbf{c}^{(z)}$ is an $(M \times 1)$ column vector.

The corresponding Fokker–Plank problem has the following form:

$$\begin{aligned} &\varpi_{\bar{t}}(t,\mathbf{z},\bar{t},\bar{\mathbf{z}}) - \sum\sum\left(\mathfrak{A}^0 + \bar{z}_i\mathfrak{A}^i\right)\varpi_{\bar{\mathbf{z}}\bar{\mathbf{z}}}(t,\mathbf{z},\bar{t},\bar{\mathbf{z}}) \\ &\quad + \left(\hat{\mathbf{b}} + \mathfrak{B}\bar{\mathbf{z}}\right) \cdot \varpi_{\bar{\mathbf{z}}}(t,\mathbf{z},\bar{t},\bar{\mathbf{z}}) + (b + c + \mathbf{c} \cdot \bar{\mathbf{z}})\,\varpi(t,\mathbf{z},\bar{t},\bar{\mathbf{z}}) = 0, \\ &\varpi(t,\mathbf{z},t,\bar{\mathbf{z}}) = \delta(\bar{\mathbf{z}} - \mathbf{z}). \end{aligned} \tag{7.18}$$

The equations for $\alpha, \boldsymbol{\delta}$ generalize the equations in (7.10). They can be written in the following form:

$$\begin{aligned} &\alpha_{\bar{t}}(t,\bar{t}) + \boldsymbol{\delta}(t,\bar{t}) \cdot \mathfrak{A}^{(0)}(t,\bar{t})\,\boldsymbol{\delta}(t,\bar{t}) + i\boldsymbol{\delta}(t,\bar{t}) \cdot \mathbf{b}(t,\bar{t}) + b(t,\bar{t}) + c(t,\bar{t}) = 0, \\ &\quad \alpha(t,t) = 0, \\ &i\delta'_i(t,\bar{t}) + \boldsymbol{\delta}(t,\bar{t}) \cdot \mathfrak{A}^{(i)}\boldsymbol{\delta}(t,\bar{t}) + i\mathfrak{B}_{ij}\delta_j(t,\bar{t}) + c_i = 0, \quad \delta_i(t,t) = m_i. \end{aligned} \tag{7.19}$$

As in the case without killing, finding an analytical solution to a multidimensional Riccati equation is generally impossible. However, in the time-independent one-dimensional case, it can be done. Solution becomes particularly simple in the special case when $\mathfrak{A}^{(0)} = 0$. The most important case is the killed one-dimensional Feller process, used, for example, to price bonds in the Cox–Ingersoll–Ross (CIR) model; see Section 8.

7.3 Example: Anomalous Kolmogorov Process

Anomalous diffusion is a phenomenon in which the random motion of particles or molecules deviates from the classical Brownian motion and, as a result, exhibits non-Gaussian probability distributions, such as power-law or exponential tails. One can distinguish between subdiffusions (slower spreading) and superdiffusions (faster spreading). Anomalous diffusion often involves long-range correlations in particle motion, meaning that the movement of a particle at a one-time step depends on its previous positions over longer time scales. Anomalous diffusion frequently displays scale-invariant properties, meaning that the statistical properties of motion remain the same across different time or spatial scales. Anomalous diffusion has applications in physics, chemistry, financial engineering, biology, and geophysics.

Fractional Brownian motion (fBm) is used to model anomalous diffusion because it possesses several relevant characteristics. In particular, it exhibits long memory, which means that the process's future values are influenced by its past values over long time scales. Additionally, fBm can produce non-Gaussian behavior while preserving scale-invariance. By adjusting the Hurst exponent and other parameters, fBm can be tailored to model different anomalous diffusions, including both subdiffusions and superdiffusions.

This section studies a fractional Kolmogorov equation of the following form:

$$\begin{aligned}
&\varpi_{\bar{t}}\left(t,x,y,\bar{t},\bar{x},\bar{y}\right) + a\left(-\frac{\partial^2}{\partial\bar{y}^2}\right)^{\nu} \varpi\left(t,x,y,\bar{t},\bar{x},\bar{y}\right) \\
&\quad + \bar{y}\varpi_{\bar{x}}\left(t,x,y,\bar{t},\bar{x},\bar{y}\right) + b\varpi_{\bar{y}}\left(t,x,y,\bar{t},\bar{x},\bar{y}\right) = 0, \qquad (7.20)\\
&\varpi\left(t,\bar{x},\bar{y},t,x,y\right) = \delta\left(\bar{x}-x\right)\delta\left(\bar{y}-y\right),
\end{aligned}$$

where $0 < \nu < 1$. The pseudo-differential operator $\left(-\partial^2/\partial\bar{y}^2\right)^{\nu}$ is defined as follows:

$$\left(-\frac{\partial^2}{\partial\bar{y}^2}\right)^{\nu}\varpi = \mathcal{F}^{-1}\left(|l|^{2\nu}\mathcal{F}\left(\varpi\right)\right). \qquad (7.21)$$

Here $\mathcal{F}$ and $\mathcal{F}^{-1}$ denote the direct and inverse Fourier transforms, respectively. Despite its complexity, problem (7.20) can be solved by using Kelvin waves.

For particular solutions of the form (3.38), (3.39), and (3.40), the corresponding characteristic equations are

$$\alpha_{\bar{t}}\left(t,\bar{t}\right) + a\left|\gamma\right|^{2\nu}\left(t,\bar{t}\right) + i\gamma_{\bar{t}}\left(t,\bar{t}\right)\bar{y} + ik\bar{y} + ib\gamma\left(t,\bar{t}\right) = 0,$$
$$\alpha\left(t,t\right) = 0, \quad \gamma\left(t,t\right) = l, \tag{7.22}$$

so that

$$\alpha_{\bar{t}}\left(t,\bar{t}\right) + a\left|\gamma\right|^{2\nu}\left(t,\bar{t}\right) + ib\gamma\left(t,\bar{t}\right) = 0, \quad \alpha\left(t,t\right) = 0,$$
$$\gamma_{\bar{t}}\left(t,\bar{t}\right) + k = 0, \quad \gamma\left(t,t\right) = l, \tag{7.23}$$

$$\gamma\left(t,\bar{t}\right) = -kT + l,$$
$$\alpha\left(t,\bar{t}\right) = -a\int_{t}^{\bar{t}}\left|-k\left(s-t\right)+l\right|^{2\nu}ds - ib\left(-\frac{kT^2}{2} + lT\right). \tag{7.24}$$

Thus,

$$\begin{aligned}\Psi &= \alpha + ik\left(\bar{x}-x\right) + i\gamma\bar{y} - ily \\ &= -a\int_{t}^{\bar{t}}\left|-k\left(s-t\right)+l\right|^{2\nu}ds \\ &\quad + ik\left(\bar{x} - x - \bar{y}T + \frac{bT^2}{2}\right) + il\left(\bar{y} - y - bT\right).\end{aligned} \tag{7.25}$$

Now, assume that $\nu = 1/2$. The key is to calculate the integral

$$\mathcal{I} = \int_{t}^{\bar{t}}\left|-k\left(s-t\right)+l\right|^{2\nu}ds = \int_{0}^{T}\left|-ks+l\right|ds, \tag{7.26}$$

for different values of (k,l). Depending on (k,l), this integral can be calculated as follows:

$$\mathcal{I}_1 = \int_{0}^{l/k}\left(-ks+l\right)ds + \int_{l/k}^{T}\left(ks-l\right)ds = \frac{kT^2}{2} - lT + \frac{l^2}{k}, \quad 0 \le k < \infty,$$
$$0 \le l \le kT,$$

$$\mathcal{I}_2 = -\frac{kT^2}{2} + lT, \quad 0 \le k < \infty, \quad kT \le l < \infty,$$

$$\mathcal{I}_3 = -\frac{kT^2}{2} + lT, \quad -\infty < k \le 0, \quad 0 \le l < \infty,$$

$$\mathcal{I}_4 = \int_{0}^{l/k}\left(ks-l\right)ds + \int_{l/k}^{T}\left(-ks+l\right)ds = -\frac{kT^2}{2} + lT - \frac{l^2}{k}, \quad -\infty < k \le 0,$$
$$kT \le l \le 0,$$

$$\mathcal{I}_5 = \frac{kT^2}{2} - lT, \ -\infty < k \le 0, \ \ -\infty < l \le kT,$$
$$\mathcal{I}_6 = \frac{kT^2}{2} - lT, \ 0 \le k < \infty, \ \ -\infty < l \le 0. \tag{7.27}$$

Thus,

$$\begin{aligned}(2\pi)^2 \mathcal{J}_1 &= \int_0^\infty \int_0^{kT} \exp\left(-a\left(\frac{kT^2}{2} - lT + \frac{l^2}{k}\right) + ikaT^2\zeta + ilaT\eta\right) dkdl \\ &= T\int_0^1 \int_0^\infty \exp\left(\left(-p + iq\right)k\right) kd\chi dk = -T\int_0^1 \frac{\partial}{\partial p}\left(\int_0^\infty \exp\left(\left(-p + iq\right)k\right) dk\right) d\chi \\ &= T\int_0^1 \frac{d\chi}{(p - iq)^2} = \frac{1}{a^2T^3}\int_0^T \frac{d\chi}{\left((\chi - f_+)(\chi - f_-)\right)^2},\end{aligned} \tag{7.28}$$

where (ζ, η) are nondimensional variables:

$$\zeta = \frac{\bar{x} - x - \bar{y}T + \frac{bT^2}{2}}{aT^2}, \quad \eta = \frac{\bar{y} - y - bT}{aT}, \tag{7.29}$$

$$l = T\chi k, \ \ p(\chi) = aT^2\left(\frac{1}{2} - \chi + \chi^2\right) > 0, \ \ q(\chi) = aT^2(\zeta + \chi\eta), \tag{7.30}$$

and $f_\pm$ are roots of the quadratic equation

$$\chi^2 - (1 + i\eta)\chi + \left(\frac{1}{2} - i\zeta\right) = 0. \tag{7.31}$$

One can check that

$$\begin{aligned}f_\pm &= \frac{(1 + i\eta) \pm \sqrt{(1 + i\eta)^2 - 2 + 4i\zeta}}{2} = \frac{(1 + i\eta) \pm i\sqrt{D}}{2}, \\ f_+f_- &= \frac{1}{2} - i\zeta, \ \ f_+ + f_- = 1 + i\eta, \ \ f_+ - f_- = i\sqrt{D},\end{aligned} \tag{7.32}$$

with

$$D = 1 + \eta^2 - 4i\zeta - 2i\eta. \tag{7.33}$$

The roots $f_\pm$ are never equal, since D does not vanish when ζ, η are real.

Thus, one has

$$\begin{aligned}(2\pi)^2 \mathcal{J}_1 &= \frac{1}{a^2T^3}\int_0^1 \frac{d\chi}{\left((\chi - f_+)(\chi - f_-)\right)^2} \\ &= \frac{1}{a^2T^3(f_+ - f_-)^2}\int_0^1 \left(\frac{1}{\chi - f_+} - \frac{1}{\chi - f_-}\right)^2 d\chi\end{aligned}$$

$$= -\frac{1}{a^2T^3(f_+ - f_-)^2}\left(\left(\left(\frac{1}{1-f_+} + \frac{1}{f_+}\right) + \left(\frac{1}{1-f_-} + \frac{1}{f_-}\right)\right)\right.$$
$$\left. + \frac{2}{(f_+ - f_-)}\ln\left(\frac{f_-(1-f_+)}{f_+(1-f_-)}\right)\right)$$
$$= \frac{1}{a^2T^3D}\left(\frac{4(D + 2i\zeta + i\eta)}{(1-2i\zeta)(1-2i\zeta-2i\eta)} - \frac{2i}{\sqrt{D}}\ln\left(\frac{2\zeta + \eta - \sqrt{D}}{2\zeta + \eta + \sqrt{D}}\right)\right). \tag{7.34}$$

By symmetry,

$$\mathcal{J}_4(\zeta,\eta) = \mathcal{J}_1(-\zeta,-\eta) = \overline{\mathcal{J}_1(\zeta,\eta)}. \tag{7.35}$$

Next,

$$(2\pi)^2\,\mathcal{J}_2 = \int_0^\infty\int_{kT}^\infty \exp\left(-a\left(-\frac{kT^2}{2} + lT\right) + ikaT^2\zeta + ilaT\eta\right)dkdl$$
$$= \frac{1}{aT(1-i\eta)}\int_0^\infty \exp\left(-\frac{kaT^2}{2} + ikaT^2(\zeta+\eta)\right)dk \tag{7.36}$$
$$= \frac{1}{a^2T^3((1-i\eta))\left(\frac{1}{2} - i(\zeta+\eta)\right)}.$$

Similarly, it is easy to show that

$$(2\pi)^2\,\mathcal{J}_3 = \int_{-\infty}^0\int_0^\infty \exp\left(-a\left(-\frac{kT^2}{2} + lT\right) + ikaT^2\zeta + ilaT\eta\right)dkdl$$
$$= \frac{1}{a^2T^3(1-i\eta)\left(\frac{1}{2} + i\zeta\right)}, \tag{7.37}$$

while, by symmetry, one gets

$$\mathcal{J}_5(\zeta,\eta) = \frac{1}{(2\pi)^2 a^2T^3(1+i\eta)\left(\frac{1}{2} + i(\zeta+\eta)\right)} = \overline{\mathcal{J}_2(\zeta,\eta)},$$
$$\mathcal{J}_6(\zeta,\eta) = \frac{1}{(2\pi)^2 a^2T^3(1+i\eta)\left(\frac{1}{2} - i\zeta\right)} = \overline{\mathcal{J}_3(\zeta,\eta)}, \tag{7.38}$$

so that

$$\varpi = \frac{1}{\pi^2 a^2 T^3}\left(\frac{1}{(1+\eta^2)}\left(\frac{(1-2\eta(\zeta+\eta))}{\left(1+4(\zeta+\eta)^2\right)}+\frac{(1+2\eta\zeta)}{(1+4\zeta^2)}\right)\right.$$
$$\left.+\mathrm{Re}\left\{\frac{1}{D}\left(\frac{2(D+2i\zeta+i\eta)}{\left(D-(2\zeta+\eta)^2\right)}-\frac{i}{\sqrt{D}}\ln\left(\frac{2\zeta+\eta-\sqrt{D}}{2\zeta+\eta+\sqrt{D}}\right)\right)\right\}\right), \tag{7.39}$$

and

$$\varpi(\bar{x},\bar{y})\,d\bar{x}d\bar{y} = \frac{1}{\pi^2 a^2}\left(\frac{1}{(1+\eta^2)}\left(\frac{(1-2\eta(\zeta+\eta))}{\left(1+4(\zeta+\eta)^2\right)}+\frac{(1+2\eta\zeta)}{(1+4\zeta^2)}\right)\right.$$
$$\left.+\mathrm{Re}\left\{\frac{1}{D}\left(\frac{2(D+2i\zeta+i\eta)}{\left(D-(2\zeta+\eta)^2\right)}-\frac{i}{\sqrt{D}}\ln\left(\frac{2\zeta+\eta-\sqrt{D}}{2\zeta+\eta+\sqrt{D}}\right)\right)\right\}\right)d\zeta d\eta \tag{7.40}$$
$$\equiv \varpi(\zeta,\eta)\,d\zeta d\eta,$$

which shows that, as expected, in the nondimensional variables there is no explicit dependence on T.[7]

A typical anomalous Kolmogorov process is depicted in Figure 9. The difference between the anomalous diffusion shown in Figure 9 and the pure diffusion shown in Figure 6 is clear.

---

[7] In a special case $a = 1$, $b = 0$, $\xi = 0$, $\theta = 0$, He *et al.* (2021) attempted to solve the problem considered previously. However, the authors made a severe error in transitioning from (2.2) to (2.3). In contrast to Kolmogorov's minor error, their error cannot be repaired. Dimensional analysis shows that the proposed solution is completely incorrect. In our notation, it has the following form:

$$\varpi(\bar{x},\bar{y})\,d\bar{x}d\bar{y} = \frac{72\sqrt{3}}{\pi^3 T^6\left(1+4\left(\frac{\bar{y}^2}{4T}+\frac{3(\bar{x}+\bar{y}T/2)^2}{T^3}\right)\right)^{7/2}}d\bar{x}d\bar{y}.$$

Introducing rescaled variables, $\zeta = \bar{x}T^{-3/2}$, $\eta = \bar{y}T^{-1/2}$, we get

$$\varpi(\zeta,\eta)\,d\zeta d\eta = \frac{72\sqrt{3}}{\pi^3 T^4\left(1+4\left(\frac{\eta^2}{4}+3\left(\zeta+\frac{\eta}{2}\right)^2\right)\right)^{7/2}}d\zeta d\eta.$$

This expression explicitly depends on T, which is impossible, since its integral must be equal to unity.

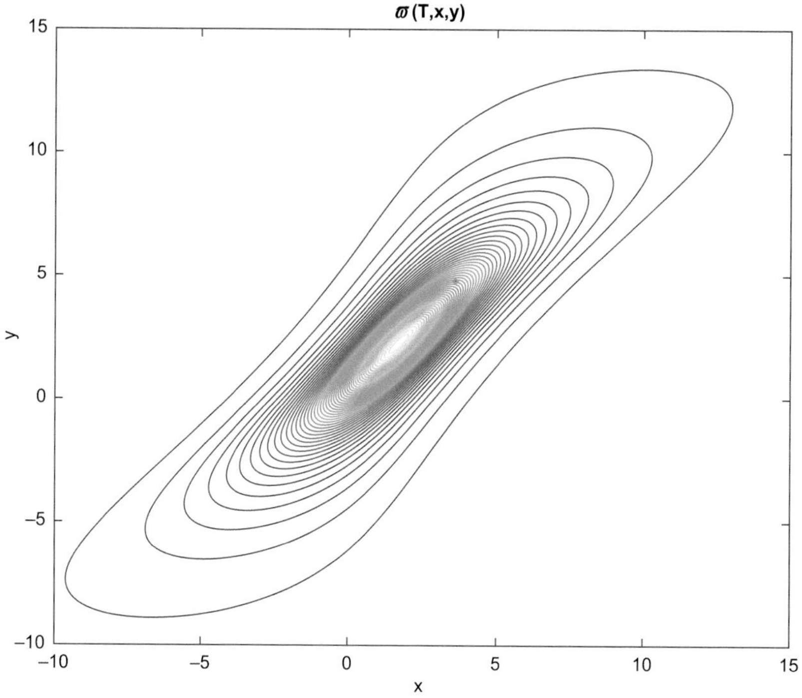

Figure 9 Contour lines of $\varpi(0,0,0,T,\tilde{x},\tilde{y})$ for an anomalous Kolmogorov process with $T = 1.5$, $a = 2.5$, $b = 1.5$. Author's graphics.

It is worth comparing Equations (7.39) and (3.28). To this end, rewrite Φ given by (3.29) in the following form:

$$\Phi = \frac{(\bar{y} - y - bT)^2}{2aT} + \frac{6\left(\bar{x} - x - \frac{(\bar{y}+y)T}{2}\right)^2}{aT^3} = \frac{\eta^2}{2} + \frac{3(2\zeta + \eta)^2}{2}, \tag{7.41}$$

where ζ, η are nondimensional variables of the form:

$$\zeta = \frac{\bar{x} - x - \bar{y}T + \frac{bT^2}{2}}{\sqrt{aT^3}}, \quad \eta = \frac{\bar{y} - y - bT}{\sqrt{aT}}, \tag{7.42}$$

and a is the diffusion coefficient; its dimension is $[a] = L^2/T^3$. Thus,

$$\varpi = \frac{\sqrt{3}}{\pi a T^2} \exp\left(-\frac{\eta^2 + 3(2\zeta + \eta)^2}{2}\right), \tag{7.43}$$

and

$$\varpi(\bar{x}, \bar{y})\, d\bar{x} d\bar{y} = \frac{\sqrt{3}}{\pi a} \exp\left(-\frac{\eta^2 + 3(2\zeta + \eta)^2}{2}\right) d\zeta d\eta \equiv \varpi(\zeta, \eta)\, d\zeta d\eta. \tag{7.44}$$

Comparing Equations (7.39) and (7.43), one can see that the scaling of ϖ and its asymptotic behavior at infinity is completely different.

7.4 Example: Feller Process

7.4.1 Feller Process

Feller Process with Constant Parameters For benchmarking purposes, it is useful to start with deriving the well-known t.p.d.f. for the Feller process with constant coefficients; see Feller (1951, 1952):

$$d\hat{y}_t = (\chi - \kappa\hat{y}_t)\,dt + \varepsilon\sqrt{\hat{y}_t}d\hat{Z}_t, \quad \hat{y}_t = y. \tag{7.45}$$

Initially, the process with time-independent parameters is considered; the time-dependent case is analyzed later in this section.

To start with, it is assumed that

$$\frac{2\chi}{\varepsilon^2} - 1 \equiv \vartheta > 0. \tag{7.46}$$

This condition guarantees that the process $\hat{y}_t$ does not hit zero, which is one of the main reasons to use the Feller process in practice; it is relaxed shortly.

The corresponding Fokker–Planck problem has the form:

$$\begin{aligned} &\varpi_{\bar{t}} - \frac{1}{2}\varepsilon^2 \left(\bar{y}\varpi\right)_{\bar{y}\bar{y}} + \left(\left(\chi - \kappa\bar{y}\right)\varpi\right)_{\bar{y}} = 0, \\ &\varpi\left(t, y, t, \bar{y}\right) = \delta\left(\bar{y} - y\right). \end{aligned} \tag{7.47}$$

This equation can be written as a conservation law:

$$\begin{aligned} &\varpi_{\bar{t}} + \mathcal{F}_{\bar{y}} = 0, \\ &\varpi\left(t, y, t, \bar{y}\right) = \delta\left(\bar{y} - y\right), \end{aligned} \tag{7.48}$$

where the probability flux $\mathcal{F}$ is given by

$$\mathcal{F} = -\frac{1}{2}\varepsilon^2 \left(\bar{y}\varpi\right)_{\bar{y}} + \left(\chi - \kappa\bar{y}\right)\varpi. \tag{7.49}$$

However, experience suggests that solving the backward Kolmogorov problem is more expedient. It can be formulated as follows:

$$\begin{aligned} &\varpi_t + \frac{1}{2}\varepsilon^2 y\varpi_{yy} + \left(\chi - \kappa y\right)\varpi_y = 0, \\ &\varpi\left(\bar{t}, y, \bar{t}, \bar{y}\right) = \delta\left(y - \bar{y}\right). \end{aligned} \tag{7.50}$$

The associated Kelvin wave function $\mathcal{K}\left(t, y, \bar{t}, \bar{y}, l\right)$ has the following form:

$$\mathcal{K} = \exp\left(\alpha\left(t, \bar{t}\right) + i\gamma\left(t, \bar{t}\right)y - il\bar{y}\right), \tag{7.51}$$

where α, γ solve the following system of backward ODEs:

$$\begin{aligned} &\alpha_t\left(t,\bar{t}\right) + \chi i\gamma\left(t,\bar{t}\right) = 0, \quad \alpha\left(\bar{t},\bar{t}\right) = 0, \\ &i\gamma_{\bar{t}}\left(t,\bar{t}\right) - \frac{1}{2}\varepsilon^2\gamma^2\left(t,\bar{t}\right) - \kappa i\gamma\left(t,\bar{t}\right) = 0, \quad \gamma\left(\bar{t},\bar{t}\right) = l. \end{aligned} \tag{7.52}$$

Thus, γ solves a nonlinear Riccati equation, which can be linearized via the standard substitution

$$\gamma\left(t,\bar{t}\right) = -\frac{2i\Omega'\left(t,\bar{t}\right)}{\varepsilon^2\Omega\left(t,\bar{t}\right)}. \tag{7.53}$$

As a result, one gets the following equations:

$$\Omega_{tt}\left(t,\bar{t}\right) - \kappa\Omega_t\left(t,\bar{t}\right) = 0, \quad \Omega\left(\bar{t},\bar{t}\right) = 1, \quad \Omega'\left(\bar{t},\bar{t}\right) = \frac{i\varepsilon^2 l}{2}, \tag{7.54}$$

$$\alpha_t\left(t,\bar{t}\right) + \frac{2\chi}{\varepsilon^2}\left(\ln\left(\Omega\left(t,\bar{t}\right)\right)\right)_t = 0, \quad \alpha\left(\bar{t},\bar{t}\right) = 0. \tag{7.55}$$

Accordingly,

$$\Omega\left(t,\bar{t}\right) = 1 - \frac{\varepsilon^2}{2}\mathsf{B}_\kappa\left(T\right)il, \tag{7.56}$$

$$\Omega'\left(t,\bar{t}\right) = \frac{\varepsilon^2}{2}\mathsf{A}_\kappa\left(T\right)il, \tag{7.57}$$

$$\gamma\left(t,\bar{t}\right) = \frac{\mathsf{A}_\kappa\left(T\right)l}{\left(1 - \frac{\varepsilon^2}{2}\mathsf{B}_\kappa\left(T\right)il\right)}, \tag{7.58}$$

$$\alpha\left(t,\bar{t}\right) = -\left(\vartheta + 1\right)\ln\left(1 - \frac{\varepsilon^2}{2}\mathsf{B}_\kappa\left(T\right)il\right), \tag{7.59}$$

and

$$\mathcal{K} = \exp\left(-\left(\vartheta + 1\right)\ln\left(1 - \frac{\varepsilon^2}{2}\mathsf{B}_\kappa\left(T\right)il\right) + \left(\frac{\frac{\varepsilon^2}{2}\mathsf{A}_\kappa\left(T\right)}{\left(1 - \frac{\varepsilon^2}{2}\mathsf{B}_\kappa\left(T\right)il\right)}y - \bar{y}\right)il\right). \tag{7.60}$$

To analyze the problem further, it is helpful to define

$$M = \frac{2}{\varepsilon^2\mathsf{B}_\kappa\left(T\right)}, \tag{7.61}$$

introduce a new variable, $l \to \hat{l}$:

$$\hat{l} = \frac{l}{2M}, \quad l = 2M\hat{l}, \tag{7.62}$$

and rescale $\mathcal{K}$, $\mathcal{K}dl \to \hat{\mathcal{K}}d\hat{l}$:

$$\hat{\mathcal{K}} = 2M\exp\left(-M\left(Y+\bar{y}\right)\right) \times \exp\left(-\left(\vartheta+1\right)\ln\left(1-2i\hat{l}\right)+M\left(\frac{Y}{1-2i\hat{l}}+\bar{y}\left(1-2i\hat{l}\right)\right)\right), \tag{7.63}$$

where M appears due to the change of variables, and

$$Y = e^{-\kappa T}y. \tag{7.64}$$

Finally,

$$\varpi\left(t,y,\bar{t},\bar{y}\right) = \frac{M}{\pi}e^{-M(\bar{y}+Y)}\int_{-\infty}^{\infty} e^{-(\vartheta+1)\ln\left(1-2i\hat{l}\right)+M\left(\frac{Y}{1-2i\hat{l}}+\bar{y}\left(1-2i\hat{l}\right)\right)}d\hat{l}. \tag{7.65}$$

Equation (7.65) allows us to understand the true meaning of condition (7.46). When this condition is satisfied, the corresponding integral converges absolutely when $\hat{l} \to \pm\infty$. A well-known formula yields

$$\varpi^{(\vartheta)}\left(t,y,\bar{t},\bar{y}\right) = Me^{-M(\bar{y}+Y)}\left(\frac{\bar{y}}{Y}\right)^{\vartheta/2} I_{\vartheta}\left(2M\sqrt{\bar{y}Y}\right). \tag{7.66}$$

See, for example, Lipton (2001) and references therein. The probability flux $\mathcal{F}$ has the form

$$\begin{aligned}\mathcal{F}^{(\vartheta)}\left(t,y,\bar{t},\bar{y}\right) &= -\frac{1}{2}\varepsilon^2\left(\bar{y}\varpi^{(\vartheta)}\left(t,y,\bar{t},\bar{y}\right)\right)_{\bar{y}} + \left(\chi-\kappa\bar{y}\right)\varpi^{(\vartheta)}\left(t,y,\bar{t},\bar{y}\right) \\ &= -\frac{1}{2}\varepsilon^2 MY\varpi^{(\vartheta+1)}\left(t,y,\bar{t},\bar{y}\right) + \left(\frac{1}{2}\varepsilon^2-\frac{\kappa}{M}\right)M\bar{y}\varpi^{(\vartheta)}\left(t,y,\bar{t},\bar{y}\right).\end{aligned} \tag{7.67}$$

It is important to note that the density $\varpi\left(\bar{y}\right)$ integrates to one:

$$\int_0^{\infty}\varpi\left(t,y,\bar{t},\bar{y}\right)d\bar{y} = \int_0^{\infty}e^{-u-v}\left(\frac{v}{u}\right)^{\vartheta/2} I_{\vartheta}\left(2\sqrt{uv}\right)dv = 1, \tag{7.68}$$

where $u = MY$, $v = M\bar{y}$. This fact is used in the following discussion.

Using the asymptotic expansion of the modified Bessel function, one can show that $\varpi^{(\vartheta)}$ and $\mathcal{F}$ vanish on the boundary, since

$$\begin{aligned}\varpi^{(\vartheta)}\left(t,y,\bar{t},\bar{y}\right) &= \frac{Me^{-MY}}{\Gamma\left(\vartheta+1\right)}\left(M\bar{y}\right)^{\vartheta}\left(1+O\left(\bar{y}\right)\right), \\ \mathcal{F}^{(\vartheta)}\left(t,y,\bar{t},\bar{y}\right) &= \left(\frac{\varepsilon^2}{2}\left(1-\frac{MY}{\left(\vartheta+1\right)}\right)-\frac{\kappa}{M}\right)Me^{-MY}\frac{\left(M\bar{y}\right)^{(\vartheta+1)}}{\Gamma\left(\vartheta+1\right)}\left(1+O\left(\bar{y}\right)\right).\end{aligned} \tag{7.69}$$

Now assume that condition (7.46) is violated, so that $-1 < \vartheta < 0$. In this case, the integral in (7.65) is no longer absolutely convergent, so one needs to regularize it. There are two ways of regularizing the corresponding integral:

(I) integration by parts, (II) change of variables. Not surprisingly, they produce different results.

Start with integration by parts and write

$$
\begin{aligned}
Int_\vartheta &\equiv \frac{1}{\pi}\int_{-\infty}^{\infty} e^{-(\vartheta+1)\ln\left(1-2i\hat{l}\right)+\frac{MY}{1-2i\hat{l}}} d\left(\frac{e^{M\bar{y}\left(1-2i\hat{l}\right)}}{-2iM\bar{y}}\right) \\
&= \frac{1}{\pi}\frac{(\vartheta+1)}{M\bar{y}}\int_{-\infty}^{\infty} e^{-(\vartheta+2)\ln\left(1-2i\hat{l}\right)+M\left(\frac{Y}{1-2i\hat{l}}+\bar{y}\left(1-2i\hat{l}\right)\right)} d\hat{l} \\
&+ \frac{1}{\pi}\frac{Y}{\bar{y}}\int_{-\infty}^{\infty} e^{-(\vartheta+3)\ln\left(1-2i\hat{l}\right)+M\left(\frac{Y}{1-2i\hat{l}}+\bar{y}\left(1-2i\hat{l}\right)\right)} d\hat{l},
\end{aligned}
\tag{7.70}
$$

where the integrals are absolutely convergent. Thus, (7.66) yields

$$
Int_\vartheta = \left(\frac{\bar{y}}{Y}\right)^{\frac{\vartheta}{2}}\left(\frac{2(\vartheta+1)}{Z} I_{\vartheta+1}(Z) + I_{\vartheta+2}(Z)\right) = \left(\frac{\bar{y}}{Y}\right)^{\frac{\vartheta}{2}} I_\vartheta(Z), \tag{7.71}
$$

where $Z = 2M\sqrt{\bar{y}Y}$, and a well-known recurrent relation for the modified Bessel functions is used; Abramowitz and Stegun (1964), Eq. 9.6.26. Thus, Equations (7.66) and (7.67) hold for $-1 < \vartheta < 0$:

$$
\varpi^{(\vartheta,I)} = \varpi^{(\vartheta)}, \quad \mathcal{F}^{(\vartheta,I)} = \mathcal{F}^{(\vartheta)}. \tag{7.72}
$$

It is important to note that $\varpi^{(\vartheta,I)}(\bar{y}\to 0)\to\infty$ when $\vartheta < 0$ (the corresponding singularity is integrable), while $\varpi^{(\vartheta)}$ is bounded at $\bar{y} = 0$, when $\vartheta > 0$. While the t.p.d.f. itself blows up at the natural boundary $\bar{y} = 0$, the probability flux $\mathcal{F}^{(\vartheta,I)}$ vanishes on the boundary, so that the total probability of staying on the positive semiaxis is conserved.

Now, use change of variables to regularize Int_ϑ. Specifically, introduce $\tilde{l}$, such that

$$
1 - 2i\hat{l} = \frac{1}{1-2i\tilde{l}}, \tag{7.73}
$$

and formally write Int_ϑ as follows:

$$
\begin{aligned}
Int_\vartheta &= \frac{1}{\pi}\int_{-\infty}^{\infty} e^{-(-\vartheta+1)\ln\left(1-2i\tilde{l}\right)+MY\left(1-2i\tilde{l}\right)+\frac{M\bar{y}}{\left(1-2i\tilde{l}\right)}} d\tilde{l} \\
&= \left(\frac{Y}{\bar{y}}\right)^{-\frac{\vartheta}{2}} I_{-\vartheta}\left(2M\sqrt{\bar{y}Y}\right) = \left(\frac{\bar{y}}{Y}\right)^{\frac{\vartheta}{2}} I_{-\vartheta}\left(2M\sqrt{\bar{y}Y}\right).
\end{aligned}
\tag{7.74}
$$

Accordingly,

$$
\varpi^{(\vartheta,II)}\left(t,y,\bar{t},\bar{y}\right) = Me^{-M(\bar{y}+Y)}\left(\frac{\bar{y}}{Y}\right)^{\frac{\vartheta}{2}} I_{-\vartheta}\left(2M\sqrt{\bar{y}Y}\right). \tag{7.75}
$$

A straightforward calculation yields

$$\mathcal{F}^{(\vartheta,II)}\left(t,y,\bar{t},\bar{y}\right) = Me^{-M(\bar{y}+Y)}\left(\frac{\bar{y}}{Y}\right)^{\vartheta/2}\left(-\frac{1}{2}\varepsilon^2 M\sqrt{\bar{y}Y}I_{-\vartheta+1}\left(2M\sqrt{\bar{y}Y}\right)\right.$$
$$\left.+\left(\frac{1}{2}\varepsilon^2\vartheta+\left(\frac{1}{2}\varepsilon^2-\frac{\kappa}{M}\right)M\bar{y}\right)I_{-\vartheta}\left(2M\sqrt{\bar{y}Y}\right)\right). \tag{7.76}$$

It is easy to see that both $\varpi^{(\vartheta,II)}$ and $\mathcal{F}^{(\vartheta,II)}$ are bounded at $\bar{y} = 0$:

$$\begin{aligned}\varpi^{(\vartheta,II)}\left(t,y,\bar{t},\bar{y}\right) &= \frac{Me^{-MY}}{\Gamma(-\vartheta+1)(MY)^{\vartheta}}(1+O(\bar{y})),\\ \mathcal{F}^{(\vartheta,II)}\left(t,y,\bar{t},\bar{y}\right) &= \frac{\varepsilon^2\vartheta Me^{-MY}}{2\Gamma(-\vartheta+1)(MY)^{\vartheta}}(1+O(\bar{y})).\end{aligned} \tag{7.77}$$

Since there is a probability flux across the natural boundary $\bar{y} = 0$, the total probability on the positive semiaxis $[0,\infty)$ is less than one.

Representative t.p.d.fs for Feller processes with different values of ϑ are illustrated in Figure 10.

Feller Process with Time-Dependent Parameters Surprisingly, studying the Feller process with time-dependent coefficients is viewed as a difficult problem, which remains an active area of research; see, for example, Masoliver (2016), Giorno and Nobile (2021), and references therein. However, using Kelvin wave formalism allows one to find an expression for the t.p.d.f. in a very natural way.

For the process with time-dependent parameters, the problem of interest has the form:

$$\begin{aligned}&\varpi_t + \frac{1}{2}\varepsilon^2(t)\,y\varpi_{yy} + (\chi(t) - \kappa(t)\,y)\,\varpi_y = 0,\\ &\varpi\left(\bar{t},y\right) = \delta(y-\bar{y}).\end{aligned} \tag{7.78}$$

Here it is assumed that the following regularity condition is satisfied:

$$\vartheta(t) = \frac{2\chi(t)}{\varepsilon^2(t)} - 1 > 0. \tag{7.79}$$

This condition guarantees that the corresponding integrals converge at infinity.

As usual, ϖ can be written as a superposition of Kelvin waves of the form

$$\mathcal{K} = \exp\left(\alpha\left(t,\bar{t}\right) + i\gamma\left(t,\bar{t}\right)y - il\bar{y}\right), \tag{7.80}$$

where α,γ solve the following system of backward ODEs:

$$\begin{aligned}&\alpha_t\left(t,\bar{t}\right) + \chi\left(t,\bar{t}\right)i\gamma\left(t,\bar{t}\right) = 0, \quad \alpha\left(\bar{t},\bar{t}\right) = 0,\\ &i\gamma_{\bar{t}}\left(t,\bar{t}\right) - \frac{1}{2}\varepsilon^2(t)\,\gamma^2\left(t,\bar{t}\right) - \kappa(t)\,i\gamma\left(t,\bar{t}\right) = 0, \quad \gamma\left(\bar{t},\bar{t}\right) = l.\end{aligned} \tag{7.81}$$

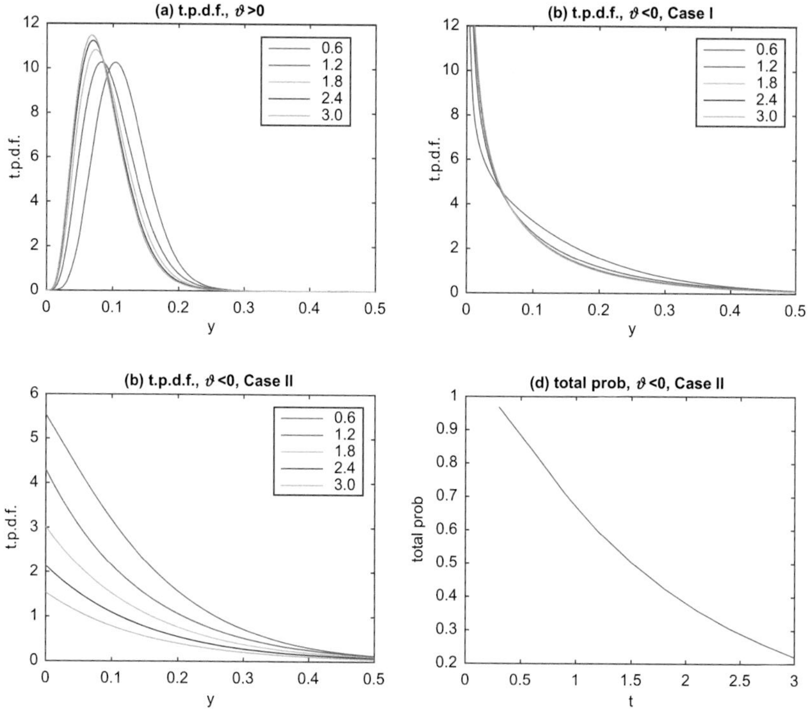

Figure 10 T.p.d.fs for three Feller processes with different parameters and regularity conditions. (a) $\chi = 0.1$, $\kappa = 1.2$, $\varepsilon = 0.2$, $y_0 = 0.15$, $\bar{t}_{max} = 3$; (b), (c) $\chi = 0.1$, $\kappa = 1.2$, $\varepsilon = 0.6$, $y_0 = 0.15$, $\bar{t}_{max} = 3$. For the first and second processes, the probability of $\bar{y} \geq 0$ is equal to one. For the third process, this probability, shown as a function of time in (d), is less than one. Author's graphics.

Introducing $\Omega\left(t, \bar{t}\right)$, such that

$$\gamma\left(t, \bar{t}\right) = -\frac{2i\Omega'\left(t, \bar{t}\right)}{\varepsilon^2(t)\,\Omega\left(t, \bar{t}\right)}, \tag{7.82}$$

one gets the following second-order equation for $\Omega\left(t, \bar{t}\right)$:

$$\Omega_{tt}\left(t, \bar{t}\right) - \left(\kappa + 2\ln\left(\varepsilon\right)'\right)\Omega_t\left(t, \bar{t}\right) = 0, \quad \Omega\left(\bar{t}, \bar{t}\right) = 1, \quad \Omega'\left(\bar{t}, \bar{t}\right) = \frac{\varepsilon^2\left(\bar{t}\right)}{2} il. \tag{7.83}$$

Solving this equation, one gets

$$\begin{aligned} \Omega\left(t, \bar{t}\right) &= 1 - \frac{\varepsilon^2(t)}{2}\bar{\mathsf{B}}_\kappa\left(t, \bar{t}\right) il, \\ \Omega_t\left(t, \bar{t}\right) &= \frac{\varepsilon^2(t)}{2}\left(\mathsf{A}_\kappa\left(t, \bar{t}\right) - \frac{2\varepsilon'(t)}{\varepsilon(t)}\bar{\mathsf{B}}_\kappa\left(t, \bar{t}\right)\right) il. \end{aligned} \tag{7.84}$$

Accordingly,

$$\gamma\left(t,\bar{t}\right)=\frac{\left(\mathsf{A}_{\kappa}\left(t,\bar{t}\right)-\frac{2\varepsilon'(t)}{\varepsilon(t)}\bar{\mathsf{B}}_{\kappa}\left(t,\bar{t}\right)\right)l}{\left(1-\frac{\varepsilon^{2}(t)}{2}\bar{\mathsf{B}}_{\kappa}\left(t,\bar{t}\right)il\right)},\tag{7.85}$$

$$\alpha\left(t,\bar{t}\right)=-\frac{2\chi\left(t\right)}{\varepsilon^{2}\left(t\right)}\ln\left(1-\frac{\varepsilon^{2}\left(t\right)}{2}\bar{\mathsf{B}}_{\kappa}\left(t,\bar{t}\right)il\right)$$

$$-\int_{t}^{\bar{t}}\left(\frac{2\chi\left(s\right)}{\varepsilon^{2}\left(s\right)}\right)'\ln\left(1-\frac{\varepsilon^{2}\left(s\right)}{2}\bar{\mathsf{B}}_{\kappa}\left(s,\bar{t}\right)il\right)ds.\tag{7.86}$$

Thus, the Kelvin wave becomes

$$\mathcal{K}=\exp\left(-\frac{2\chi\left(t\right)}{\varepsilon^{2}\left(t\right)}\ln\left(1-\frac{\varepsilon^{2}\left(t\right)}{2}\bar{\mathsf{B}}_{\kappa}\left(t,\bar{t}\right)il\right)\right.$$

$$-\int_{t}^{\bar{t}}\left(\frac{2\chi\left(s\right)}{\varepsilon^{2}\left(s\right)}\right)'\ln\left(1-\frac{\varepsilon^{2}\left(s\right)}{2}\bar{\mathsf{B}}_{\kappa}\left(s,\bar{t}\right)il\right)ds$$

$$\left.+\left(\frac{\left(\mathsf{A}_{\kappa}\left(t,\bar{t}\right)-\frac{2\varepsilon'(t)}{\varepsilon(t)}\bar{\mathsf{B}}_{\kappa}\left(t,\bar{t}\right)\right)}{\left(1-\frac{\varepsilon^{2}(t)}{2}\bar{\mathsf{B}}_{\kappa}\left(t,\bar{t}\right)il\right)}y-\bar{y}\right)il\right).\tag{7.87}$$

By analogy with (7.61), (7.62), and (7.63), define

$$M\left(t,\bar{t}\right)=\frac{2}{\varepsilon^{2}\left(t\right)\mathsf{B}_{\kappa}\left(t,\bar{t}\right)},\quad \hat{l}=\frac{l}{2M\left(t,\bar{t}\right)},\quad l=2M\left(t,\bar{t}\right)\hat{l}\tag{7.88}$$

and represent $\hat{\mathcal{K}}$ as follows:

$$\hat{\mathcal{K}}\left(t,y,\bar{t},\bar{y},\hat{l}\right)=2M\exp\left(-M\left(t,\bar{t}\right)\left(Y+\bar{y}\right)\right)\exp\left(-\frac{2\chi\left(t\right)}{\varepsilon^{2}\left(t\right)}\ln\left(1-2i\hat{l}\right)\right.$$

$$\left.-\int_{t}^{\bar{t}}\left(\frac{2\chi\left(s\right)}{\varepsilon^{2}\left(s\right)}\right)'\ln\left(1-\frac{M\left(t,\bar{t}\right)}{M\left(s,\bar{t}\right)}2i\hat{l}\right)ds+M\left(t,\bar{t}\right)\left(\frac{Y}{\left(1-2i\hat{l}\right)}+\bar{y}\left(1-2i\hat{l}\right)\right)\right),\tag{7.89}$$

where

$$Y=\left(\mathsf{A}_{\kappa}\left(t,\bar{t}\right)-\frac{4\varepsilon'\left(t\right)}{\varepsilon^{3}\left(t\right)M\left(t,\bar{t}\right)}\right)y.\tag{7.90}$$

Finally,

$$\varpi\left(t,y,\bar{t},\bar{y}\right)=\frac{1}{2\pi}\int_{-\infty}^{\infty}\hat{\mathcal{K}}\left(t,y,\bar{t},\bar{y},\hat{l}\right)d\hat{l}.\tag{7.91}$$

Therefore, finding $\varpi\left(t,y,\bar{t},\bar{y}\right)$ is reduced to solving some very simple ODEs and calculating a one-dimensional integral, which is theoretically appealing and numerically efficient.

Feller Process with Jumps Consider a jump-diffusion process $\hat{y}_t$ with constant coefficients governed by the following equation:

$$d\hat{y}_t = (\chi - \kappa\hat{y}_t)\,dt + \varepsilon\sqrt{\hat{y}_t}d\hat{Z}_t + Jd\hat{\Pi}_t, \quad \hat{y}_t = y, \tag{7.92}$$

where $\hat{Z}_t$ is a standard Wiener process, and $\hat{\Pi}_t$ is a Poisson process with intensity λ. To preserve tractability, it is assumed that jumps are positive and exponentially distributed with parameter ϕ; for additional insights, see Lipton and Shelton (2012).

The backward Kolmogorov problem can be written as

$$\begin{aligned}
&\varpi_t + \frac{1}{2}\varepsilon^2 y\varpi_{yy} + (\chi - \kappa y)\,\varpi_y + \lambda\left(\phi\int_0^\infty \varpi(t,y+J)e^{-\phi J}dJ - \varpi(t,y)\right) = 0,\\
&\varpi\left(\bar{t},y,\bar{t},\bar{y}\right) = \delta\left(y-\bar{y}\right).
\end{aligned} \tag{7.93}$$

The corresponding Kelvin wave has the familiar form:

$$\mathcal{K}\left(t,y,\bar{t},\bar{y},l\right) = \exp\left\{\alpha\left(t,\bar{t}\right) + i\gamma\left(t,\bar{t}\right)y - il\bar{y}\right\}, \tag{7.94}$$

where α, γ satisfy the following system of ODEs:

$$\begin{aligned}
&\alpha_t\left(t,\bar{t}\right) + \chi i\gamma\left(t,\bar{t}\right) + \frac{\lambda i\gamma\left(t,\bar{t}\right)}{\phi - i\gamma\left(t,\bar{t}\right)}, \quad \alpha\left(\bar{t},\bar{t}\right) = 0,\\
&i\gamma_{\bar{t}}\left(t,\bar{t}\right) - \frac{1}{2}\varepsilon^2\gamma^2\left(t,\bar{t}\right) - \kappa i\gamma\left(t,\bar{t}\right) = 0, \quad \gamma(\bar{t},\bar{t}) = l.
\end{aligned} \tag{7.95}$$

The expression for γ is given by (7.58), while α can be split as follows:

$$\alpha\left(t,\bar{t}\right) = \alpha_0\left(t,\bar{t}\right) + \lambda\alpha_1\left(t,\bar{t}\right). \tag{7.96}$$

In this setting, α_0 has the familiar form:

$$\alpha_0\left(t,\bar{t}\right) = -(\vartheta+1)\ln\left(1 - \frac{\varepsilon^2}{2}\bar{\mathsf{B}}_\kappa\left(T\right)il\right), \tag{7.97}$$

while α_1 can be represented as follows:

$$\begin{aligned}
\alpha_1\left(t,\bar{t}\right) &= \int_t^{\bar{t}} \frac{\mathsf{A}_\kappa\left(\bar{t}-s\right)il}{\phi - \left(\frac{\phi\varepsilon^2}{2}\bar{\mathsf{B}}_\kappa\left(\bar{t}-s\right) + \mathsf{A}_\kappa\left(\bar{t}-s\right)\right)il}ds\\
&= \frac{1}{\left(\kappa - \frac{\phi\varepsilon^2}{2}\right)}\ln\left(\frac{\phi - \left(\frac{\phi\varepsilon^2}{2}\bar{\mathsf{B}}_\kappa\left(T\right) + \mathsf{A}_\kappa\left(T\right)\right)il}{\phi - il}\right).
\end{aligned} \tag{7.98}$$

Thus, jumps do profoundly affect the dynamics of the underlying stochastic process.

7.4.2 Augmented Feller Process, I

This section studies the joint dynamics of a Feller process $\hat{y}_t$ and its integral $\hat{x}_t$. The corresponding combined process is described by the following equations:

$$d\hat{x}_t = \hat{y}_t dt, \quad \hat{x}_t = x,$$
$$d\hat{y}_t = (\chi - \kappa\hat{y}_t)\,dt + \varepsilon\sqrt{\hat{y}_t}d\hat{Z}_t, \quad \hat{y}_t = y. \tag{7.99}$$

Depending on the interpretation, these equations can describe the joint evolution of a particle's position and its velocity, the integral of variance and variance, among other possibilities.

The forward Fokker–Planck has the following form:

$$\varpi_{\bar{t}} - \frac{1}{2}\varepsilon^2\left(\bar{y}\varpi\right)_{\bar{y}\bar{y}} + \bar{y}\varpi_{\bar{x}} + \left(\left(\chi - \kappa\bar{y}\right)\varpi\right)_{\bar{y}} = 0,$$
$$\varpi\left(t,x,y,t,\bar{x},\bar{y}\right) = \delta\left(\bar{x}-x\right)\delta\left(\bar{y}-y\right), \tag{7.100}$$

while the backward Kolmogorov problem can be written as follows:

$$\varpi_t + \frac{1}{2}\varepsilon^2 y\varpi_{yy} + y\varpi_x + \left(\chi - \kappa y\right)\varpi_y = 0$$
$$\varpi\left(\bar{t},x,y,\bar{t},\bar{x},\bar{y}\right) = \delta\left(x-\bar{x}\right)\delta\left(y-\bar{y}\right). \tag{7.101}$$

In the following discussion the backward problem is considered, which allows one to derive the desired formula more efficiently. The corresponding function $\mathcal{K}$ has the following form:

$$\mathcal{K} = \exp\left(\alpha\left(t,\bar{t}\right) + ik\left(x-\bar{x}\right) + i\gamma\left(t,\bar{t}\right)y - il\bar{y}\right), \tag{7.102}$$

where

$$\alpha_t\left(t,\bar{t}\right) + i\chi\gamma\left(t,\bar{t}\right) = 0, \quad \alpha\left(\bar{t},\bar{t}\right) = 0,$$
$$i\gamma_t\left(t,\bar{t}\right) - \frac{1}{2}\varepsilon^2\gamma^2\left(t,\bar{t}\right) - i\kappa\gamma\left(t,\bar{t}\right) + ik = 0, \quad \gamma\left(\bar{t},\bar{t}\right) = l. \tag{7.103}$$

As before, one can linearize the Riccati equation for γ by using substitution given by (7.53), with $\Omega\left(t,\bar{t}\right)$ solving the second-order equation of the following form:

$$\Omega_{tt}\left(t,\bar{t}\right) - \kappa\Omega_t\left(t,\bar{t}\right) + \frac{i\varepsilon^2 k}{2}\Omega\left(t,\bar{t}\right) = 0, \quad \Omega\left(\bar{t},\bar{t}\right) = 1, \quad \Omega'\left(\bar{t},\bar{t}\right) = \frac{i\varepsilon^2 l}{2}. \tag{7.104}$$

One can represent $\Omega\left(t,\bar{t}\right)$ in the following form:

$$\Omega\left(t,\bar{t}\right)=\omega_{+}e^{\lambda_{+}\left(\bar{t}-t\right)}+\omega_{-}e^{\lambda_{+}\left(\bar{t}-t\right)},\tag{7.105}$$

where $\lambda_{\pm}$ are solutions of the characteristic equation:

$$\lambda^{2}+\kappa\lambda+\frac{i\varepsilon^{2}k}{2}=0,\tag{7.106}$$

and $\omega_{\pm}$ satisfy the following system of linear equations:

$$\begin{aligned}\omega_{+}+\omega_{-}&=1,\\ \lambda_{+}\omega_{+}+\lambda_{-}\omega_{-}&=-\frac{i\varepsilon^{2}l}{2}.\end{aligned}\tag{7.107}$$

Thus,

$$\begin{aligned}\lambda_{\pm}&=\mu\pm\zeta,\\ \mu&=-\frac{\kappa}{2},\quad\zeta=\frac{\sqrt{\kappa^{2}-2i\varepsilon^{2}k}}{2},\end{aligned}\tag{7.108}$$

$$\omega_{+}=-\frac{\left(2\lambda_{-}+i\varepsilon^{2}l\right)}{4\zeta},\quad\omega_{-}=\frac{\left(2\lambda_{+}+i\varepsilon^{2}l\right)}{4\zeta}.\tag{7.109}$$

It is useful to note that

$$\lambda_{+}\lambda_{-}=\mu^{2}-\zeta^{2}=\frac{i\varepsilon^{2}k}{2}.\tag{7.110}$$

For the sake of brevity, notation (6.122) is used:

$$\Omega\left(t,\bar{t}\right)=\frac{\mathsf{E}_{0}\left(-\left(2\lambda_{-}+i\varepsilon^{2}l\right)\mathsf{E}_{+}+\left(2\lambda_{+}+i\varepsilon^{2}l\right)\mathsf{E}_{-}\right)}{4\zeta},\tag{7.111}$$

$$\Omega_{t}\left(t,\bar{t}\right)=\frac{\mathsf{E}_{0}\left(\lambda_{+}\left(2\lambda_{-}+i\varepsilon^{2}l\right)\mathsf{E}_{+}-\lambda_{-}\left(2\lambda_{+}+i\varepsilon^{2}l\right)\mathsf{E}_{-}\right)}{4\zeta},\tag{7.112}$$

$$\gamma=\frac{2i\left(\lambda_{+}\left(2\lambda_{-}+i\varepsilon^{2}l\right)\mathsf{E}_{+}-\lambda_{-}\left(2\lambda_{+}+i\varepsilon^{2}l\right)\mathsf{E}_{-}\right)}{\varepsilon^{2}\left(\left(2\lambda_{-}+i\varepsilon^{2}l\right)\mathsf{E}_{+}-\left(2\lambda_{+}+i\varepsilon^{2}l\right)\mathsf{E}_{-}\right)},\tag{7.113}$$

$$\alpha=\frac{\chi\kappa T}{\varepsilon^{2}}-(\vartheta+1)\ln\left(\frac{-\left(2\lambda_{-}+i\varepsilon^{2}l\right)\mathsf{E}_{+}+\left(2\lambda_{+}+i\varepsilon^{2}l\right)\mathsf{E}_{-}}{4\zeta}\right).\tag{7.114}$$

Accordingly, $\mathcal{K}$ can be written in the following form:

$$\begin{aligned}\mathcal{K}=\exp\Bigg(&\frac{\chi\kappa T}{\varepsilon^{2}}+ik(x-\bar{x})\\ &-(\vartheta+1)\ln\left(\frac{2\left(-\lambda_{-}\mathsf{E}_{+}+\lambda_{+}\mathsf{E}_{-}\right)-i\varepsilon^{2}l\left(\mathsf{E}_{+}-\mathsf{E}_{-}\right)}{4\zeta}\right)\\ &+\frac{2\left(2\lambda_{+}\lambda_{-}\left(\mathsf{E}_{+}-\mathsf{E}_{-}\right)+i\varepsilon^{2}l\left(\lambda_{+}\mathsf{E}_{+}-\lambda_{-}\mathsf{E}_{-}\right)\right)}{\varepsilon^{2}\left(2\left(-\lambda_{-}\mathsf{E}_{+}+\lambda_{+}\mathsf{E}_{-}\right)-i\varepsilon^{2}l\left(\mathsf{E}_{+}-\mathsf{E}_{-}\right)\right)}y-il\bar{y}\Bigg).\end{aligned}\tag{7.115}$$

Define a new variable $\hat{l}$, such that

$$\hat{l} = \frac{l}{2M}, \quad l = 2M\hat{l}, \tag{7.116}$$

where

$$M = \frac{2\left(-\lambda_- \mathsf{E}_+ + \lambda_+ \mathsf{E}_-\right)}{\varepsilon^2 \left(\mathsf{E}_+ - \mathsf{E}_-\right)}. \tag{7.117}$$

Rescaled $\hat{\mathcal{K}}$ can be factorized as follows:

$$\hat{\mathcal{K}} = \hat{\mathcal{K}}_1 \hat{\mathcal{K}}_2, \tag{7.118}$$

where

$$\begin{aligned} \hat{\mathcal{K}}_1 &= \exp\left(\frac{\chi\kappa T}{\varepsilon^2} + ik\left(x - \bar{x}\right) - (\vartheta + 1)\ln\left(\frac{-\lambda_- \mathsf{E}_+ + \lambda_+ \mathsf{E}_-}{2\zeta}\right)\right. \\ &\quad \left. + \frac{2\lambda_+\lambda_-\left(\mathsf{E}_+ - \mathsf{E}_-\right)}{\varepsilon^2\left(-\lambda_- \mathsf{E}_+ + \lambda_+ \mathsf{E}_-\right)} y\right), \\ \hat{\mathcal{K}}_2 &= 2M\exp\left(-M\left(Y + \bar{y}\right)\right) \\ &\quad \times \exp\left(-(\vartheta + 1)\ln\left(1 - 2i\hat{l}\right) + M\left(\frac{Y}{1 - 2i\hat{l}} + \bar{y}\left(1 - 2i\hat{l}\right)\right)\right), \end{aligned} \tag{7.119}$$

with

$$Y = \frac{4\zeta^2}{\left(-\lambda_- \mathsf{E}_+ + \lambda_+ \mathsf{E}_-\right)^2} y. \tag{7.120}$$

Integration with respect to $\hat{l}$ can be done analytically:

$$\frac{M}{\pi}\int_{-\infty}^{\infty} \hat{\mathcal{K}}_2 d\hat{l} = Me^{-M(\bar{y}+Y)}\left(\frac{\bar{y}}{Y}\right)^{\frac{\vartheta}{2}} I_\vartheta\left(2M\sqrt{\bar{y}Y}\right), \tag{7.121}$$

which allows one to calculate ϖ via a single inverse Fourier transform:

$$\begin{aligned} \varpi &= \frac{1}{2\pi}\int_{-\infty}^{\infty} \exp\left(\frac{\chi\kappa T}{\varepsilon^2} + ik\left(x - \bar{x}\right) - (\vartheta + 1)\ln\left(\frac{-\lambda_- \mathsf{E}_+ + \lambda_+ \mathsf{E}_-}{2\zeta}\right)\right. \\ &\quad \left. + \frac{2\lambda_+\lambda_-\left(\mathsf{E}_+ - \mathsf{E}_-\right)}{\varepsilon^2\left(-\lambda_- \mathsf{E}_+ + \lambda_+ \mathsf{E}_-\right)} y\right) Me^{-M(\bar{y}+Y)}\left(\frac{\bar{y}}{Y}\right)^{\frac{\vartheta}{2}} I_\vartheta\left(2M\sqrt{\bar{y}Y}\right) dk. \end{aligned} \tag{7.122}$$

A typical t.p.d.f. for a degenerate augmented Feller process is illustrated in Figure 11.

Since the integral over $\bar{y}$ is equal to one, one can represent the marginal distribution of $\bar{x}$ in the following form:

$$\varpi^{(x)}\left(t, x, y, \bar{t}, \bar{x}\right) = \frac{1}{2\pi}\int_{-\infty}^{\infty} \mathsf{F}\left(t, y, \bar{t}, k\right) e^{ik(x-\bar{x})} dk, \tag{7.123}$$

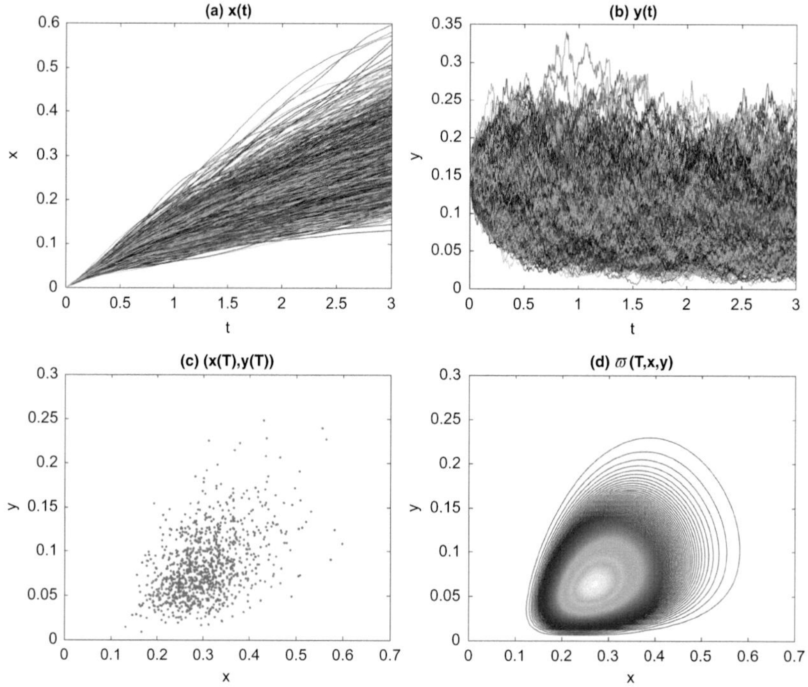

Figure 11 A thousand trajectories of a representative t.p.d.f. for the degenerate augmented Feller process. Parameters are $T = 3$, $dt = 0.01$, $\chi = 0.1$, $\kappa = 1.2$, $\varepsilon = 0.2$, $x = 0$; $y_0 = 0.15$. (a) $x(t)$, (b) $y(t)$, (c) $(\bar{x}(T), \bar{y}(T))$, (d) contour lines of $\varpi(0, 0.15, 0, T, \bar{x}, \bar{y})$. Author's graphics.

where

$$F\left(t, y, \bar{t}, k\right) = \exp\left(\frac{\chi\kappa T}{\varepsilon^2} - (\vartheta + 1)\ln\left(\frac{-\lambda_- \mathsf{E}_+ + \lambda_+ \mathsf{E}_-}{2\zeta}\right) + \frac{2\lambda_+\lambda_-(\mathsf{E}_+ - \mathsf{E}_-)}{\varepsilon^2(-\lambda_- \mathsf{E}_+ + \lambda_+ \mathsf{E}_-)}y\right), \tag{7.124}$$

with μ, ζ given by the equations in (7.106). It is easy to check that $\varpi^{(x)}\left(t, x, y, \bar{t}, \bar{x}\right)$ integrates to one:

$$\int_{-\infty}^{\infty} \varpi^{(x)}\left(t, x, y, \bar{t}, \bar{x}\right) d\bar{x} = \frac{1}{2\pi}\int_{-\infty}^{\infty}\int_{-\infty}^{\infty} F\left(t, y, \bar{t}, k\right)\exp\left(ik(x - \bar{x})\right) dk d\bar{x}$$
$$= \int_{-\infty}^{\infty} F\left(t, y, \bar{t}, k\right)\delta(k)\, dk = F\left(t, y, \bar{t}, 0\right) = \exp\left(\frac{\chi\kappa T}{\varepsilon^2} - \frac{2\chi}{\varepsilon^2}\frac{\kappa T}{2}\right) = 1. \tag{7.125}$$

The expected value of $\bar{x}$ has the following form:

$$X = \int_{-\infty}^{\infty} \varpi^{(x)}\left(t, x, y, \bar{t}, \bar{x}\right)\bar{x} d\bar{x} = x + \int_{-\infty}^{\infty} \varpi^{(x)}\left(t, x, y, \bar{t}, \bar{x}\right)(\bar{x} - x)\, d\bar{x}$$
$$= x + \frac{1}{2\pi}\int_{-\infty}^{\infty}\int_{-\infty}^{\infty} F\left(t, y, \bar{t}, k\right)\exp\left(ik(\bar{x} - x)\right)(\bar{x} - x)\, dk d\bar{x}$$

$$= x + \lim_{\epsilon \to 0} \left(\frac{d}{d\epsilon} \left(\frac{1}{2\pi} \int_{-\infty}^{\infty} \int_{-\infty}^{\infty} F\left(t, y, \bar{t}, k\right) \exp\left(\left(ik + \epsilon\right)\left(\bar{x} - x\right)\right) dk d\bar{x} \right) \right)$$

$$= x + \lim_{\epsilon \to 0} \left(\frac{d}{d\epsilon} \left(\int_{-\infty}^{\infty} F\left(t, y, \bar{t}, k\right) \delta\left(k - i\epsilon\right) dk \right) \right)$$

$$= x + \frac{d}{d\epsilon} F\left(t, y, \bar{t}, i\epsilon\right) \Big|_{\epsilon = 0}. \tag{7.126}$$

A calculation left to the reader yields

$$X = x + \frac{\chi}{\kappa} T - \bar{\mathsf{B}}_{\kappa}(T) \left(\frac{\chi}{\kappa} - y \right), \tag{7.127}$$

which agrees with (6.115).

It is worth noting that $\varpi^{(x)}\left(\bar{t}, \bar{x}\right)$ has fat tails, since some of the exponential moments of $\bar{x}$ have finite-time explosions; see Andersen and Piterbarg (2007), Friz and Keller-Ressel (2010), and references therein.[8] Specifically, one needs to analyze if $\mathcal{I}_p\left(t, \bar{t}\right)$ of the following form:

$$\begin{aligned}
\mathcal{I}_p\left(t, \bar{t}\right) &= \int_{-\infty}^{\infty} \varpi^{(x)}\left(t, x, y, \bar{t}, \bar{x}\right) e^{p\bar{x}} d\bar{x} \\
&= \frac{e^{px}}{2\pi} \int_{-\infty}^{\infty} \int_{-\infty}^{\infty} F\left(t, y, \bar{t}, k\right) \exp\left(ik\left(x - \bar{x}\right) - p\left(x - \bar{x}\right)\right) dk d\bar{x} \\
&= e^{px} \int_{-\infty}^{\infty} F\left(t, y, \bar{t}, k\right) \delta\left(ik - p\right) dk = e^{px} F\left(t, y, \bar{t}, -ip\right),
\end{aligned} \tag{7.128}$$

blows up for some finite $\bar{t} > t$. Indeed,

$$\begin{aligned}
&F\left(t, y, \bar{t}, -ip\right) \\
&= \exp\left(\frac{\chi \kappa T}{\varepsilon^2} - (\vartheta + 1) \ln\left(\frac{-\lambda_- \mathsf{E}_+ + \lambda_+ \mathsf{E}_-}{2\zeta} \right) + \frac{2\lambda_+ \lambda_- \left(\mathsf{E}_+ - \mathsf{E}_-\right)}{\varepsilon^2 \left(-\lambda_- \mathsf{E}_+ + \lambda_+ \mathsf{E}_-\right)} y \right),
\end{aligned} \tag{7.129}$$

[8] Of course, it is not surprising that such explosions exist since Riccati equations are well-known to have solutions exploding in finite time. Consider the following Riccati initial-value problem

$$f' + af^2 + bf + c = 0, \quad f(\tau) = d,$$

and assume that $b^2 - 4ac < 0$. The solution of this initial-value problem has the form

$$f(\tau, t) = -\frac{|\zeta|}{a} \tan\left(|\zeta| (t - \tau) - \arctan\left(\frac{2ad + b}{2|\zeta|} \right) \right) - \frac{b}{2a},$$

where $|\zeta| = \sqrt{4ac - b^2} \big/ 2$. The corresponding blow-up time t^* has the form

$$t^* = \tau + \frac{\pi}{2|\zeta|} + \frac{1}{|\zeta|} \arctan\left(\frac{2ad + b}{2|\zeta|} \right).$$

where

$$\lambda_\pm = \mu \pm \zeta,$$
$$\mu = -\frac{\kappa}{2}, \quad \zeta = \frac{\sqrt{\kappa^2 - 2\varepsilon^2 p}}{2}, \tag{7.130}$$
$$\lambda_+\lambda_- = \frac{\varepsilon^2 p}{2}.$$

Thus, when $\zeta > 0$ is real:

$$\mathcal{I}_p = \left(\frac{2\zeta}{-\mu \sinh(|\zeta| T) + \zeta \cosh(|\zeta| T)}\right)^{(\vartheta+1)}$$
$$\exp\left(\frac{\chi\kappa T}{\varepsilon^2} + px + \frac{p \sinh(\zeta T)}{(-\mu \sinh(|\zeta| T) + \zeta \cosh(|\zeta| T))} y\right), \tag{7.131}$$

and, when $\zeta = i|\zeta|$ is imaginary:

$$\mathcal{I}_p = \left(\frac{|\zeta|}{-\mu \sin(|\zeta| T) + |\zeta| \cos(|\zeta| T)}\right)^{(\vartheta+1)}$$
$$\exp\left(\frac{\chi\kappa T}{\varepsilon^2} + px + \frac{p \sin(|\zeta| T)}{(-\mu \sin(|\zeta| T) + |\zeta| \cos(|\zeta| T))} y\right). \tag{7.132}$$

For $p \in [-\infty, \hat{p}]$, ζ is real, and for $p \in [\hat{p}, \infty]$, it is imaginary. Here

$$\hat{p} = \frac{\kappa^2}{2\varepsilon^2} > 0. \tag{7.133}$$

There is no blowup when ζ is real. When ζ is imaginary, the blowup time t^* is the smallest positive root of the equation

$$\kappa \sin\left(\sqrt{2\varepsilon^2 p - \kappa^2}\,(t^* - t)\right) + \sqrt{2\varepsilon^2 p - \kappa^2} \cos\left(\sqrt{2\varepsilon^2 p - \kappa^2}\,(t^* - t)\right) = 0, \tag{7.134}$$

$$t^* = t + \frac{\pi - \arctan\left(\frac{\sqrt{2\varepsilon^2 p - \kappa^2}}{\kappa}\right)}{\sqrt{2\varepsilon^2 p - \kappa^2}}. \tag{7.135}$$

It is clear that $\mathcal{I}_{-1}$ does not blow up. This fact in used in the next section.

The marginal distribution of $\bar{y}$, $\varpi^{(y)}\left(\bar{t}, \bar{y}\right)$ is the standard Feller distribution given by (7.66).

7.4.3 Augmented Feller Process, II

This section studies the joint dynamics of an arithmetic Brownian $\hat{x}_t$ whose stochastic variance is driven by a Feller process $\hat{y}_t$, and considers the following system of affine SDEs:

$$d\hat{x}_t = \sqrt{\hat{y}_t} d\hat{W}_t, \quad \hat{x}_t = x,$$
$$d\hat{y}_t = (\chi - \kappa \hat{y}_t) dt + \varepsilon \sqrt{\hat{y}_t} d\hat{Z}_t, \quad \hat{y}_t = y. \tag{7.136}$$

Studying such a process is very helpful for finding option prices and solving other important problems in the financial engineering context.

The associated forward Fokker–Planck problem can be written as follows:

$$\varpi_{\bar{t}} - \frac{1}{2} \bar{y} \varpi_{\bar{x}\bar{x}} - \rho\varepsilon \left(\bar{y}\varpi\right)_{\bar{x}\bar{y}} - \frac{1}{2}\varepsilon^2 \left(\bar{y}\varpi\right)_{\bar{y}\bar{y}} + \left(\left(\chi - \kappa\bar{y}\right)\varpi\right)_{\bar{y}} = 0,$$
$$\varpi\left(t, x, y, t, \bar{x}, \bar{y}\right) = \delta\left(\bar{x} - x\right)\delta\left(\bar{y} - y\right), \tag{7.137}$$

while the backward Kolmogorov problem has the following form:

$$\varpi_t + \frac{1}{2} y \varpi_{xx} + \rho\varepsilon y \varpi_{xy} + \frac{1}{2}\varepsilon^2 y \varpi_{yy} + \left(\chi - \kappa y\right)\varpi_y = 0,$$
$$\varpi\left(\bar{t}, x, y, \bar{t}, \bar{x}, \bar{y}\right) = \delta\left(x - \bar{x}\right)\delta\left(y - \bar{y}\right). \tag{7.138}$$

As before, concentrate on problem (7.138).

The Kelvin function $\mathcal{K}$ has the form (7.102). The governing ODEs for α, γ are as follows:

$$\alpha_t\left(t, \bar{t}\right) + i\chi\gamma\left(t, \bar{t}\right) = 0, \quad \alpha\left(\bar{t}, \bar{t}\right) = 0,$$
$$i\gamma_t\left(t, \bar{t}\right) - \frac{1}{2}\varepsilon^2\gamma^2\left(t, \bar{t}\right) - \left(\kappa - i\rho\varepsilon k\right) i\gamma\left(t, \bar{t}\right) - \frac{1}{2}k^2 = 0, \quad \gamma\left(\bar{t}, \bar{t}\right) = l. \tag{7.139}$$

Formulas (7.111)–(7.114) hold; however, the corresponding characteristic equation is

$$\lambda^2 + \left(\kappa - i\rho\varepsilon k\right)\lambda - \frac{\varepsilon^2}{4}k^2 = 0, \tag{7.140}$$

so that

$$\lambda_\pm = \mu \pm \zeta,$$
$$\mu = -\frac{1}{2}\left(\kappa - i\rho\varepsilon k\right), \quad \zeta = \frac{1}{2}\sqrt{\varepsilon^2\bar{\rho}^2 k^2 - 2i\rho\varepsilon\kappa k + \kappa^2}, \tag{7.141}$$
$$\lambda_+\lambda_- = \mu^2 - \zeta^2 = -\frac{\varepsilon^2}{4}k^2,$$

where $\bar{\rho}^2 = 1 - \rho^2$. Subsequent calculations are very similar to the ones performed in the previous subsection, so they are omitted for brevity. The final expressions for ϖ and $\varpi^{(x)}$ are given by Equations (7.122), (7.123), and

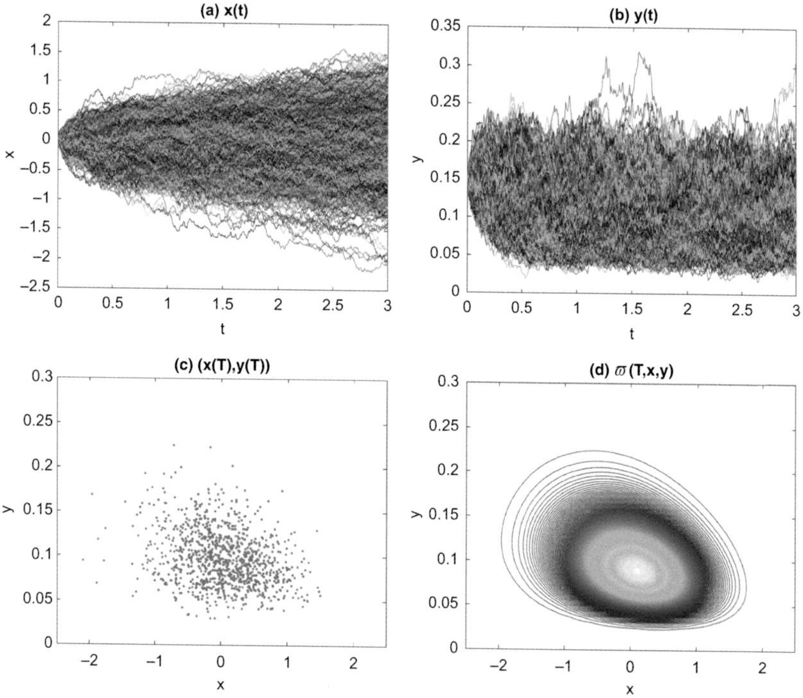

Figure 12 A thousand trajectories of a representative nondegenerate augmented Feller process. Parameters are $T = 3$, $dt = 0.01$, $\chi = 0.2$, $\kappa = 2.0$, $\varepsilon = 0.2$, $\rho = -0.5$, $x = 0$, $y_0 = 0.15$. (a) $x(t)$, (b) $y(t)$, (c) $(\bar{x}(T), \bar{y}(T))$, (d) contour lines of $\varpi(0, 0.15, 0, T, \tilde{x}, \tilde{y})$. Author's graphics.

(7.124), with μ, ζ given by the equations in (7.141). These expressions are similar to the formulas originally derived by Lipton as part of his analysis of the Heston stochastic volatility model; see Lipton (2001).[9]

A typical t.p.d.f. for a nondegenerate augmented Feller process is shown in Figure 12.

As before, $\varpi^{(x)}\left(t, x, y, \bar{t}, \bar{x}\right)$ has fat tails. Consider $\mathcal{I}_p\left(t, \bar{t}\right)$ given by (7.128). The corresponding $\lambda_\pm$ have the following form:

$$\begin{aligned} \lambda_\pm &= \mu \pm \zeta, \\ \mu &= -\frac{1}{2}\left(\kappa - \rho\varepsilon p\right), \quad \zeta = \frac{1}{2}\sqrt{-\varepsilon^2\bar{\rho}^2 p^2 - 2\rho\varepsilon\kappa p + \kappa^2}, \\ \lambda_+\lambda_- &= \mu^2 - \zeta^2 = \frac{\varepsilon^2}{4}p^2. \end{aligned} \quad (7.142)$$

[9] Despite the fact that these formulas were originally derived by Lipton (2001), they are frequently mistakenly attributed to Dragulescu and Yakovenko (2002).

Thus, when $\zeta > 0$ is real,

$$\mathcal{I}_p = \left(\frac{\zeta}{-\mu\sinh(\zeta T) + \zeta\cosh(\zeta T)}\right)^{(\vartheta+1)}$$
$$\exp\left(\frac{2\chi\mu T}{\varepsilon^2} + px + \frac{p(p-1)\sinh(\zeta T)}{2(-\mu\sinh(\zeta T) + \zeta\cosh(\zeta T))}y\right), \tag{7.143}$$

and when $\zeta = i|\zeta|$ is imaginary,

$$\mathcal{I}_p = \left(\frac{|\zeta|}{-\mu\sin(|\zeta|T) + |\zeta|\cos(|\zeta|T)}\right)^{(\vartheta+1)}$$
$$\exp\left(\frac{2\chi\mu T}{\varepsilon^2} + px + \frac{p(p-1)\sin(|\zeta|T)}{2(-\mu\sin(|\zeta|T) + |\zeta|\cos(|\zeta|T))}y\right). \tag{7.144}$$

One needs to determine when ζ becomes imaginary. The corresponding quadratic equation has the form:

$$\bar{\rho}^2\varepsilon^2p^2 + 2\rho\varepsilon\kappa p - \kappa^2 = 0, \tag{7.145}$$

its roots are as follows:

$$p_\pm = \frac{-\rho\varepsilon\kappa \pm \sqrt{\rho^2\varepsilon^2\kappa^2 + \bar{\rho}^2\varepsilon^2\kappa^2}}{\bar{\rho}^2\varepsilon^2} = \frac{(-\rho \pm 1)\kappa}{\bar{\rho}^2\varepsilon}, \tag{7.146}$$

so that

$$p_+ > 1, \quad p_- < 1. \tag{7.147}$$

For $p \in [p_-, p_+]$, ζ is real, for $p \notin [p_-, p_+]$, it is imaginary. There is no blowup when ζ is real. When ζ is imaginary, the blowup time t^* is the smallest positive root of the equation

$$-\mu\sin(|\zeta|(t^* - t)) + |\zeta|\cos(|\zeta|(t^* - t)) = 0, \tag{7.148}$$

$$t^* = \begin{cases} t + \dfrac{\arctan\left(\frac{|\zeta|}{|\mu|}\right)}{|\zeta|}, & \mu > 0, \\ t + \dfrac{\pi - \arctan\left(\frac{|\zeta|}{|\mu|}\right)}{|\zeta|}, & \mu < 0. \end{cases} \tag{7.149}$$

7.5 Example: Path-Dependent Process

Let $\hat{y}_t$ be a stochastic process and $\hat{x}_t$ be its moving average. Then

$$\hat{x}_t = \kappa\int_{-\infty}^{t} e^{-\kappa(t-s)}\hat{y}_s ds. \tag{7.150}$$

A simple calculation yields

$$d\hat{x}_t = \kappa(\hat{y}_t - \hat{x}_t)\,dt. \tag{7.151}$$

The process $\hat{y}_t$ is path-dependent, because its volatility $\hat{\sigma}_t$ depends on its moving average $\hat{x}_t$:

$$\hat{\sigma}_t = \sqrt{a_0 + a_1 (\hat{y}_t - \hat{x}_t)}, \tag{7.152}$$

where $a_0 > 0$, $a_1 < 0$, in order to capture the effect of leverage. Thus, one can write the governing degenerate system of SDEs as follows:

$$\begin{aligned} d\hat{x}_t &= \kappa (\hat{y}_t - \hat{x}_t)\, dt, \quad \hat{x}_t = x, \\ d\hat{y}_t &= \sqrt{a_0 + a_1 (\hat{y}_t - \hat{x}_t)} d\hat{W}_t, \quad \hat{y}_t = y. \end{aligned} \tag{7.153}$$

The Fokker–Planck and Kolmogorov problems are

$$\begin{aligned} &\varpi_{\bar{t}} - \frac{1}{2}\left((a_0 + a_1 (\bar{y} - \bar{x}))\, \varpi\right)_{\bar{y}\bar{y}} + \left(\kappa (\bar{y} - \bar{x})\, \varpi\right)_{\bar{x}} = 0, \\ &\varpi (t, x, y, t, \bar{x}, \bar{y}) = \delta (\bar{x} - x)\, \delta (\bar{y} - y), \end{aligned} \tag{7.154}$$

$$\begin{aligned} &\varpi_t + \frac{1}{2}(a_0 + a_1 (y - x))\, \varpi_{yy} + \kappa (y - x)\, \varpi_x = 0, \\ &\varpi \left(\bar{t}, x, y, \bar{t}, \bar{x}, \bar{y}\right) = \delta (x - \bar{x})\, \delta (y - \bar{y}), \end{aligned} \tag{7.155}$$

respectively.

A representative Kelvin mode has the following form:

$$\mathcal{K} = \exp\left(\alpha\left(t, \bar{t}\right) + i\beta\left(t, \bar{t}\right) x - ik\bar{x} + i\gamma\left(t, \bar{t}\right) y - il\bar{y}\right). \tag{7.156}$$

The system of backward ODEs for α, γ, β is as follows:

$$\begin{aligned} &\alpha_t\left(t, \bar{t}\right) - \frac{a_0}{2}\gamma^2\left(t, \bar{t}\right) = 0, \quad \alpha\left(\bar{t}, \bar{t}\right) = 0, \\ &i\beta_t\left(t, \bar{t}\right) + \frac{a_1}{2}\gamma^2\left(t, \bar{t}\right) - i\kappa\beta\left(t, \bar{t}\right) = 0, \quad \beta\left(\bar{t}, \bar{t}\right) = k, \\ &i\gamma_t\left(t, \bar{t}\right) - \frac{a_1}{2}\gamma^2\left(t, \bar{t}\right) + i\kappa\beta\left(t, \bar{t}\right) = 0, \quad \gamma\left(\bar{t}, \bar{t}\right) = l. \end{aligned} \tag{7.157}$$

The equations in (7.157) are matrix Riccati equations, as opposed to the scalar Riccati equations considered earlier. In general, such equations are very difficult to solve. However, the case under consideration is one of the relatively rare instances when a matrix Riccati equation can be solved explicitly. Start with an observation:

$$\gamma_t\left(t, \bar{t}\right) + \beta_t\left(t, \bar{t}\right) = 0, \tag{7.158}$$

so that

$$\beta\left(t, \bar{t}\right) = -\gamma\left(t, \bar{t}\right) + k + l. \tag{7.159}$$

Accordingly,

$$i\gamma_t\left(t,\bar{t}\right)-\frac{a_1}{2}\gamma^2\left(t,\bar{t}\right)-i\kappa\gamma\left(t,\bar{t}\right)+i\kappa\left(k+l\right)=0,\quad \gamma\left(\bar{t},\bar{t}\right)=l. \tag{7.160}$$

One can use Equations (7.111)–(7.113) with (β, k) replaced by (γ, l), and

$$\lambda^2+\kappa\lambda+\frac{ia_1\kappa\left(k+l\right)}{2}=0, \tag{7.161}$$

so that

$$\lambda_\pm=\mu\pm\zeta, \tag{7.162}$$

$$\mu=-\frac{\kappa}{2},\quad \zeta=\frac{\sqrt{\kappa^2-2ia_1\kappa\left(k+l\right)}}{2}.$$

Equation (7.159) yields

$$\beta\left(t,\bar{t}\right)=\frac{2i\Omega'\left(t,\bar{t}\right)}{a_1\Omega\left(t,\bar{t}\right)}+k+l, \tag{7.163}$$

and

$$\begin{aligned}\gamma^2\left(t,\bar{t}\right)&=\frac{2i}{a_1}\left(\gamma_t\left(t,\bar{t}\right)+\kappa\beta\left(t,\bar{t}\right)\right)\\&=\frac{2i}{a_1}\left(\gamma_t\left(t,\bar{t}\right)-\kappa\gamma\left(t,\bar{t}\right)+\kappa\left(\kappa+k\right)\right).\end{aligned} \tag{7.164}$$

Thus,

$$\alpha_t\left(t,\bar{t}\right)=\frac{ia_0}{a_1}\left(\gamma_t\left(t,\bar{t}\right)-\kappa\gamma\left(t,\bar{t}\right)+\kappa\left(k+l\right)\right),\quad \alpha\left(\bar{t},\bar{t}\right)=0. \tag{7.165}$$

Accordingly,

$$\alpha\left(t,\bar{t}\right)=\frac{ia_0}{a_1}\left(\gamma\left(t,\bar{t}\right)-l\right)-\frac{2a_0\kappa}{a_1^2}\ln\left(\Omega\left(t,\bar{t}\right)\right)+\frac{a_0\kappa T}{a_1}i\left(k+l\right). \tag{7.166}$$

Finally,

$$\begin{aligned}\mathcal{K}&=\exp\left(\alpha+i\beta\left(t,\bar{t}\right)x-ik\bar{x}+i\gamma\left(t,\bar{t}\right)y-il\bar{y}\right)\\&=\exp\left(-\frac{2a_0\kappa}{a_1^2}\ln\left(\Omega\left(t,\bar{t}\right)\right)+i\gamma\left(t,\bar{t}\right)\left(y-x+\frac{a_0}{a_1}\right)\right.\\&\left.\quad+il\left(x-\bar{y}+\frac{a_0}{a_1}\left(\kappa T-1\right)\right)+ik\left(x-\bar{x}+\frac{a_0\kappa T}{a_1}\right)\right).\end{aligned} \tag{7.167}$$

To make sure that $\hat{\sigma}_t$ given by (7.152) and the integrand (7.167) are well defined, it is assumed that

$$a_0+a_1\left(y-x\right)>0,\quad a_0+a_1\left(\bar{y}-\bar{x}\right)>0. \tag{7.168}$$

7.6 Example: OU-Like Process

This section considers several instances when an OU-inspired process becomes non-Gaussian. This can happen for a variety of reasons, such as effects of anomalous diffusion, the presence of jumps, effects of augmentation, and the likes.

7.6.1 Anomalous OU Process

This section considers a mean-reverting process driven by a non-Gaussian anomalous diffusion. For brevity, it is assumed that coefficients are time-independent. The fractional forward Fokker–Planck and backward Kolmogorov problems can be written as follows:

$$\begin{aligned} &\varpi_{\bar{t}} + a\left(-\frac{\partial^2}{\partial \bar{y}^2}\right)^{1/2} \varpi + \left(\left(\chi - \kappa \bar{y}\right)\varpi\right)_{\bar{y}} = 0, \\ &\varpi\left(t, y, t, \bar{y}\right) = \delta\left(\bar{y} - y\right), \end{aligned} \tag{7.169}$$

$$\begin{aligned} &\varpi_{t} - a\left(-\frac{\partial^2}{\partial y^2}\right)^{1/2} \varpi + \left(\chi - \kappa y\right)\varpi_{y} = 0, \\ &\varpi\left(\bar{t}, y, \bar{t}, \bar{y}\right) = \delta\left(y - \bar{y}\right), \end{aligned} \tag{7.170}$$

respectively. Here $a > 0$ is the anomalous diffusion coefficient.

As before, one can use Kelvin waves to solve (7.170) by choosing a particular solution of the form (7.51). The corresponding (α, γ) satisfy the following ODEs:

$$\begin{aligned} &\alpha_t\left(t, \bar{t}\right) - a\left|\gamma\left(t, \bar{t}\right)\right| + i\chi\gamma\left(t, \bar{t}\right) = 0, \quad \alpha\left(\bar{t}, \bar{t}\right) = 0, \\ &\gamma_t\left(t, \bar{t}\right) - \kappa\gamma\left(t, \bar{t}\right) = 0, \quad \gamma\left(\bar{t}, \bar{t}\right) = l, \end{aligned} \tag{7.171}$$

so that

$$\begin{aligned} &\alpha\left(t, \bar{t}\right) = -\bar{\mathsf{B}}_\kappa\left(T\right)\left(a\left|l\right| - i\chi l\right), \\ &\gamma\left(t, \bar{t}\right) = e^{-\kappa T} l. \end{aligned} \tag{7.172}$$

Accordingly,

$$\begin{aligned} \varpi\left(t, y, \bar{t}, \bar{y}\right) &= \frac{1}{2\pi}\int_{-\infty}^{\infty} \exp\left(-\bar{\mathsf{B}}_\kappa\left(T\right) a\left|l\right| + \left(\bar{\mathsf{B}}_\kappa\left(T\right)\chi + e^{-\kappa T} y - \bar{y}\right) il\right) dl \\ &= \frac{1}{\pi}\frac{\bar{\mathsf{B}}_\kappa\left(T\right) a}{\left(\left(\bar{\mathsf{B}}_\kappa\left(T\right) a\right)^2 + \left(e^{-\kappa T}\left(y - \frac{\chi}{\kappa}\right) - \left(\bar{y} - \frac{\chi}{\kappa}\right)\right)^2\right)}. \end{aligned} \tag{7.173}$$

Thus, in sharp contrast to the classical OU process, which is described by a Gaussian distribution, the fractional OU process is described by a Cauchy distribution. This distribution has fat tails and no first and second moments.

7.6.2 Non-Gaussian Augmented OU Process, I

On occasion, problems seemingly not of the type given by (7.11) can be cast in the proper form via a suitable trick. Consider, for example, the following system of SDEs:

$$d\hat{x}_t = \hat{y}_t^2 dt, \quad \hat{x}_t = x, \qquad (7.174)$$
$$d\hat{y}_t = (\chi - \kappa \hat{y}_t)\, dt + \varepsilon d\hat{Z}_t, \quad \hat{y}_t = y.$$

Superficially, it does not belong to the class of processes studied earlier. However, by introducing new variables $z_1 = x$, $z_2 = y^2$, $z_3 = y$, one can augment the equations in (7.127) as follows:

$$\begin{aligned}
d\hat{z}_{1,t} &= \hat{z}_{2,t} dt, \quad \hat{z}_{1,t} = x \equiv z_1, \\
d\hat{z}_{2,t} &= \left(\varepsilon^2 - 2\kappa \hat{z}_{2,t} + 2\chi \hat{z}_{3,t}\right) + 2\varepsilon \hat{z}_{3,t} d\hat{Z}_t, \quad \hat{z}_{2,t} = y^2 \equiv z_2, \qquad (7.175) \\
d\hat{z}_{3,t} &= \left(\chi - \kappa \hat{z}_{3,t}\right) dt + \varepsilon d\hat{Z}_t, \quad \hat{z}_{3,t} = z_3 \equiv y.
\end{aligned}$$

These equations are "almost" in the suitable form. The only snag is that one cannot claim that $\hat{z}_{3,t} = \sqrt{\hat{z}_{2,t}}$ since $\hat{z}_{3,t}$ is not always positive.

The corresponding Fokker–Planck and Kolmogorov problems can be written as follows:

$$\begin{aligned}
&\varpi_{\bar{t}} - 2\varepsilon^2 \left(\bar{z}_2 \varpi\right)_{\bar{z}_2 \bar{z}_2} - 2\varepsilon^2 \left(\bar{z}_3 \varpi\right)_{\bar{z}_2 \bar{z}_3} - \frac{1}{2}\varepsilon^2 \varpi_{\bar{z}_3 \bar{z}_3} \\
&\quad + \bar{z}_2 \varpi_{\bar{z}_1} + \left(\left(\varepsilon^2 - 2\kappa \bar{z}_2 + 2\chi \bar{z}_3\right) \varpi\right)_{\bar{z}_2} + \left(\left(\chi - \kappa \bar{z}_3\right) \varpi\right)_{\bar{z}_3} = 0, \qquad (7.176) \\
&\varpi\left(t, x, y^2, y, t, \bar{z}_1, \bar{z}_2, \bar{z}_3\right) = \delta\left(\bar{z}_1 - x\right) \delta\left(\bar{z}_2 - y^2\right) \delta\left(\bar{z}_3 - y\right), \\
&\quad \varpi_t + 2\varepsilon^2 z_2 \varpi_{z_2 z_2} + 2\varepsilon^2 z_3 \varpi_{z_2 z_3} + \frac{1}{2}\varepsilon^2 \varpi_{z_3 z_3} \\
&\quad + z_2 \varpi_{z_1} + \left(\varepsilon^2 - 2\kappa z_2 + 2\chi z_3\right) \varpi_{z_2} + \left(\chi - \kappa z_3\right) \varpi_{z_3} = 0, \qquad (7.177) \\
&\varpi\left(\bar{t}, z_1, z_2, z_3, \bar{t}, \bar{z}_1, \bar{z}_3^2, \bar{z}_3\right) = \delta\left(z_1 - \bar{z}_1\right) \delta\left(z_2 - \bar{z}_3^2\right) \delta\left(z_3 - \bar{z}_3\right).
\end{aligned}$$

As usual, $\mathcal{K}$ has the form:

$$\begin{aligned}
&\mathcal{K}\left(t, \bar{t}, \mathbf{z}, \mathbf{m}\right) \\
&= \exp\left(\alpha\left(t, \bar{t}\right) + i m_1\left(z_1 - \bar{z}_1\right) + i\delta_2\left(t, \bar{t}\right) z_2 - i m_2 \bar{z}_3^2 + i\delta_3\left(t, \bar{t}\right) z_3 - i m_3 \bar{z}_3\right).
\end{aligned} \qquad (7.178)$$

The corresponding set of ODEs for $\alpha, \delta_2, \delta_3$ is as follows:

$$\begin{aligned}
&\alpha_t\left(t,\bar{t}\right) - \frac{\varepsilon^2}{2}\delta_3^2\left(t,\bar{t}\right) + i\varepsilon^2\delta_2\left(t,\bar{t}\right) + i\chi\delta_3\left(t,\bar{t}\right) = 0, \quad \alpha\left(\bar{t},\bar{t}\right) = 0,\\
&i\delta_2'\left(t,\bar{t}\right) - 2\varepsilon^2\delta_2^2\left(t,\bar{t}\right) - 2i\kappa\delta_2\left(t,\bar{t}\right) + im_1 = 0, \quad \delta_2\left(\bar{t},\bar{t}\right) = m_2,\\
&i\delta_3'\left(t,\bar{t}\right) - 2\varepsilon^2\delta_2\left(t,\bar{t}\right)\delta_3\left(t,\bar{t}\right) + 2i\chi\delta_2\nu - i\kappa\delta_3\left(t,\bar{t}\right) = 0, \quad \delta_3\left(\bar{t},\bar{t}\right) = m_3.
\end{aligned} \tag{7.179}$$

These are matrix Riccati equations.

Once again, the corresponding matrix Riccati equation can be solved explicitly. Since the second equation is separable and hence can be viewed as a scalar Riccati equation, one can start with a familiar ansatz and use Equations (7.111)–(7.113) with (γ, l) replaced by (δ_2, m_2), and the corresponding characteristic equation is as follows:

$$\lambda^2 + 2\kappa\lambda + 2i\varepsilon^2 m_1 = 0, \tag{7.180}$$

and its solutions have the familiar form:

$$\begin{aligned}
&\lambda_\pm = \mu \pm \zeta,\\
&\mu = -\kappa, \quad \zeta = \sqrt{\kappa^2 - 2i\varepsilon^2 m_1}.
\end{aligned} \tag{7.181}$$

To linearize the equations in (7.179) as a whole, use the following ansatz:

$$\begin{aligned}
&\Omega = \mathsf{E}_0\left(\omega_+\mathsf{E}_+ + \omega_-\mathsf{E}_-\right),\\
&\alpha = -\frac{1}{2}\ln\left(\Omega\right) + \frac{\mathsf{E}_0\left(a_0 + a_+\mathsf{E}_+ + a_-\mathsf{E}_-\right)}{\Omega} + g\left(\bar{t} - t\right),\\
&\delta_2 = \frac{\mathsf{E}_0\left(b_+\mathsf{E}_+ + b_-\mathsf{E}_-\right)}{\Omega}, \quad \delta_3 = \frac{\mathsf{E}_0\left(c_0 + c_+\mathsf{E}_+ + c_-\mathsf{E}_-\right)}{\Omega},
\end{aligned} \tag{7.182}$$

where $a_0, a_\pm, b_0, b_\pm$, and g are constants to be determined. This ansatz is useful since terms proportional to $\sim \mathsf{E}_0, \mathsf{E}_+, \mathsf{E}_-$ balance each other, which allows us to find the coefficients explicitly. Initial conditions complete the picture. The actual calculation is omitted for brevity. The result is as follows:

$$\begin{aligned}
&\omega_\pm = \mp\frac{\left(\lambda_\mp + 2i\varepsilon^2 m_2\right)}{2\zeta}, \quad b_\pm = \frac{i\lambda_\pm\omega_\pm}{2\varepsilon^2},\\
&c_\pm = \pm\frac{i\chi\lambda_\pm\omega_\pm}{\varepsilon^2\zeta}, \quad c_0 = m_3 - c_+ - c_-, \quad g = \frac{\chi^2\lambda_+\lambda_-}{2\varepsilon^2\zeta^2},\\
&a_0 = -\frac{i\kappa\chi c_0}{\zeta^2}, \quad a_\pm = -\omega_\pm a_0 \mp \left(\frac{\varepsilon^2 c_0^2}{4\zeta} + \frac{\chi^2\kappa^2\omega_+\omega_-}{\varepsilon^2\zeta^3}\right),
\end{aligned} \tag{7.183}$$

where $\lambda_\pm$ are given by the equations in (7.181). These expressions can be substituted in the function $\mathcal{K}$ to obtain the corresponding t.p.d.f.

7.6.3 Non-Gaussian Augmented OU Process, II

This section studies an affine process of the following form:

$$d\hat{x}_t = \hat{y}_t d\hat{W}_t, \quad \hat{x}_t = x, \qquad (7.184)$$
$$d\hat{y}_t = (\chi - \kappa\hat{y}_t)\, dt + \varepsilon d\hat{Z}_t, \quad \hat{y}_t = y.$$

The killed process is studied in Section 8 in the context of the Stein–Stein model.

Precisely as before, one can introduce the new variables $z_1 = x$, $z_2 = y^2$, $z_3 = y$, and expand the equations in (7.184) as follows:

$$\begin{aligned} d\hat{z}_{1,t} &= \hat{z}_{3,t} d\hat{W}_t, \quad \hat{z}_{1,t} = x \equiv z_1, \\ d\hat{z}_{2,t} &= \left(\varepsilon^2 - 2\kappa\hat{z}_{2,t} + 2\chi\hat{z}_{3,t}\right) + 2\varepsilon\hat{z}_{3,t} d\hat{Z}_t, \quad \hat{z}_{2,t} = y^2 \equiv z_2, \\ d\hat{z}_{3,t} &= \left(\chi - \kappa\hat{z}_{3,t}\right) dt + \varepsilon d\hat{Z}_t, \quad \hat{z}_{3,t} = z_3 \equiv y. \end{aligned} \qquad (7.185)$$

It is clear that the equations in (7.185) are affine.

The corresponding Fokker–Planck and Kolmogorov problems can be written as follows:

$$\begin{aligned} &\varpi_{\bar{t}} - \frac{1}{2}\bar{z}_2 \varpi_{\bar{z}_1\bar{z}_1} - 2\rho\varepsilon\left(\bar{z}_2\varpi\right)_{\bar{z}_1\bar{z}_2} - \rho\varepsilon\left(\bar{z}_3\varpi\right)_{\bar{z}_1\bar{z}_3} \\ &\quad - 2\varepsilon^2\left(\bar{z}_2\varpi\right)_{\bar{z}_2\bar{z}_2} - 2\varepsilon^2\left(\bar{z}_3\varpi\right)_{\bar{z}_2\bar{z}_3} - \frac{1}{2}\varepsilon^2\varpi_{\bar{z}_3\bar{z}_3} \\ &\quad + \left(\left(\varepsilon^2 - 2\kappa\bar{z}_2 + 2\chi\bar{z}_3\right)\varpi\right)_{\bar{z}_2} + \left(\left(\chi - \kappa\bar{z}_3\right)\varpi\right)_{\bar{z}_3} = 0, \\ &\varpi\left(t, x, y^2, y, t, \bar{z}_1, \bar{z}_2, \bar{z}_3\right) = \delta\left(\bar{z}_1 - x\right)\delta\left(\bar{z}_2 - y^2\right)\delta\left(\bar{z}_3 - y\right), \end{aligned} \qquad (7.186)$$

$$\begin{aligned} &\varpi_t + \frac{1}{2}z_2\varpi_{z_1z_1} + 2\rho\varepsilon z_2\varpi_{z_1z_2} + \rho\varepsilon z_3\varpi_{z_1z_3} \\ &\quad + 2\varepsilon^2 z_2\varpi_{z_2z_2} + 2\varepsilon^2 z_3\varpi_{z_2z_3} + \frac{1}{2}\varepsilon^2\varpi_{z_3z_3} \\ &\quad + \left(\varepsilon^2 - 2\kappa z_2 + 2\chi z_3\right)\varpi_{z_2} + \left(\chi - \kappa z_3\right)\varpi_{z_3} = 0, \\ &\varpi\left(\bar{t}, z_1, z_2, z_3, \bar{t}, \bar{z}_1, \bar{z}_3^2, \bar{z}_3\right) = \delta\left(z_1 - \bar{z}_1\right)\delta\left(z_2 - \bar{z}_3^2\right)\delta\left(z_3 - \bar{z}_3\right). \end{aligned} \qquad (7.187)$$

One can use $\mathcal{K}$ given by (7.178) and write the set of ODEs for $\alpha, \delta_2, \delta_3$ as follows:

$$\begin{aligned} &\alpha_t\left(t, \bar{t}\right) - \frac{\varepsilon^2}{2}\delta_3^2\left(t, \bar{t}\right) + i\varepsilon^2\delta_2\left(t, \bar{t}\right) + i\chi\delta_3\left(t, \bar{t}\right) = 0, \quad \alpha\left(\bar{t}, \bar{t}\right) = 0, \\ &i\delta_2'\left(t, \bar{t}\right) - 2\varepsilon^2\delta_2^2\left(t, \bar{t}\right) - 2i\left(\kappa - i\rho\varepsilon m_1\right)\delta_2\left(t, \bar{t}\right) - \frac{1}{2}m_1^2 = 0, \quad \delta_2\left(\bar{t}, \bar{t}\right) = m_2, \\ &i\delta_3'\left(t, \bar{t}\right) - 2\varepsilon^2\delta_2\left(t, \bar{t}\right)\delta_3\left(t, \bar{t}\right) + 2i\chi\delta_2\left(t, \bar{t}\right) - i\left(\kappa - i\rho\varepsilon m_1\right)\delta_3\left(t, \bar{t}\right) = 0, \\ &\delta_3\left(\bar{t}, \bar{t}\right) = m_3. \end{aligned} \qquad (7.188)$$

As before, this system can be linearized and solved analytically, which was pointed out by Stein and Stein (1991), Schöbel and Zhu (1999). One can repeat the result obtained in the previous section verbatim, except for (7.181). The corresponding characteristic equation has the following form:

$$\lambda^2 + 2\left(\kappa - i\rho\varepsilon m_1\right)\lambda - \varepsilon^2 m_1^2 = 0, \tag{7.189}$$

and its solutions can be written as follows:

$$\lambda_{\pm} = \mu \pm \zeta,$$
$$\mu = -\left(\kappa - i\rho\varepsilon m_1\right), \quad \zeta = \sqrt{\bar{\rho}^2\varepsilon^2 m_1^2 - 2i\rho\varepsilon\kappa m_1 + \kappa^2}. \tag{7.190}$$

The rest of the formal analysis is the same. But the asymptotic behavior of the t.p.d.f. is, of course, different.

8 Pricing of Financial Instruments

8.1 Background

The formulas derived in Sections 6 and 7 can be used to solve numerous problems of financial engineering within a consistent framework based on Kelvin waves. Here are some representative examples.

Payoffs of European options depend solely on the terminal value of $\bar{S} = \hat{S}_{\bar{t}}$ of the underlying price at the option's maturity. The most common European options are calls and puts, but, on occasion, binary options and other types are traded as well. Since the hedging and speculation needs of market participants cannot be satisfied by European options alone, the whole industry emerged to design, price, and hedge the so-called exotic options, with payoffs depending on the entire price trajectory between inception and maturity.

Prices of the fundamental financial instruments, such as forwards and European calls and puts, depend on the underlying prices only at maturity. However, the prices of many other instruments depend on the entire underlying price history between the instrument's inception and maturity. Typical examples are barrier, American, Asian, lookback, and passport options; see, for example, Lipton-Lifschitz (1999), Lipton (2001), and references therein. Moreover, the prices of bonds also depend on the history of the interest rates and credit spreads throughout their life. This section shows how to price some path-dependent financial instruments using the methodology developed in the previous sections.

8.2 The Underlying Processes

The original approach to modeling financial assets was developed by Bachelier, who assumed that prices $\hat{S}_t$ of such instruments are governed by an arithmetic Brownian motion; see Bachelier (1900):

$$d\hat{S}_t = r\hat{S}_t dt + \hat{\sigma} d\hat{W}_t, \quad \hat{S}_t = S. \tag{8.1}$$

Here, r is the risk-neutralized drift, $\hat{\sigma}$ is the volatility, and $\hat{W}_t$ is a Wiener process; r, $\hat{\sigma}$ are dimensional quantities, $[r] = T^{-1}$, $[\sigma] = \$T^{-1/2}$. The process for $\hat{S}_t$ given by (8.1) is affine; in fact, it is an OU process with zero mean and mean-repulsion instead of mean-reversion.

Subsequently, the academic community concluded that using a geometric Brownian motion as a driver is more appropriate; see Boness (1964), Samuelson (1965), Black and Scholes (1973), and Merton (1973). At present, the basic assumption is that the price $\hat{S}_t$ of an underlying financial instrument follows a geometric Brownian motion process with constant coefficients:

$$\frac{d\hat{S}_t}{\hat{S}_t} = rdt + \sigma d\hat{W}_t, \quad \hat{S}_t = S. \tag{8.2}$$

Here, r is the risk-neutralized drift, and σ is the volatility. These are dimensional quantities, $[r] = T^{-1}$, $[\sigma] = T^{-1/2}$.

The choice between using the Bachelier and the Black–Scholes models often depends on the nature of the underlying asset and the market's specific characteristics. Since the Bachelier model assumes that the underlying asset prices follow a normal distribution, it can be more appropriate for assets whose price changes are additive and can theoretically go below zero, like interest rates, some commodities, or certain types of bonds. Generally, the price movements of the underlying asset are relatively small for short periods, so the Bachelier model provides a good description of these movements. The Bachelier model is often used for pricing commodities, some interest-rate derivatives, and studying the optimal execution. In markets with relatively low volatility, the Bachelier model's assumption of additive price movements can provide a better fit for pricing and hedging derivatives than the multiplicative approach of the Black–Scholes model.

It was realized, very soon after the seminal paper by Black and Scholes (1973) was published, that in practice it provides a rather poor description of reality. Hence, considerable efforts were dedicated to developing more adequate models. Such models include the jump-diffusion, local volatility, path-dependent volatility, stochastic volatility, local-stochastic volatility, rough volatility, and culminate in the universal volatility model; see Merton (1976), Stein and Stein (1991), Bick and Reisman (1993), Heston (1993), Derman and Kani (1994), Dupire (1994), Rubinstein (1994), Hobson and Rogers (1998), Jex *et al.* (1999), Lewis (2000), Lipton (2000, 2001), Boyarchenko and Levendorsky (2002), Hagan *et al.* (2002), Lipton (2002), Bergomi (2015), Reghai (2015), Gatheral *et al.* (2018), Gershon *et al.* (2022), and references therein.

Replacing constant volatility for a geometric Brownian motion with stochastic volatility driven by a Feller process results in the popular Heston model; see Heston (1993). This model has numerous applications, particularly for pricing equity and foreign exchange derivatives. The governing SDEs are as follows:

$$\begin{aligned} &\frac{d\hat{S}_t}{\hat{S}_t} = rdt + \sqrt{\hat{v}_t}d\hat{W}_t, \quad \hat{S}_t = S, \\ &d\hat{v}_t = (\chi - \kappa\hat{v}_t)\,dt + \varepsilon\sqrt{\hat{v}_t}d\hat{Z}_t, \quad \hat{v}_t = v, \end{aligned} \tag{8.3}$$

where $d\hat{W}_t d\hat{Z}_t = \rho dt$. The logarithmic change of variables, given by (8.3), yields the equations of (7.136).

Replacing constant volatility with stochastic volatility driven by an OU process results in the (less popular) Stein–Stein model; see Schöbel and Zhu (1999); Stein and Stein (1991). The corresponding SDEs have the form:

$$\begin{aligned} &\frac{d\hat{S}_t}{\hat{S}_t} = rdt + \hat{\sigma}_t d\hat{W}_t, \quad \hat{S}_t = S, \\ &d\hat{\sigma}_t = (\chi - \kappa\hat{\sigma}_t)\,dt + \varepsilon d\hat{Z}_t, \quad \hat{v}_t = v, \end{aligned} \tag{8.4}$$

Stein and Stein (1991) considered the special case of zero correlation, $d\hat{W}_t d\hat{Z}_t = 0$, while Schöbel and Zhu (1999) studied the general case of arbitrary correlation, $d\hat{W}_t d\hat{Z}_t = \rho dt$.

Now, it is shown how to use formulas derived in Sections 6 and 7 in the context of financial engineering.

8.3 European Derivatives

8.3.1 Forwards, Calls, Puts, and Covered Calls

The most basic derivatives are forwards. Recall that a forward contract obligates the buyer (seller) to buy (to sell) an underlying asset for an agreed price at a specified future date. These contracts are not standardized and are traded over-the-counter (OTC), not on exchanges. Typical underlying assets are commodities, currencies, and financial instruments. The choice of an asset depends on the needs of the contracting parties. The price agreed upon in a forward contract is called the forward price. This price is derived based on the spot price of the underlying asset, adjusted for factors like time to maturity, interest rates, and dividends. Forward contracts are primarily used for hedging price fluctuations of the underlying asset or speculation. The payoff of a forward contract with maturity $\bar{t}$ and strike K has the following form:

$$U^{(F)}\left(\bar{S}, K\right) = \bar{S} - K, \tag{8.5}$$

where the strike is chosen in such a way that today's price of the forward contract is equal to zero. This price can be found without knowing the actual stochastic process $\hat{S}$. The hedging argument shows that the only way to deliver the price of a non-dividend-paying stock at maturity $\bar{t}$ is to buy it outright at inception t. Similarly, to deliver the strike K at time $\bar{t}$, one has to buy a zero coupon bond at time t. Let $\mathrm{Z}_{t,\bar{t}}$ be the price of a bond paying unity at maturity $\bar{t}$. Then

$$F_{t,\bar{t}} \equiv K = \frac{S}{\mathrm{Z}_{t,\bar{t}}}. \tag{8.6}$$

In contrast to forwards, a European call option grants the holder the right, but imposes no obligation, to buy an underlying asset at the option maturity for a predetermined strike price. Similarly, a European put option grants the holder the right to sell an underlying asset. Theoretically, buyers utilize calls and puts to hedge future risks; however, they often buy options for speculative purposes. American options can be exercised at any time of the buyer's choice before the option's maturity. Bermudan options are exercisable at fixed times between their inception and maturity. A call option is a contract between two parties – a buyer and a seller. Typically, the buyer takes the long position on the underlying (i.e., she expects that at maturity, the underlying price will exceed the strike price) and does not hedge her position. On the other hand, the seller or writer of the option (typically a bank) does hedge and, hence, maintains a market-neutral position. The seller receives cash up-front but incurs potential liabilities at option maturity if the option is exercised. In contrast, the buyer pays money up front in exchange for the potential for future gains. For a put option, the buyer takes a short position, while the seller is still market-neutral.

Payoffs of call and put options with maturity $\bar{t}$ and strike K have the form

$$\begin{aligned} U^{(C)}\left(\bar{S},K\right) &= \max\left\{\bar{S}-K,0\right\}, \\ U^{(P)}\left(\bar{S},K\right) &= \max\left\{K-\bar{S},0\right\}, \\ U^{(C,P)}\left(\bar{S},K\right) &= \max\left\{\phi\left(\bar{S}-K\right),0\right\}, \end{aligned} \tag{8.7}$$

where $\phi = 1$ for a call, and $\phi = -1$ for a put. Put-call parity implies that their difference is linear in $\bar{S}$ and represents a forward contract:

$$U^{(C)}\left(\bar{S},K\right) - U^{(P)}\left(\bar{S},K\right) = \bar{S} - K. \tag{8.8}$$

Several popular models, including Bachelier, Black–Scholes, Heston, and Stein–Stein, are considered below. While the Bachelier model is not scale invariant, all the other models are. A general driver for a scale-invariant model can be written as follows:

$$\frac{d\hat{S}_t}{\hat{S}_t} = rdt + \sigma_t d\hat{W}_t + \upsilon d\hat{\Pi}_t, \quad \hat{S}_t = S, \tag{8.9}$$

where, potentially, the volatility $\hat{\sigma}_t$ and the intensity $\hat{\lambda}_t$ of the Poisson process $\hat{\Pi}_t$ are driven by SDEs of their own. For such models, it is convenient to decompose call and put payoffs (8.43) into parts, which are easier to study via Kevin waves; see Lipton (2001, 2002). To this end, introduce the covered call with the payoff of the form

$$U^{(CC)}\left(\bar{S},K\right) = \min\left(\bar{S},K\right). \tag{8.10}$$

The call and put payoffs can be decomposed as follows:

$$U^{(C)}\left(\bar{S},K\right) = \bar{S} - U^{(CC)}\left(\bar{S},K\right), \quad U^{(P)}\left(\bar{S},K\right) = K - U^{(CC)}\left(\bar{S},K\right) \tag{8.11}$$

Thus, the call price is the difference between the forward price and the covered call price, while the put price is the difference between the bond price and the covered call price. In both cases, the covered call is the source of optionality.

8.3.2 Black–Scholes Model

For the standard log-normal process, the backward pricing problem for covered calls can be written as follows:

$$\begin{aligned} &U_t + \frac{1}{2}\sigma^2 S^2 U_{SS} + rU_S - rU = 0, \\ &U\left(\bar{t},S\right) = \min\{S,K\}. \end{aligned} \tag{8.12}$$

It is helpful to rewrite it by using forward rather than spot prices:

$$\begin{aligned} &\hat{U}_t + \frac{1}{2}\sigma^2 F^2 \hat{U}_{FF} = 0, \\ &\hat{U}\left(\bar{t},F\right) = \min\{F,K\}, \end{aligned} \tag{8.13}$$

where

$$\hat{F}_{t,\bar{t}} = e^{r(\bar{t}-t)}\hat{S}_t, \quad \hat{U}(t,F) = e^{r(\bar{t}-t)}U(t,S). \tag{8.14}$$

Change of variables,

$$\hat{F}_{t,\bar{t}} \to \hat{x}_{t,\bar{t}}, \quad \hat{F}_{t,\bar{t}} = Ke^{\hat{x}_{t,\bar{t}}}, \tag{8.15}$$

results in the following process for $\hat{x}_t$:

$$d\hat{x}_{t,\bar{t}} = -\frac{1}{2}\sigma^2 dt + \sigma d\hat{W}_t, \quad \hat{x}_{t,\bar{t}} = x = \ln\left(\frac{F_{t,\bar{t}}}{K}\right). \tag{8.16}$$

The t.p.d.f. for this process is Gaussian:

$$\varpi\left(t,x,\bar{t},\bar{x}\right) = \frac{1}{\sqrt{2\pi\sigma^2 T}}\exp\left(-\frac{\left(\bar{x}-x+\sigma^2/2T\right)^2}{2\sigma^2 T}\right). \tag{8.17}$$

Since the the nondimensional payoff of the covered call has the form

$$\tilde{U}^{(CC)}(x) = \min\{e^x, 1\}, \tag{8.18}$$

where $\tilde{U} = \hat{U}/K$, one obtains the following expression for $\tilde{U}^{(CC)}$:

$$\tilde{U}^{(CC)}(t,x) = e^x \mathrm{N}\left(-\frac{x}{\sigma\sqrt{T}} - \frac{\sigma\sqrt{T}}{2}\right) + \mathrm{N}\left(\frac{x}{\sigma\sqrt{T}} - \frac{\sigma\sqrt{T}}{2}\right), \tag{8.19}$$

where N (.) is the cumulative normal function.

By using (8.19), one can represent call and put prices as follows:

$$\begin{aligned} \hat{U}^{(C,P)}(t,F_T) &= \phi\left(F_T \mathrm{N}(\phi d_+) - K\mathrm{N}(\phi d_-)\right), \\ d_\pm &= \frac{\ln(F_T/K)}{\sigma\sqrt{T}} \pm \frac{\sigma\sqrt{T}}{2}. \end{aligned} \tag{8.20}$$

See Black (1976).

Returning to the original variables, write the classical Black and Scholes (1973) closed-form formula for the time t prices of calls and puts in its original form:

$$\begin{aligned} U^{(C,P)}(t,S) &= \phi\left(S\mathrm{N}(\phi d_+) - e^{-rT}K\mathrm{N}(\phi d_-)\right), \\ d_\pm &= \frac{\ln\left(e^{rT}S/K\right)}{\sigma\sqrt{T}} \pm \frac{\sigma\sqrt{T}}{2}. \end{aligned} \tag{8.21}$$

Further transforming,

$$\tilde{U}^{(CC)}(t,x) = e^{x/2}V^{(CC)}(t,x), \tag{8.22}$$

yields the following backward problem:

$$\begin{aligned} &V_t^{(CC)} + \frac{1}{2}\sigma^2 V_{xx}^{(CC)} - \frac{1}{8}\sigma^2 V^{(CC)} = 0, \\ &V^{(CC)}\left(\bar{t},x\right) = e^{-|x|/2}, \end{aligned} \tag{8.23}$$

with symmetric "peakon" payoff, which is proportional to the Laplace distribution density. This transform removes the drift in the x direction at the expense of adding killing with intensity $\sigma^2/8$. Equation (8.19) implies

$$V(t,x) = e^{x/2}\mathrm{N}\left(-\frac{x}{\sigma\sqrt{T}} - \frac{\sigma\sqrt{T}}{2}\right) + e^{-x/2}\mathrm{N}\left(\frac{x}{\sigma\sqrt{T}} - \frac{\sigma\sqrt{T}}{2}\right). \tag{8.24}$$

The Fourier transform of the "peakon" payoff yields

$$\int_{-\infty}^{\infty} e^{-|x|/2-ikx}dx = \frac{1}{k^2+1/4}. \tag{8.25}$$

By using this formula, one can derive an alternative expression for $U^{(C,P)}$ based on Kelvin waves; see Lipton (2002). It is clear that Kelvin waves associated with the killed arithmetic Brownian motion described by (8.16) are the standard Fourier waves of the following form:

$$\mathcal{K}(t,x,k) = e^{-\left(k^2+1/4\right)\sigma^2 T/2+ikx}. \tag{8.26}$$

Equations (8.25) and (8.26) yield the following alternative expression for the price of covered calls given by (8.24):

$$V^{(CC)}(t,x) = \frac{1}{2\pi}\int_{-\infty}^{\infty} \frac{e^{-\left(k^2+1/4\right)\sigma^2 T/2+ikx}}{k^2+1/4}dk. \tag{8.27}$$

See Lipton (2002). Equation (8.27) is central for the subsequent developments. For a single strike, this formula is less efficient than its classical counterpart; however, for a set of strikes, it is faster, because all the prices can be computed in one go, via the Fast Fourier Transform.

As one shall see shortly, these formulas help to handle affine pricing models very naturally.

8.3.3 Heston Model

The transformed forward pricing problem for the Heston model with the "peakon" payoff has the following form:

$$\begin{aligned} &V_t^{(CC)} + \frac{1}{2}y\left(V_{xx}^{(CC)} + 2\rho\varepsilon V_{xy}^{(CC)} + \varepsilon^2 V_{yy}^{(CC)}\right) \\ &\qquad + (\chi - \hat{\kappa}y)\,V_y^{(CC)} - \frac{y}{8}V^{(CC)} = 0, \\ &V^{(CC)}\left(\bar{t},x,y\right) = e^{-|x|/2}, \end{aligned} \tag{8.28}$$

where $\hat{\kappa} = \kappa - \rho\varepsilon/2$. Thus, one is dealing with the killed stochastic process given by the equations in (7.136). Adapting the corresponding equations to accommodate the updated mean-reversion rate and the presence of the killing term, one gets the following system of ODEs for the corresponding Kelvin wave parameters:

$$\alpha_t\left(t,\bar{t}\right) + i\chi\gamma\left(t,\bar{t}\right) = 0, \quad \alpha\left(\bar{t},\bar{t}\right) = 0,$$
$$i\gamma_t\left(t,\bar{t}\right) - \frac{1}{2}\varepsilon^2\gamma^2\left(t,\bar{t}\right) - \left(\hat{\kappa} - i\rho\varepsilon k\right) i\gamma\left(t,\bar{t}\right) - \frac{1}{2}\left(k^2 + \frac{1}{4}\right) = 0, \quad \gamma\left(\bar{t},\bar{t}\right) = 0. \tag{8.29}$$

Formulas (7.111)–(7.114) are still applicable. However, the corresponding characteristic equation and its solution are:

$$\lambda^2 + \left(\hat{\kappa} - i\rho\varepsilon k\right)\lambda - \frac{\varepsilon^2}{4}\left(k^2 + \frac{1}{4}\right) = 0, \tag{8.30}$$

$$\lambda_\pm = \mu \pm \zeta,$$
$$\mu = -\frac{\left(\hat{\kappa} - i\rho\varepsilon k\right)}{2}, \quad \zeta = \frac{\sqrt{\bar{\rho}^2\varepsilon^2 k^2 - 2i\rho\varepsilon k + \hat{\kappa}^2 + \varepsilon^2/4}}{2}. \tag{8.31}$$

It is convenient to write (α, γ) as follows:

$$\alpha\left(T,k\right) = -\frac{2\chi}{\varepsilon^2}\left(\left(\mu + \zeta\right)T + \ln\left(\frac{-\mu + \zeta + \left(\mu + \zeta\right)e^{-2\zeta T}}{2\zeta}\right)\right), \tag{8.32}$$

$$\gamma\left(T,k\right) = \left(k^2 + \frac{1}{4}\right)\frac{i\left(1 - e^{-2\zeta T}\right)}{2\left(-\mu + \zeta + \left(\mu + \zeta\right)e^{-2\zeta T}\right)} \equiv \left(k^2 + \frac{1}{4}\right)i\varsigma\left(T,k\right). \tag{8.33}$$

Hence, the price of the "peakon" has the following form:

$$V^{(CC)}\left(t,x,y\right) = \frac{1}{2\pi}\int_{-\infty}^{\infty}\frac{e^{\alpha(T,k) - \left(k^2 + 1/4\right)\varsigma(T,k)y + ikx}}{k^2 + 1/4}dk. \tag{8.34}$$

Equation (8.34) is frequently called the Lewis–Lipton formula; see, for example, Lewis (2000), Lipton (2000), Lewis (2001), Lipton (2001, 2002), Schmelzle (2010), Janek *et al.* (2011).

The implied volatility surface generated by a representative Heston model is shown in Figure 13. Recall that the implied volatility $\Sigma\left(T,K\right)$ is the volatility one must substitute into the Black–Scholes formula to reproduce the market price of a call (or put) option with maturity T and strike K. Thus, the deviation of the volatility surface from the flat surface $\Sigma\left(T,K\right) = \Sigma_0$ shows how far a given market (or model) is from the idealized Black–Scholes framework.

8.3.4 Stein–Stein Model

The transformed forward pricing problem for the Stein–Stein model with the "peakon" payoff has the following form:

$$V_t^{(CC)} + \frac{1}{2}z_2 V_{z_1 z_1}^{(CC)} + 2\rho\varepsilon z_2 V_{z_1 z_2}^{(CC)} + \rho\varepsilon z_3 V_{z_1 z_3}^{(CC)}$$
$$+ 2\varepsilon^2 z_2 V_{z_2 z_2}^{(CC)} + 2\varepsilon^2 z_3 V_{z_2 z_3}^{(CC)} + \frac{1}{2}\varepsilon^2 V_{z_3 z_3}^{(CC)}$$

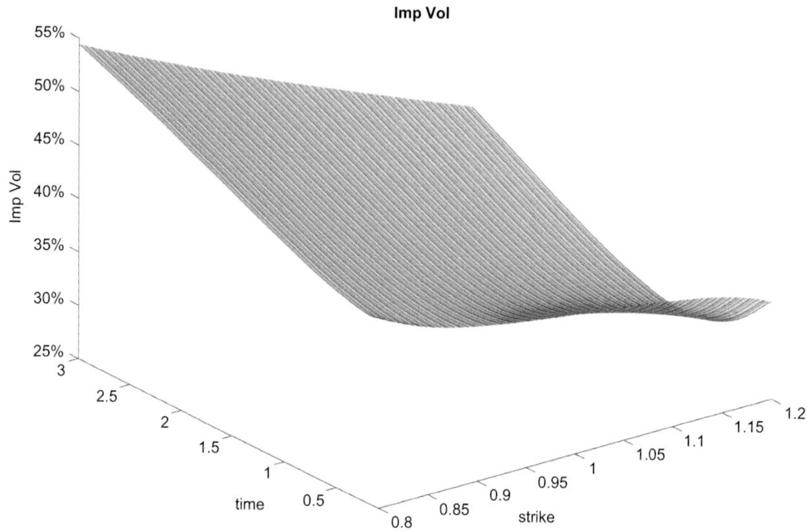

Figure 13 A representative implied volatility surface generated by the Heston model. Parameters are the same as in Figure 12. Author's graphics.

$$
\begin{aligned}
&+\left(\varepsilon^2 - 2\hat{\kappa} z_2 + 2\chi z_3\right) V^{(CC)}_{z_2} + \left(\chi - \hat{\kappa} z_3\right) V^{(CC)}_{z_3} - \frac{z_2}{8} V^{(CC)} = 0, \quad (8.35)\\
&V^{(CC)}\left(\bar{t}, z_1, z_2, z_3\right) = e^{-|z_1|/2},
\end{aligned}
$$

which corresponds to the killed stochastic process described by the equations in (7.184). By incorporating the killing term, one gets the following set of ODEs for the Kelvin wave parameters

$$
\begin{aligned}
&\alpha_t\left(t,\bar{t}\right) - \frac{\varepsilon^2}{2}\delta_3^2\left(t,\bar{t}\right) + i\varepsilon^2\delta_2\left(t,\bar{t}\right) + i\chi\delta_3\left(t,\bar{t}\right) = 0, \quad \alpha\left(\bar{t},\bar{t}\right) = 0,\\
&i\delta_2'\left(t,\bar{t}\right) - 2\varepsilon^2\delta_2^2\left(t,\bar{t}\right) - 2i\left(\hat{\kappa} - i\rho\varepsilon m_1\right)\delta_2\left(t,\bar{t}\right)\\
&\qquad - \frac{1}{2}\left(m_1^2 + \frac{1}{4}\right) = 0, \quad \delta_2\left(\bar{t},\bar{t}\right) = 0,\\
&i\delta_3'\left(t,\bar{t}\right) - 2\varepsilon^2\delta_2\left(t,\bar{t}\right)\delta_3\left(t,\bar{t}\right) + 2i\chi\delta_2\left(t,\bar{t}\right)\\
&\qquad - i\left(\hat{\kappa} - i\rho\varepsilon m_1\right)\delta_3\left(t,\bar{t}\right) = 0, \quad \delta_3\left(\bar{t},\bar{t}\right) = 0. \qquad (8.36)
\end{aligned}
$$

The corresponding solution has the form given by the equations in (7.182) with

$$
\begin{aligned}
&\lambda_\pm = \mu \pm \zeta,\\
&\mu = -\left(\hat{\kappa} - i\rho\varepsilon m_1\right), \quad \zeta = \sqrt{\bar{\rho}^2\varepsilon^2 m_1^2 - 2i\rho\varepsilon\kappa m_1 + \kappa^2 + \varepsilon^2/4},\\
&\omega_\pm = \mp\frac{\lambda_\mp}{2\zeta}, \quad b_\pm = \frac{i\lambda_\pm\omega_\pm}{2\varepsilon^2}, \qquad (8.37)
\end{aligned}
$$

$$c_\pm = \pm\frac{i\chi\lambda_\pm\omega_\pm}{\varepsilon^2\zeta}, \quad c_0 = -c_+ - c_-, \quad g = \frac{\chi^2\lambda_+\lambda_-}{2\varepsilon^2\zeta^2},$$

$$a_0 = -\frac{i\kappa\chi c_0}{\zeta^2}, \quad a_\pm = -\omega_\pm a_0 \mp \left(\frac{\varepsilon^2 c_0^2}{4\zeta} + \frac{\chi^2\kappa^2\omega_+\omega_-}{\varepsilon^2\zeta^3}\right).$$

The generic expression for the price of the “peakon” has the following form:

$$V^{(CC)}\left(\bar{t}, z_1, z_3^2, z_3\right) = \frac{1}{2\pi}\int_{-\infty}^{\infty} \frac{e^{\alpha(T,m_1)+i\delta_2(T,m_1)z_3^2+i\delta_3(T,m_1)z_3+im_1z_1}}{m_1^2+1/4} dm_1. \quad (8.38)$$

It is clear that this price is a function of $\bar{t}, z_1, z_3$.

8.3.5 Path-Dependent Volatility Model

Hobson and Rogers (1998) initially proposed path-dependent volatility models; subsequently, they were studied by many authors; see Davis (2004), Di Francesco and Pascucci (2004, 2005), Guyon (2014), and Lipton and Reghai (2023), among others. They present a viable alternative to the more popular local volatility models developed by Bick and Reisman (1993), Derman and Kani (1994), Dupire (1994), and Rubinstein (1994).

The main advantage of path-dependent volatility models compared to their local volatility brethren is that the former deal with volatility functions depending on a nondimensional argument, such as $\hat{S}_t/\hat{A}_t$, where $\hat{S}_t$ is the stock price, and $\hat{A}_t$ is its average, say, $\sigma = \sigma(\hat{S}_t/\hat{A}_t)$, while the latter use volatilities depending on a dimensional argument $\hat{S}_t$, $\sigma = \sigma(\hat{S}_t)$, which is conceptually unsound and results in model dynamics deviating from the one observed in the market. The problem with path-dependent models is that building an analytically tractable path-dependent model is exceedingly tricky, so gaining the necessary intuition or benchmarking numerical solutions is complicated. However, this section develops such a model using results derived in Section 7.3.

Here, an original path-dependent model with a semianalytical solution is presented for the first time. The dynamics is adapted from Section 7.3, Equation (7.153) as follows:

$$\hat{A}_t = \exp\left(\kappa\int_{-\infty}^{t} e^{-\kappa(t-t')}\ln\hat{S}_{t'}dt'\right), \quad \hat{A}_t = A,$$
$$\frac{d\hat{S}_t}{\hat{S}_t} = \sqrt{c_0 + c_1\ln\left(\frac{\hat{S}_t}{\hat{A}_t}\right)}d\hat{W}_t, \quad \hat{S}_t = S. \quad (8.39)$$

It is not necessary to describe in detail how $\hat{S}_{\tilde{t}}$, and, hence, $\hat{A}_{\tilde{t}}$, behave when $\tilde{t} < t$, since it becomes unimportant provided that κT is sufficiently large. For instance, one can assume that $\hat{S}_{\bar{t}} \equiv A$, when $\bar{t} < t$, then $A = S$. Additionally, it is assumed that $r = 0$, so that spot and forward prices coincide, $\hat{S}_t = \hat{F}_{t,\bar{t}}$.

In logarithmic variables $\hat{x}_t = \ln\left(\hat{A}_t\right)$, $\hat{y}_t = \ln\left(\hat{S}_t\right)$, the equations in (8.39) assume the form given by the equations in (7.153). Accordingly, the pricing equation for the path-dependent model with the symmetric "peakon" payoff can be written as follows:

$$
\begin{aligned}
&V_t^{(CC)} + \frac{1}{2}\left(a_0 + a_1\left(y - x\right)\right)\left(V_{yy}^{(CC)} - \frac{1}{4}V^{(CC)}\right) + \kappa\left(y - x\right)V_x^{(CC)} = 0,\\
&V^{(CC)}\left(\bar{t}, x, y\right) = e^{-|y|/2}.
\end{aligned}
\tag{8.40}
$$

The Kelvin wave parameters are governed by the equations of the following form:

$$
\begin{aligned}
&\alpha_t\left(t,\bar{t}\right) - \frac{a_0}{2}\left(\gamma^2\left(t,\bar{t}\right) + \frac{1}{4}\right) = 0, \quad \alpha\left(\bar{t},\bar{t}\right) = 0,\\
&i\beta_t\left(t,\bar{t}\right) + \frac{a_1}{2}\left(\gamma^2\left(t,\bar{t}\right) + \frac{1}{4}\right) - i\kappa\beta\left(t,\bar{t}\right) = 0, \quad \beta\left(\bar{t},\bar{t}\right) = 0,\\
&i\gamma_t\left(t,\bar{t}\right) - \frac{a_1}{2}\left(\gamma^2\left(t,\bar{t}\right) + \frac{1}{4}\right) + i\kappa\beta\left(t,\bar{t}\right) = 0, \quad \gamma\left(\bar{t},\bar{t}\right) = l.
\end{aligned}
\tag{8.41}
$$

8.3.6 Bachelier Model

In the Bachelier model, the corresponding discounted t.p.d.f. is given by a modified (6.96):

$$
\varpi\left(t, S, \bar{t}, \bar{S}\right) = \frac{1}{\sqrt{2\pi\Sigma^2\left(t,\bar{t}\right)}}\exp\left(-\frac{\left(\bar{S} - F_T\right)^2}{2\Sigma^2\left(t,\bar{t}\right)}\right),
\tag{8.42}
$$

where

$$
\Sigma^2\left(t,\bar{t}\right) = \frac{\hat{\sigma}^2\left(e^{2rT} - 1\right)}{2r}.
\tag{8.43}
$$

By virtue of (8.7), one can price European calls and puts as follows:

$$
V(t, F_T) = e^{-rT}\left(\phi\left(F_T - K\right)\mathrm{N}\left(\phi\frac{F_T - K}{\Sigma\left(T\right)}\right) + \Sigma\left(T\right)\mathrm{n}\left(\frac{F_T - K}{\Sigma\left(T\right)}\right)\right),
\tag{8.44}
$$

or, in spot terms:

$$
V(t, S) = \phi\left(S - e^{-rT}K\right)\mathrm{N}\left(\phi\frac{S - e^{-rT}K}{\tilde{\Sigma}\left(T\right)}\right) + \tilde{\Sigma}\left(T\right)\mathrm{n}\left(\frac{S - e^{-rT}K}{\tilde{\Sigma}\left(T\right)}\right),
\tag{8.45}
$$

where

$$
\tilde{\Sigma}^2\left(T\right) = \frac{\hat{\sigma}^2\left(1 - e^{-2rT}\right)}{2r}.
\tag{8.46}
$$

See Bachelier (1900), Schachermayer & Teichmann (2008), and Terakado (2019) for further details.

8.4 Asian Options with Arithmetic and Geometric Averaging

The most basic path-dependent options are fixed strike Asian calls and puts, whose payoff depends on the underlying value averaged between the inception and maturity. Such options are popular for commodity and energy trading and in many other circumstances. The average $\hat{A}_{t,\bar{t}}$ on the interval $\left[t,\bar{t}\right]$ can be defined in several ways. The simplest and, as a result, the most popular is an arithmetic average:

$$\hat{A}_{t,\bar{t}} = \frac{1}{T}\int_t^{\bar{t}} \hat{S}_s ds. \tag{8.47}$$

A less frequent, but technically easier to deal with, alternative is a geometric average:

$$\hat{A}_{t,\bar{t}} = \exp\left(\frac{1}{T}\int_t^{\bar{t}} \ln\left(\hat{S}_s\right) ds\right). \tag{8.48}$$

The payoff of an Asian option with maturity $\bar{t}$ and fixed strike K is

$$U\left(\bar{A}_{t,\bar{t}}\right) = \max\left\{\phi\left(\bar{A}_{t,\bar{t}} - K\right), 0\right\}, \tag{8.49}$$

as before, $\phi = 1$ for a call, and $\phi = -1$ for a put. For the floating strike, the payoff is

$$U\left(\bar{S}_{\bar{t}}, \bar{A}_{t,\bar{t}}\right) = \max\left\{\phi\left(\bar{S}_{\bar{t}} - k\bar{A}_{t,\bar{t}}\right), 0\right\}, \tag{8.50}$$

where the nondimensional parameter k is called weighting; typically, $k = 1$.

Start with the Bachelier model. Equations for pricing Asian Options with an arithmetic average are as follows:

$$\begin{aligned} d\hat{A}_t &= \hat{S}_t dt, \quad \hat{A}_t = 0, \\ d\hat{S}_t &= r\hat{S}_t dt + \sigma d\hat{W}_t, \quad \hat{S}_t = S. \end{aligned} \tag{8.51}$$

Thus, (6.114) and (6.115) are applicable. All one needs is the marginal distribution for $\bar{A}_{t,\bar{t}}$, which is Gaussian:

$$\varpi\left(\bar{A}\right) \sim \mathrm{N}\left(R, \Sigma^2\right), \tag{8.52}$$

where

$$R = \mathsf{B}_{-r}(T)S, \quad \Sigma^2 = \frac{\sigma^2}{r}\left(\mathsf{B}_0(T) - 2\mathsf{B}_{-r}(T) + \mathsf{B}_{-2r}(T)\right). \tag{8.53}$$

Consider the discounted payoff of the Asian call option (say):

$$U(t,\bar{A}) = \left(\frac{\bar{A}}{T} - K\right)_+ . \tag{8.54}$$

The corresponding calculation is straightforward:

$$\begin{aligned} U(t,S) &= e^{-rT} \int_{TK}^{\infty} \frac{\left(\frac{\bar{A}}{T} - K\right) e^{-\frac{(\bar{A}-R)^2}{2\Sigma^2}}}{\sqrt{2\pi\Sigma^2}} d\bar{A} \\ &= \frac{e^{-rT}\Sigma}{T} \int_{\frac{(TK-R)}{\Sigma}}^{\infty} \frac{\eta e^{-\frac{\eta^2}{2}}}{\sqrt{2\pi}} d\eta - \frac{e^{-rT}(TK-R)}{T} \int_{\frac{(TK-R)}{\Sigma}}^{\infty} \frac{e^{-\frac{\eta^2}{2}}}{\sqrt{2\pi}} d\eta \\ &= \frac{e^{-rT}\Sigma}{T} \mathrm{n}\left(\frac{R-TK}{\Sigma}\right) - \frac{e^{-rT}(TK-R)}{T} \mathrm{N}\left(\frac{R-TK}{\Sigma}\right). \end{aligned} \tag{8.55}$$

Analytical pricing of Asian options with arithmetic averaging for the Black–Scholes model is notoriously tricky; see Geman and Eydeland (1995), Rogers and Shi (1995), and Lipton (1999, 2001). At the same time, pricing Asian options with geometric averaging can be done quickly; see Barrucci *et al.* (2001), Lipton (2001), and Di Francesco and Pascucci (2005), and references therein. Such options can be priced using formula (6.45) derived in Section 6. An alternative approach based on the path integral method is discussed in Devreese *et al.* (2010). Define

$$\hat{x}_t = \int_t^t \hat{y}_s ds, \quad \hat{y}_t = \ln\left(\hat{S}_t\right). \tag{8.56}$$

Then

$$\begin{aligned} d\hat{x}_t &= \hat{y}_t dt, \quad \hat{x}_t = 0, \\ d\hat{y}_t &= \left(r - \frac{\sigma^2}{2}\right) dt + \sigma d\hat{W}_t, \quad \hat{y}_t = \ln\left(\hat{S}_t\right) \equiv y. \end{aligned} \tag{8.57}$$

The value of the option can be written as follows:

$$U(t,S) = e^{-rT} \int_{x^*}^{\phi\infty} \varpi(\bar{x}) \left(\exp\left(\frac{\bar{x}}{T}\right) - \exp(\ln K)\right) d\bar{x}, \tag{8.58}$$

where

$$x^* = T \ln K. \tag{8.59}$$

Since (8.57) is a special case of (6.74), one can use the equations in (6.81) to obtain the marginal distribution for $\bar{x}$, which is a Gaussian distribution of the form:

$$\varpi(\bar{x}) = \frac{\exp\left(-\frac{(\bar{x}-p)^2}{2\sigma_x^2}\right)}{\sqrt{2\pi\sigma_x^2}},$$
$$\sigma_x^2 = \frac{\sigma^2 T^3}{3}, \quad p = \ln(S)\,T + \frac{1}{2}\left(r - \frac{\sigma^2}{2}\right)T^2. \tag{8.60}$$

Thus,

$$U(t,S) = \mathcal{J}_1(t,S) - \mathcal{J}_2(t,S), \tag{8.61}$$

where

$$\mathcal{J}_1(t,S) = e^{-rT}\int_{x^*}^{\phi\infty} \frac{\exp\left(-\frac{(\bar{x}-p)^2}{2\sigma_x^2} + \frac{\bar{x}}{T}\right)}{\sqrt{2\pi\sigma_x^2}} d\bar{x} = \phi e^{-\frac{1}{2}\left(r+\frac{\sigma^2}{6}\right)T} S\mathrm{N}(\phi d_+),$$
$$\mathcal{J}_2(t,S) = e^{-rT}\int_{x^*}^{\phi\infty} \frac{\exp\left(-\frac{(\bar{x}-p)^2}{2\sigma_x^2} + \ln(K)\right)}{\sqrt{2\pi\sigma_x^2}} d\bar{x} = \phi e^{-rT} K\mathrm{N}(\phi d_-), \tag{8.62}$$

where

$$d_\pm = \frac{\ln(S/K) + \frac{1}{2}\left(r - \frac{\sigma^2}{6} \pm \frac{\sigma^2}{3}\right)T}{\sqrt{\sigma^2 T/3}}. \tag{8.63}$$

Finally, one obtains a well-known formula for the price of a fixed strike Asian option with geometric averaging:

$$U(t,S) = \phi\left(e^{-\frac{1}{2}\left(r+\frac{\sigma^2}{6}\right)T} S\mathrm{N}(\phi d_+) - e^{-rT} K\mathrm{N}(\phi d_-)\right). \tag{8.64}$$

Of course, a similar formula holds when r, σ are time-dependent. The derivation, although very simple, seems to be new.

8.5 Volatility and Variance Swaps and Swaptions

8.5.1 Volatility Swaps and Swaptions

Recall that the Stein–Stein stochastic volatility model assumes that the volatility is driven by an OU process; see Stein and Stein (1991). One needs to find Green's function associated with the following augmented SDEs:

$$
\begin{aligned}
d\hat{x}_t &= \hat{y}_t dt, \quad \hat{x}_t = 0, \\
d\hat{y}_t &= \left(\chi^{(Vol)} - \kappa^{(Vol)}\hat{y}_t\right) dt + \varepsilon^{(Vol)} d\hat{W}_t, \quad \hat{y}_t = y^{(Vol)},
\end{aligned}
\tag{8.65}
$$

or, equivalently,

$$
\begin{aligned}
d\hat{x}_t &= \hat{y}_t dt, \quad \hat{x}_t = 0, \\
d\hat{y}_t &= \kappa^{(Vol)} \left(\theta^{(Vol)} - \hat{y}_t\right) dt + \varepsilon^{(Vol)} d\hat{W}_t, \quad \hat{y}_t = y^{(Vol)},
\end{aligned}
\tag{8.66}
$$

which describe the evolution of the volatility $\hat{\sigma}_t \equiv \hat{y}_t$ and its integral $\hat{x}_t$; the equations of (8.65) are identical to the equations of (6.98).

It can be shown that the pair $(\bar{x}, \bar{y})$ has the bivariate Gaussian distribution with the covariance matrix $\mathfrak{H}$ given by (6.113), and mean (p, q) given by (6.114):

$$
\begin{pmatrix} p \\ q \end{pmatrix} = \begin{pmatrix} T\theta^{(Vol)} + \bar{\mathsf{B}}_{\kappa^{(Vol)}}(T)\left(y^{(Vol)} - \theta^{(Vol)}\right) \\ \theta^{(Vol)} + \mathsf{A}_{\kappa^{(Vol)}}(T)\left(y^{(Vol)} - \theta^{(Vol)}\right) \end{pmatrix}.
\tag{8.67}
$$

Since the marginal distribution of $\hat{x}_t$ given by (6.115) is Gaussian, the fair strike of a volatility swap with maturity t is simply the expected value of $\hat{x}_t/T$:

$$
VolSwap = \theta^{(Vol)} + \left(y^{(Vol)} - \theta^{(Vol)}\right) \frac{\bar{\mathsf{B}}_{\kappa^{(Vol)}}(T)}{T}.
\tag{8.68}
$$

Here

$$
[VolSwap] = \left[\frac{\chi^{(Vol)}}{\kappa^{(Vol)}}\right] = \left[\theta^{(Vol)}\right] = [y] = \frac{1}{T^{1/2}}.
\tag{8.69}
$$

Of course, one can calculate the expected value of $\hat{x}_t/T$ via more straightforward means. To this end, (8.68) can be derived directly by taking expectations of SDE (8.65). However, as we shall see in the following subsection, (6.115) for the marginal distribution $\varpi^{(x)}\left(t, y^{(Vol)}, \bar{t}, \bar{x}\right)$ allows one to solve more interesting problems, such as calculating prices of bonds and bond options; see the discussion that follows.

Moreover, by using this equation, one can price volatility swaptions with payoffs of the form:

$$
U\left(\bar{t}, \bar{x}\right) = \max\left\{\phi\left(\bar{x} - x^*\right), 0\right\}.
\tag{8.70}
$$

The price $U\left(t, y^{(Vol)}\right)$ becomes:

$$
\begin{aligned}
U\left(t, y^{(Vol)}\right) &= e^{-rT}\phi \int_{x^*}^{\phi\infty} (\bar{x} - x^*)\, \varpi^{(x)}\left(t, y^{(Vol)}, \bar{t}, \bar{x}\right) d\bar{x} \\
&= \frac{e^{-rT}\phi}{\sqrt{2\pi h_0\,(t, \bar{t})}} \int_{x^*}^{\phi\infty} (\bar{x} - x^*) \exp\left(\frac{(\bar{x} - p)^2}{2h_0}\right) d\bar{x} \qquad (8.71) \\
&= e^{-rT}\left(\phi\,(p - x^*)\,\mathrm{N}\left(\phi\frac{(p - x^*)}{\sqrt{h_0}}\right) + \sqrt{h_0}\,\mathrm{n}\left(\frac{(p - x^*)}{\sqrt{h_0}}\right)\right).
\end{aligned}
$$

It is clear that formula (8.71) is a variant of the Bachelier formula (8.44).

8.5.2 Variance Swaps and Swaptions

In contrast to volatility, which, despite common misconceptions, can be negative, variance must be nonnegative since it is a square of a real-valued quantity. Accordingly, the easiest way to model it is by using the augmented Feller process with $\vartheta > 0$; see (7.99).

Using (7.127), one can immediately obtain the following expression for the fair value of a variance swap for the Feller process:

$$
VarSwap = \theta^{(Var)} + \left(y^{(Var)} - \theta^{(Var)}\right)\frac{\bar{\mathsf{B}}_{\kappa^{(Var)}}(T)}{T}, \qquad (8.72)
$$

where $\theta^{(Var)} = \chi^{(Var)}/\kappa^{(Var)}$. Here

$$
[VarSwap] = \left[\theta^{(Var)}\right] = \left[y^{(Var)}\right] = \frac{1}{T}. \qquad (8.73)
$$

While formulas (8.68) and (8.72) look the same but deal with the volatility and variance, respectively, the corresponding parameters have different meanings.

Alternatively, one can use the degenerate augmented OU process, sec the equations of (7.174). Averaging away stochastic terms, one gets the following formula for the fair price of the variance swap:

$$
VarSwap = \left(\theta^{(Vol)}\right)^2 + \left(\left(y^{(Vol)}\right)^2 - \left(\theta^{(Vol)}\right)^2\right)\frac{\bar{\mathsf{B}}_{\kappa^{(Vol)}}(T)}{T}. \qquad (8.74)
$$

It is clear that Equations (8.72) and (8.74) provide different fair values for a variance swap, although these values asymptotically agree. This fact reflects the so-called model risk – by using different models, one gets different answers to the same question.

Equation (7.123) can be used to calculate the price of a variance swaption:

$$\begin{aligned}
U\left(t, y^{(Var)}\right) &= \frac{1}{2\pi}\int_{x^*}^{\phi\infty}\int_{-\infty}^{\infty}\phi\,(\bar{x}-x^*)F\left(\bar{t},k\right)e^{ik\bar{x}}dkd\bar{x} \\
&= \frac{1}{2\pi}\int_{-\infty}^{\infty}F\left(\bar{t},k\right)\left(\phi\int_{x^*}^{\phi\infty}(\bar{x}-x^*)\,e^{ik\bar{x}}d\bar{x}\right)dk \\
&= \frac{1}{2\pi}\lim_{\epsilon\to 0}\int_{-\infty}^{\infty}F\left(\bar{t},k\right)e^{ikx^*}\left(-\frac{\partial}{\partial\epsilon}\int_{x^*}^{\phi\infty}e^{(ik-\phi\epsilon)\bar{x}}d\bar{x}\right) \\
&= \frac{1}{2\pi}\lim_{\epsilon\to 0}\int_{-\infty}^{\infty}\frac{F\left(\bar{t},k\right)e^{ikx^*}}{(ik-\phi\epsilon)^2}dk,
\end{aligned} \tag{8.75}$$

where $F\left(\bar{t},k\right)$ is given by (7.124).

8.6 Automated Market Makers

Variance and volatility swaps had long occupied a specific niche within the financial product landscape. Recently, they experienced an unexpected surge in interest due to the influence of cryptocurrency trading. These swaps have proven effective in hedging impermanent loss, a phenomenon generated by automated market makers; see Lipton and Hardjono (2021), Lipton and Treccani (2021), Lipton and Sepp (2022), Cartea *et al.* (2023), Fukasawa *et. al* (2023), and others. This section closely follows Lipton and Hardjono (2021).

Let us consider a smart contract (SC), called an automated market maker (AMM) designed to facilitate exchanges of two tokens, TN_1 and TN_2. The analytical formula for the price of the second token in terms of the first defines the nature of the contract. AMMs have gained significant traction in recent years. Initially, anyone can participate as a market maker and liquidity provider by depositing TN_1 and TN_2 simultaneously and in the correct ratio into the collateral pool. Subsequently, participants can withdraw one token from the pool by delivering the other token according to the rules established by the underlying SC. While AMMs excel in facilitating stablecoin swaps, they can easily accommodate the exchange of various tokens, such as swapping a stablecoin, say USDT, for ethereum (ETH).

The actual exchange rate is determined by rules that rely on prior agreement. The available options are the constant sum, constant product, and mixture rules. Sources including Angeris *et al.* (2019), Egorov (2019), Zhang *et al.* (2018), Lipton and Hardjono (2021), Lipton and Sepp (2022), and references therein offer detailed coverage of AMMs and comprehensive insights into their mechanisms.

Assuming that initially tokens TN_1, TN_2 are equal in value, one can define a constant sum AMM:

$$X + Y = \Sigma_0, \quad X_0 = Y_0 = N, \quad \Sigma_0 = 2N. \tag{8.76}$$

Here X, Y are the quantities of TN_1, TN_2 in the pool. Equation (8.76) yields

$$Y = \Sigma_0 - X, \quad \left|\frac{dY}{dX}\right| = 1. \tag{8.77}$$

As per (8.77), the pool reaches depletion at $X = \Sigma_0$, as it becomes advantageous for an arbitrageur to increase X from N to $2N$ when TN_2 surpasses TN_1 in value. The marginal price of TN_2 relative to TN_1, as expressed in the second equation (8.77), remains consistent and equal to one. A constant price is optimal for a constant sum AMM, particularly when dealing with stablecoins like TN_1 and TN_2, whose prices fluctuate mildly around their equilibrium values. Depleting the pool is rational in scenarios where transaction fees are nonexistent, even with a minimal deviation from equilibrium. However, under more realistic conditions with nonzero transaction fees, arbitrage becomes profitable only if the deviation surpasses a certain threshold.

The constant product rule defines more intricate and, importantly, practical AMMs:

$$XY = \Pi_0, \quad X_0 = Y_0 = N, \quad \Pi_0 = N^2. \tag{8.78}$$

It is clear that

$$Y = \frac{\Pi_0}{X}, \quad \left|\frac{dY}{dX}\right| = \frac{\Pi_0}{X^2}. \tag{8.79}$$

Consequently, an arbitrageur is unable to deplete such a pool, allowing it to persist indefinitely. In this scenario, it becomes evident that the price of TN_2 relative to TN_1 is no longer steady; instead, it rises (or falls) as X decreases (or increases).

To make liquidity provision more attractive to potential market makers, one can generalize the constant sum and constant product rules. Expressions (8.76) and (8.78) representing these rules can be formulated as follows:

$$\begin{aligned} &\left(\frac{\Sigma}{\Sigma_0} - 1\right) = 0, \quad X_0 = Y_0 = N, \quad \Sigma_0 = 2N, \\ &\left(\frac{\Pi_0}{\Pi} - 1\right) = 0, \quad X_0 = Y_0 = N, \quad \Pi_0 = N^2. \end{aligned} \tag{8.80}$$

where $\Sigma = X + Y$, $\Pi = XY$ are the current sum and product, respectively. These rules can be combined as follows:

$$\left(\frac{\Pi_0}{\Pi} - 1\right) + \alpha\left(\frac{\Sigma}{\Sigma_0} - 1\right) = 0,$$
$$X_0 = Y_0 = N, \quad \Sigma_0 = 2N, \quad \Pi_0 = N^2. \tag{8.81}$$

Here, $\alpha > 0$ is an adaptive parameter, characterizing the transition from the constant product to the constant sum rule. The product Π is in the denominator to avoid the possibility of exhausting the entire pool and ensuring that

$$Y(X) \underset{X \to 0}{\to} \infty, \qquad X(Y) \underset{Y \to 0}{\to} \infty. \tag{8.82}$$

Certainly, when AMM liquidity providers are exposed to arbitragers, they face potential losses stemming from a decline in collateral value below its buy-and-hold threshold. In financial terms, an AMM liquidity provider is an option seller experiencing negative convexity, so that they must impose transaction fees to offset these losses. The losses incurred by AMMs are (somewhat misleadingly) termed "impermanent" because they tend to vanish under the assumption of mean reversion. However, the validity of the mean-reversion assumption in real-world scenarios can vary. Introducing variables x and y where $X = Nx$ and $Y = Ny$, one can express the constant sum rule described by Equations (8.76) and (8.77) as follows:

$$x + y = 2, \quad x_0 = y_0 = 1, \tag{8.83}$$
$$y(x) = 2 - x, \quad \left|\frac{dy}{dx}\right| = 1. \tag{8.84}$$

In terms of x and y, the constant product rule given by Equations (8.78) and (8.79) can be written in the following form:

$$xy = 1, \quad x_0 = y_0 = 1, \tag{8.85}$$
$$y(x) = \frac{1}{x}, \quad \left|\frac{dy}{dx}\right| = \frac{1}{x^2}. \tag{8.86}$$

Finally, the mixed-rule equations of (8.81) written in terms of x and y become

$$\left(\frac{1}{xy} - 1\right) + \alpha\left(\frac{x+y}{2} - 1\right) = 0, \quad x_0 = y_0 = 1. \tag{8.87}$$

Straightforward algebra yields

$$y_\alpha = \frac{1}{2\alpha}\left(-(2(1-\alpha)+\alpha x) + \left((2(1-\alpha)+\alpha x)^2 + \frac{8\alpha}{x}\right)^{1/2}\right),$$

$$\frac{dy_\alpha}{dx} = \frac{1}{2}\left(-1 + \frac{2(1-\alpha)+\alpha x - 4/x^2}{\left((2(1-\alpha)+\alpha x)^2 + \frac{8\alpha}{x}\right)^{1/2}}\right), \tag{8.88}$$

$$\frac{d^2 y_\alpha}{dx^2} = \frac{1}{2}\left(\frac{\alpha + 8/x^3}{\left((2(1-\alpha)+\alpha x)^2 + \frac{8\alpha}{x}\right)^{1/2}} - \frac{\alpha\left(2(1-\alpha)+\alpha x - 4/x^2\right)}{\left((2(1-\alpha)+\alpha x)^2 + \frac{8\alpha}{x}\right)^{3/2}}\right).$$

Assume that the external exchange price S of TN_2 expressed in terms of TN_1 moves away from its equilibrium value $S_0 = 1$. Let $S > 1$. For the constant sum contract, an arbitrageur can choose a number x, $1 < x \leq 2$, and deliver $(x-1)$ of TN_1 tokens to the pool in exchange for getting $(x-1)$ of TN_2 tokens. The profit or loss ($P\&L$) is given by

$$\Omega(x) = (S-1)(x-1). \tag{8.89}$$

Since Ω is a linear function of x, it is rational to exhaust the entire pool by choosing the following optimal values (x^*, y^*, Ω^*):

$$x^* = 2, \quad y^* = 0, \quad \Omega^* = (S-1). \tag{8.90}$$

Similarly, when $S < 1$:

$$x^* = 0, \quad y^* = 2, \quad \Omega^* = -(S-1). \tag{8.91}$$

The arbitraged portfolio's value is $\pi^*(S)$, where

$$\pi^*(S) = \begin{cases} 2, & S \geq 1, \\ 2S, & S < 1. \end{cases}, \tag{8.92}$$

while the buy-and-hold portfolio's value is $(S+1)$. The difference ω has the form

$$\omega = (S+1) - \pi^*(S) = |S-1|. \tag{8.93}$$

In the DeFi parlance, ω is termed as impermanent loss. However, this description can be misleading as the loss can swiftly become permanent when S moves away from its assumed "equilibrium" value of one. The percentage loss in the actual portfolio compared to the buy-and-hold portfolio is structured as follows:

$$\lambda = 1 - \frac{|S-1|}{S+1}. \tag{8.94}$$

A similar calculation can be performed for the constant product contract. When S deviates from one, an arbitrageur can choose a number $x > 1$ and deliver $(x - 1)$ tokens TN_1 to the pool, while taking $(1 - y)$ tokens TN_2 from the pool, where $y = 1/x$. The $P\&L$ has the form:

$$\Omega(x) = \left(S\left(1 - \frac{1}{x}\right) - (x - 1)\right). \tag{8.95}$$

The optimality condition has the form

$$\Omega'(x) = \left(\frac{S}{x^2} - 1\right) = 0, \tag{8.96}$$

so that the corresponding optimal values (x^*, y^*, Ω^*) are

$$x^* = \sqrt{S}, \quad y^* = \frac{1}{\sqrt{S}}, \quad \Omega^* = \left(\sqrt{S} - 1\right)^2. \tag{8.97}$$

Hence, a constant product collateral pool remains inexhaustible. Throughout each phase, the ideal quantities of TN_1 and TN_2 maintained in the portfolio are both $\sqrt{S}$. As both tokens' values within the portfolio must equate, the suggested optimal value of TN_2 in terms of TN_1 is $S^* = x^*/y^* = S$. The value of the arbitrage-driven portfolio stands at $\pi^* = 2\sqrt{S}$, whereas the value of the buy-and-hold portfolio amounts to $(S + 1)$. The difference is given by

$$\omega = (S + 1) - 2\sqrt{S} = \left(\sqrt{S} - 1\right)^2. \tag{8.98}$$

The corresponding percentage loss is

$$\lambda = 1 - \frac{2\sqrt{S}}{(S + 1)} = \frac{\left(\sqrt{S} - 1\right)^2}{(S + 1)}. \tag{8.99}$$

For the mixed-rule AMM, the arbitrageur's profit for $S > 1$ has the form

$$\Omega(x) = (S(1 - y_\alpha(x)) - (x - 1)), \tag{8.100}$$

with the optimum achieved at $x_\alpha^*, y_\alpha^*, \Omega_\alpha^*$ of the form

$$y'_\alpha\left(x_\alpha^*\right) = -\frac{1}{S}, \quad y_\alpha^* = y_\alpha\left(x_\alpha^*\right), \quad \Omega_\alpha^* = \left(S\left(1 - y_\alpha^*\right) - \left(x_\alpha^* - 1\right)\right), \tag{8.101}$$

with the optimal x_α^* via the Newton–Raphson method starting with a suitable $x_\alpha^{(0)}$:

$$x_\alpha^{(n+1)} = x_\alpha^{(n)} - \frac{y'_\alpha\left(x_\alpha^{(n)}\right) + \frac{1}{S}}{y''_\alpha\left(x_\alpha^{(n)}\right)}. \tag{8.102}$$

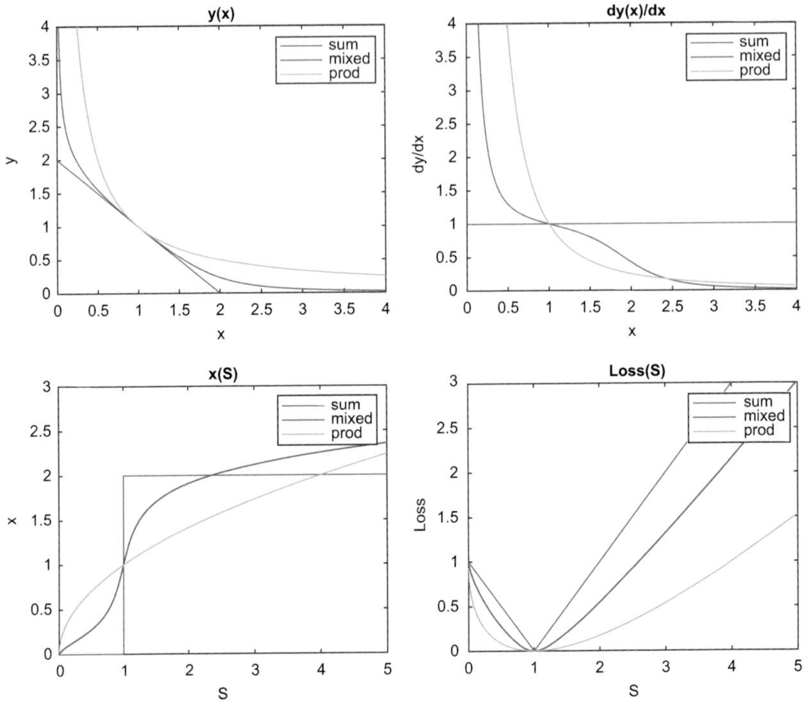

Figure 14 The constant sum, constant product, and mixed-rule curves, along with the relative prices of TN_2 in terms of TN_1 and the associated impermanent losses; $\alpha = 10$. Author's graphics.

Here y'_α, y''_α are given by the equations of (8.88). Due to quadratic convergence of the Newton–Raphson method, ten iterations provide machine accuracy, so that one can set $x^*_\alpha = x^{(10)}_\alpha$. The value of the arbitraged portfolio is

$$\pi^* = x^*_\alpha + Sy_\alpha\left(x^*_\alpha\right). \tag{8.103}$$

Figure 14 shows the constant sum, constant product, and mixed-rule curves, along with the relative prices of TN_2 in terms of TN_1 and the associated impermanent losses. It demonstrates that deviations from the tokens' equilibrium values result in losses for the market maker. Impermanent loss is relatively minor for the constant product rule, moderate for the mixed rule, and notably high for the constant sum rule. Even when the price S sways by a factor of five from its equilibrium, the impermanent loss within the constant product rule remains manageable, especially compared to the mixed rule.

One can use variance swaps to hedge impermanent loss. For brevity, consider the constant product rule. The corresponding impermanent loss, shown in Figure 14, is given by (8.98). It can be viewed as a payoff of a nonstandard

European option. The hedging approach is straightforward – one approximates this payoff with payoffs of options, which can be priced explicitly. Specifically, one can use two such options: the log and entropy contracts. The corresponding payoffs are as follows:

$$U^{LC}(S) = c^{LC}(S - 1 - \ln(S)), \tag{8.104}$$
$$U^{EC}(S) = c^{EC}(S\ln(S) - (S - 1)). \tag{8.105}$$

The prefactors c^{LC}, c^{EC} are chosen in such a way that the value of the impermanent loss (8.98) and the hypothetical payoffs (8.104) and ((8.105)) agree at the point $S = 1$ up to the third derivative, so that

$$c^{LC} = c^{EC} = \frac{1}{2}. \tag{8.106}$$

Assuming that S is driven by the geometric Brownian motion with stochastic volatility, one can find the value of the log and entropy contracts at time t at the point $S = 1$, by solving the following problems:

$$U_t + \frac{1}{2}v\left(S^2 U_{SS} + 2\varepsilon\rho S U_{Sv} + \varepsilon^2 U_{vv}\right) + (\chi - \kappa v)\, U_v = 0, \tag{8.107}$$

supplied with terminal conditions of the form

$$U^{LC}\left(\bar{t}, S, v\right) = (S - 1 - \ln(S)), \tag{8.108}$$

and

$$U^{EC}\left(\bar{t}, S, v\right) = (S\ln(S) - (S - 1)), \tag{8.109}$$

respectively.

The corresponding solutions are well-known and easy to find. One can present $U^{LC}(t, S)$ as follows:

$$U^{LC}\left(t, S, v, \bar{t}\right) = \Phi^{LC}\left(t, v, \bar{t}\right) + (S - 1 - \ln(S)), \tag{8.110}$$

where

$$\begin{aligned} &\Phi_t^{LC} + \frac{1}{2}v\left(1 + \varepsilon^2\Phi_{vv}^{LC}\right) + (\chi - \kappa v)\,\Phi_v^{LC} = 0,\\ &\Phi^{LC}\left(\bar{t}, v, \bar{t}\right) = 0. \end{aligned} \tag{8.111}$$

Accordingly,

$$\Phi^{LC}\left(t, v, \bar{t}\right) = \alpha^{LC}\left(t, \bar{t}\right) + \beta^{LC}\left(t, \bar{t}\right) v, \tag{8.112}$$

where

$$\alpha_t^{LC}(t,\bar{t}) + \chi\beta^{LC}(t,\bar{t}) = 0, \quad \alpha^{LC}(\bar{t},\bar{t}) = 0,$$
$$\beta_t^{LC}(t,\bar{t}) - \kappa\beta^{LC}(t,\bar{t}) + \frac{1}{2} = 0, \quad \beta^{LC}(\bar{t},\bar{t}) = 0. \tag{8.113}$$

Thus,

$$\alpha^{LC}(t,\bar{t}) = \frac{\chi}{2\kappa}\left(T - \bar{\mathsf{B}}_\kappa(T)\right),$$
$$\beta^{LC}(t,\bar{t}) = \frac{\bar{\mathsf{B}}_\kappa(T)}{2}, \tag{8.114}$$

so that

$$U^{LC}(t,S,v,\bar{t}) = \frac{1}{2}\left(\frac{\chi T}{\kappa} + \left(v - \frac{\chi}{2\kappa}\right)\bar{\mathsf{B}}_\kappa(T)\right) + (S - 1 - \ln(S)). \tag{8.115}$$

It is clear that $U^{LC}(t,1,v,\bar{t})$ is in agreement with (8.72).

One can calculate $U^{EC}(t,S,v)$ in a similar fashion by representing it in the form:

$$U^{EC}(t,S,v,\bar{t}) = \Phi^{EC}(t,v,\bar{t})\,S + (S\ln(S) - (S-1)), \tag{8.116}$$

where, once the common factor S is omitted,

$$\Phi_t^{EC} + \frac{1}{2}v\left(1 + 2\varepsilon\rho\Phi_v^{EC} + \varepsilon^2\Phi_{vv}^{EC}\right) + (\chi - \kappa v)\,\Phi_v^{EC} = 0,$$
$$\Phi^{LC}(\bar{t},v,\bar{t}) = 0. \tag{8.117}$$

As before,

$$\Phi^{EC}(t,v,\bar{t}) = \alpha^{EC}(t,\bar{t}) + \beta^{EC}(t,\bar{t})\,v, \tag{8.118}$$

where

$$\alpha_t^{EC}(t,\bar{t}) + \chi\beta^{EC}(t,\bar{t}) = 0, \quad \alpha^{EC}(\bar{t},\bar{t}) = 0,$$
$$\beta_t^{EC}(t,\bar{t}) - (\kappa - \varepsilon\rho)\,\beta^{EC}(t,\bar{t}) + \frac{1}{2} = 0, \quad \beta^{EC}(\bar{t},\bar{t}) = 0. \tag{8.119}$$

Thus,

$$\alpha^{EC}(t,\bar{t}) = \frac{\chi}{2(\kappa - \varepsilon\rho)}\left(T - \bar{\mathsf{B}}_{\kappa-\varepsilon\rho}(T)\right), \tag{8.120}$$

$$\beta^{EC}(t,\bar{t}) = \frac{\bar{\mathsf{B}}_{\kappa-\varepsilon\rho}(T)}{2},$$
$$U^{EC}(t,S,v,\bar{t}) = \frac{1}{2}\left(\frac{\chi T}{\kappa_1} + \left(v - \frac{\chi}{2\kappa_1}\right)\bar{\mathsf{B}}_{\kappa_1}(T)\right)S + (S\ln(S) - (S-1)). \tag{8.121}$$

where $\kappa_1 = \kappa - \varepsilon\rho$. Equations (8.115) and (8.121) allow us to estimate the amount a liquidity provider needs to collect to cover the expected impermanent loss.

However, it turns out (which comes as a surprise, at least to the present author) that one can solve the pricing problem (8.107) with the exact terminal condition (8.98) *explicitly*, since the impermanent loss does not have any optionality and is a linear combination of the so-called power contracts with payoffs of the form $S, \sqrt{S}, 1$.[10]

Thus, by using an appropriate Kelvin wave, one can solve the problem (8.107) with the power terminal condition:

$$U^{(\nu)}(S) = S^{\nu}. \tag{8.122}$$

Of course, for $\nu = 0, 1$, the solution is trivial; for other values of ν, additional efforts are needed. To be concrete, it is assumed that $0 < \nu < 1$; for other values of ν, the solution can blow up in finite time. The price of the power contract with the payoff S^{ν} (even when the interest rate $r \neq 0$) is given by a Kelvin wave:

$$V\left(t, S, \bar{t}\right) = e^{\alpha(t,\bar{t}) + \beta(t,\bar{t})\nu} S^{\nu}, \tag{8.123}$$

where $\alpha(t), \beta(t)$ solve the following system of ODEs:

$$\begin{gathered}\alpha_t\left(t,\bar{t}\right) + \chi\beta\left(t,\bar{t}\right) = 0, \quad \alpha\left(\bar{t},\bar{t}\right) = 0, \\ \beta_t\left(t,\bar{t}\right) + \frac{\varepsilon^2}{2}\beta^2\left(t,\bar{t}\right) - (\kappa - \nu\rho\varepsilon)\beta\left(t,\bar{t}\right) + \frac{\nu(\nu-1)}{2} = 0, \quad \beta\left(\bar{t},\bar{t}\right) = 0,\end{gathered} \tag{8.124}$$

which has an explicit solution given by Equations (7.111)–(7.114) with

$$\lambda_{\pm}^2 + (\kappa - \nu\rho\varepsilon)\lambda_{\pm} + \frac{\varepsilon^2\nu(\nu-1)}{4} = 0, \tag{8.125}$$

$$\lambda_{\pm} = \mu \pm \zeta,$$

$$\mu = -\frac{(\kappa - \nu\rho\varepsilon)}{2}, \quad \zeta = \frac{\sqrt{(\kappa - \nu\rho\varepsilon)^2 - \varepsilon^2\nu(\nu-1)}}{2}. \tag{8.126}$$

Thus, both μ and ζ are real. Accordingly, one can represent α and β as follows:

$$\begin{gathered}\alpha(T) = -\frac{2\chi}{\varepsilon^2}\left(-\frac{(\kappa - \nu\rho\varepsilon)T}{2} + \ln\left(\frac{\zeta\cosh(T) - \mu\sinh(T)}{\zeta}\right)\right), \\ \beta(T) = \frac{\nu(\nu-1)(\sinh(T))}{2(\zeta\cosh(T) - \mu\sinh(T))}.\end{gathered} \tag{8.127}$$

The exact impermanent loss and its approximations are shown in Figure 15. This figure shows that $\max\left(U^{LC}, U^{EC}\right)$ strictly dominates the exact solution

[10] This fact is true even for nonzero interest rates.

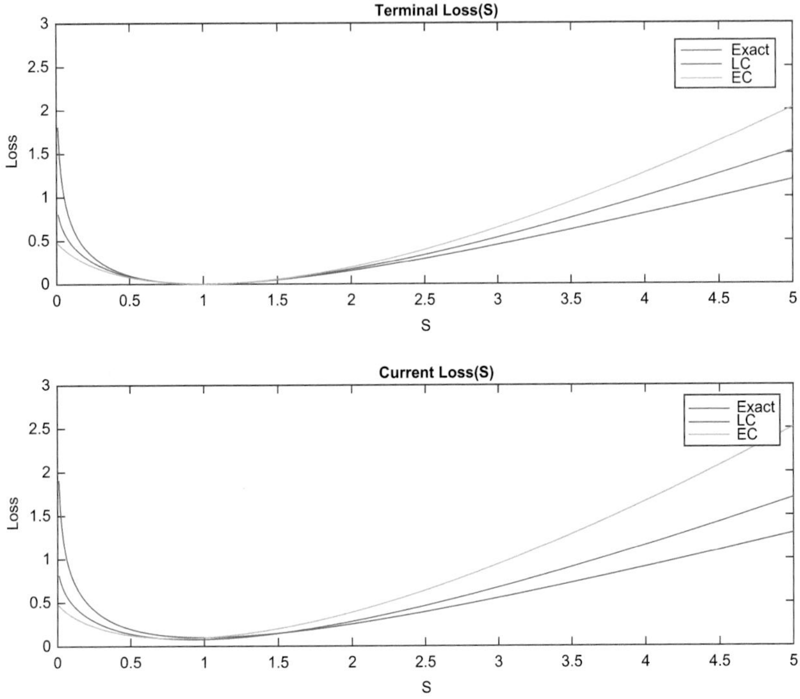

Figure 15 The exact impermanent loss and its approximations via log and enthropy contracts. The corresponding parameters are $T = 3$, $dt = 0.01$, $\chi = 0.2$, $\kappa = 2.0$, $\varepsilon = 0.2$, $\rho = -0.5$, $v = 0.15$. Author's graphics.

U^{EX}, but, as time of liquidity provision grows, the corresponding upper bound becomes inaccurate.

The calculation of the mixed-rule impermanent loss and its approximations is left to the reader as a difficult exercise.

In *P&L* modeling for AMMs, the primary aim is to ensure that the liquidity provider makes a profit or, at least, does not incur a loss. This profit stems from transaction fees charged by the pool, which must exceed the impermanent loss caused by collateral value dropping below its buy-and-hold threshold. These fees must exceed the impermanent loss. An arbitrageur needs to add more tokens to the pool than the rule dictates to account for transaction fees. In the presence of nonzero transaction costs, the actual composition of the pool is time- and path-dependent. Given the stochastic nature of the log price, the analysis of $\overline{P\&L}$ can only be conducted probabilistically through Monte Carlo simulations; see Lipton and Hardjono (2021) and Lipton and Sepp (2022). For the parameter selection used by these authors, automated liquidity provision is profitable on average. This profitability arises because the AMM accumulates more tokens by the process's conclusion than initially possessed.

8.7 Bonds and Bond Options

8.7.1 Background

We now use the machinery developed in Sections 6 and 7 for pricing bonds and bond options in some popular fixed-income models, including Vasicek–Hull–White and Cox–Ingersoll–Ross.

8.7.2 Vasicek Model

One can use formulas derived in the previous subsection to price bonds and bond options in the popular Vasicek and Hull–White models; see Hull and White (1990); Vasicek (1977). Recall that Vasicek postulated the following dynamics for the short interest rate $\hat{y}_t$:

$$d\hat{y}_t = (\chi - \kappa \hat{y}_t)\, dt + \varepsilon d\hat{W}_t, \quad \hat{y}_t = y, \tag{8.128}$$

or, alternatively,

$$d\hat{y}_t = \kappa (\theta - \hat{y}_t)\, dt + \varepsilon d\hat{W}_t, \quad \hat{y}_t = y, \tag{8.129}$$

where $\kappa\theta = \chi$.

At time t, the price of a bond maturing at time $\bar{t}$, which is denoted by $\mathsf{Z}\left(t, y, \bar{t}\right)$, boils down to solving the following classical backward problem:

$$\begin{aligned} &\mathsf{Z}_t\left(t, y, \bar{t}\right) + (\chi - \kappa y)\, \mathsf{Z}_y\left(t, y, \bar{t}\right) + \frac{1}{2}\varepsilon^2 \mathsf{Z}_{yy}\left(t, y, \bar{t}\right) - y\mathsf{Z}\left(t, y, \bar{t}\right) = 0, \\ &\mathsf{Z}\left(\bar{t}, y, \bar{t}\right) = 1. \end{aligned} \tag{8.130}$$

The standard affine ansatz yields

$$\begin{aligned} \mathsf{Z}\left(t, y, \bar{t}\right) &= \exp\left(\mathsf{C} - \mathsf{B}_\kappa y\right) \\ \mathsf{C} &= \left(\theta - \frac{\varepsilon^2}{2\kappa^2}\right)(\mathsf{B}_\kappa - T) - \frac{\varepsilon^2}{4\kappa}\mathsf{B}_\kappa^2 \\ &= (\mathsf{B}_\kappa - T)\,\theta + \frac{h_0}{2}, \end{aligned} \tag{8.131}$$

where h_0 is given by (6.114).

One can use formulae derived in the previous section to come up with an alternative derivation. Introduce $\hat{x}_t = \int_t^t \hat{y}_s ds$. The distribution of $(\hat{x}_t, \hat{y}_t)$ is given by (6.45) with the covariance matrix $\mathfrak{H}$, given by (6.114) and the expected value $\mathbf{r}$ given by (6.115). Accordingly, the price of a bond can be written as follows:

$$\mathsf{Z}\left(t,y,\bar{t}\right) = \mathbb{E}\left\{e^{-\bar{x}}\right\} = \frac{1}{\sqrt{2\pi h_0}}\int_{-\infty}^{\infty} e^{-\bar{x}-\frac{(\bar{x}-p)^2}{2h_0}}\,d\bar{x}$$
$$= e^{-p+\frac{h_0}{2}} = \exp\left(\mathsf{C}\left(T\right) - \mathsf{B}_\kappa\left(T\right)y\right), \tag{8.132}$$

so that Equations (8.131) and (8.132) are in agreement.

Knowing the joint Gaussian distribution for $(\hat{x}_t, \hat{y}_t)$, one can price an option on zero coupon bond maturing at time $\breve{t} > t, \breve{t} - t = \breve{T}$. The payoff of a European option with strike K has the form:

$$U\left(\bar{t},\bar{y}\right) = \max\left\{\phi\left(\exp\left(\mathsf{C}\left(\breve{T}\right) - \mathsf{B}_\kappa\left(\breve{T}\right)\bar{y}\right) - \exp\left(\ln K\right)\right), 0\right\}. \tag{8.133}$$

At maturity $\bar{t}$, the payoff is independent of $\bar{x}$; however, at inception it does depend on the realized value of $\bar{x}$. By using Equations (6.45), (6.114), and (6.115), one can write $U(t,y)$ (recall that here $x = 0$) as follows:

$$U(t,y) = \mathcal{J}_1(t,y) - \mathcal{J}_2(t,y), \tag{8.134}$$

where

$$\mathcal{J}_1(t,y) = \frac{1}{2\pi\det(\mathfrak{H})^{1/2}}\int_{-\infty}^{\infty}\int_{-\phi\infty}^{\mathsf{y}^*}\exp\left(-\Lambda(\bar{x},\bar{y}) - \bar{x} + \mathsf{C}\left(\breve{T}\right) - \mathsf{B}_\kappa\left(\breve{T}\right)\bar{y}\right)d\bar{x}d\bar{y}, \tag{8.135}$$

$$\mathcal{J}_2(t,y) = \frac{1}{2\pi\det(\mathfrak{H})^{1/2}}\int_{-\infty}^{\infty}\int_{-\phi\infty}^{\mathsf{y}^*}\exp\left(-\Lambda(\bar{x},\bar{y}) - \bar{x} + \ln K\right)d\bar{x}d\bar{y}, \tag{8.136}$$

$$\Lambda(\bar{x},\bar{y}) = \frac{\left(h_2(\bar{x}-p)^2 - 2h_1(\bar{x}-p)(\bar{y}-q) + h_0(\bar{y}-q)^2\right)}{2\det(\mathfrak{H})}, \tag{8.137}$$

with h_i given by (6.114), $\det(\mathfrak{H}) = h_0h_2 - h_1^2$. Here y^* is defined as follows:

$$\mathsf{y}^* = \frac{\mathsf{C}\left(\breve{T}\right) - \ln K}{\mathsf{B}_\kappa\left(\breve{T}\right)}. \tag{8.138}$$

First, consider $\mathcal{J}_1$. Completing the square, one gets

$$-\Lambda(\bar{x},\bar{y}) - \bar{x} + \mathsf{C}\left(\breve{T}\right) - \mathsf{B}_\kappa\left(\breve{T}\right)\bar{y}$$
$$= -\frac{\left(h_2\left((\bar{x}-p) - \frac{\Xi(y)}{\sqrt{h_2}}\right)^2 - \Xi^2(\bar{y}) + h_0(\bar{y}-q)^2\right)}{2\det(\mathfrak{H})}$$
$$-\mathsf{B}_\kappa\left(\breve{T}\right)(\bar{y}-q) - p + \mathsf{C}\left(\breve{T}\right) - \mathsf{B}_\kappa\left(\breve{T}\right)q, \tag{8.139}$$

where

$$\Xi(\bar{y}) = \frac{(h_1(\bar{y}-q) - \det(\mathfrak{H}))}{\sqrt{h_2}}. \tag{8.140}$$

Integrating over $\bar{x}$, one obtains the following expression for $\mathcal{J}_1$:

$$\mathcal{J}_1(t,y) = \frac{e^{-p+\mathsf{C}(\breve{T})-\mathsf{B}_\kappa(\breve{T})q}}{\sqrt{2\pi h_2}} \int_{-\phi\infty}^{\mathsf{y}^*} \exp\left(-\frac{\left(-\Xi^2(\bar{y})+h_0(\bar{y}-q)^2+2\det(\mathfrak{H})\,\mathsf{B}_\kappa\left(\breve{T}\right)(\bar{y}-q)\right)}{2\det(\mathfrak{H})}\right)d\bar{y}. \tag{8.141}$$

Completing the square one more time, one gets:

$$-\frac{-\Xi^2+h_0(\bar{y}-q)^2+2\det(\mathfrak{H})\,\mathsf{B}_\kappa\left(\breve{T}\right)(\bar{y}-q)}{2\det(\mathfrak{H})} \tag{8.142}$$
$$= -\frac{\left(\bar{y}-q+h_1+\mathsf{B}_\kappa\left(\breve{T}\right)h_2\right)^2}{2h_2} + \frac{h_0}{2} + \mathsf{B}_\kappa\left(\breve{T}\right)h_1 + \frac{\mathsf{B}_\kappa^2\left(\breve{T}\right)h_2}{2},$$

so that

$$\mathcal{J}_1(t,y) = \frac{e^{-p+\mathsf{C}(\breve{T})-\mathsf{B}_\kappa(\breve{T})q+\frac{h_0}{2}+\mathsf{B}_\kappa(\breve{T})h_1+\frac{\mathsf{B}_\kappa^2(\breve{T})h_2}{2}}}{\sqrt{2\pi h_2(t,t)}} \int_{-\phi\infty}^{\mathsf{y}^*} \exp\left(-\frac{\left(\bar{y}-q+h_1+\mathsf{B}_\kappa\left(\breve{T}\right)h_2\right)^2}{2h_2}\right)d\bar{y}$$
$$= \phi e^{-p+\mathsf{C}(\breve{T})-\mathsf{B}_\kappa(\breve{T})q+\frac{h_0}{2}+\mathsf{B}_\kappa(\breve{T})h_1+\frac{\mathsf{B}_\kappa^2(\breve{T})h_2}{2}} \mathrm{N}\left(\frac{\phi\left(\mathsf{y}^*-q+h_1+\mathsf{B}_\kappa\left(\breve{T}\right)h_2\right)}{\sqrt{h_2}}\right). \tag{8.143}$$

It is easy to see that $\mathsf{Z}\left(t,y,\breve{t}\right)$ is given by (8.143) with $\phi = 1$ and $\mathsf{y}^* = \infty$, so that

$$\mathsf{Z}\left(t,y,\breve{t}\right) = e^{-p+\mathsf{C}(\breve{T})-\mathsf{B}_\kappa(\breve{T})q+\frac{h_0}{2}+\mathsf{B}_\kappa(\breve{T})h_1+\frac{\mathsf{B}_\kappa^2(\breve{T})h_2}{2}}. \tag{8.144}$$

Thus,

$$\mathcal{J}_1(t,y) = \phi \mathsf{Z}\left(t,y,\breve{t}\right) \mathrm{N}\left(\frac{\phi\left(\mathsf{C}\left(\breve{T}\right) - \ln K - \mathsf{B}_\kappa\left(\breve{T}\right) q + \mathsf{B}_\kappa\left(\breve{T}\right) h_1 + \mathsf{B}_\kappa^2\left(\breve{T}\right) h_2\right)}{\sqrt{h_2}\mathsf{B}_\kappa\left(\breve{T}\right)}\right). \tag{8.145}$$

Direct verification of (8.143) is left to the reader as a useful exercise. By using this equation, it is easy but tedious to show that

$$\mathcal{J}_1(t,y) = \phi \mathsf{Z}\left(t,y,\breve{t}\right) \mathrm{N}\left(\phi d_+\right), \tag{8.146}$$

$$d_+ = \frac{\ln\left(\frac{\mathsf{Z}(t,y,\breve{t})}{\mathsf{Z}(t,y,\bar{t})K}\right)}{\Sigma\left(t,\bar{t},\breve{t}\right)} + \frac{\Sigma\left(t,\bar{t},\breve{t}\right)}{2},$$

where

$$\Sigma\left(t,\bar{t},\breve{t}\right) = \sqrt{h_2}\mathsf{B}_\kappa\left(\breve{T}\right). \tag{8.147}$$

Second, consider $\mathcal{J}_2$, proceed in the same way as before, and represent $\mathcal{J}_2(t,y)$ in the following form:

$$\mathcal{J}_2(t,y) = \phi \mathsf{Z}\left(t,y,\bar{t}\right) \mathrm{N}\left(\phi d_-\right), \tag{8.148}$$

$$d_- = \frac{\ln\left(\frac{\mathsf{Z}(t,y,\breve{t})}{\mathsf{Z}(t,y,\bar{t})K}\right)}{\Sigma\left(t,\bar{t},\breve{t}\right)} - \frac{\Sigma\left(t,\bar{t},\breve{t}\right)}{2}.$$

Finally, one arrives at the following familiar expression for the bond option price:

$$U(t,y) = \phi\left(\mathsf{Z}\left(t,y,\breve{t}\right) \mathrm{N}\left(\phi d_+\right) - \mathsf{Z}\left(t,y,\bar{t}\right) K \mathrm{N}\left(\phi d_-\right)\right). \tag{8.149}$$

8.7.3 CIR Model

The CIR model postulates that the short rate follows the Feller process; see Cox *et al.* (1985). Accordingly, the bond price can be calculated by using (7.123) with $x = 0$, and $k = -i$:

$$\begin{aligned} \mathsf{Z}\left(t,y,\bar{t}\right) &= \int_{-\infty}^{\infty} \varpi^{(x)}\left(t,y,\bar{t},\bar{x}\right) e^{-\bar{x}} d\bar{x} \\ &= \frac{1}{2\pi} \int_{-\infty}^{\infty}\int_{-\infty}^{\infty} F\left(t,y,\bar{t},k\right) e^{(ik-1)\bar{x}} dk d\bar{x} = F\left(t,y,\bar{t},-i\right), \end{aligned} \tag{8.150}$$

where

$$F\left(t,y,\bar{t},-i\right) = \exp\left(\frac{2\chi\mu T}{\varepsilon^2} - \frac{2\chi}{\varepsilon^2}\ln\left(\frac{-\lambda_- \mathsf{E}_+ + \lambda_+ \mathsf{E}_-}{2\zeta}\right) + \frac{2\lambda_+\lambda_-\left(\mathsf{E}_+ - \mathsf{E}_-\right) y}{\varepsilon^2\left(-\lambda_- \mathsf{E}_+ + \lambda_+ \mathsf{E}_-\right)}\right), \tag{8.151}$$

with

$$\lambda_\pm = \mu \pm \zeta, \qquad \mu = -\frac{\kappa}{2}, \quad \zeta = \frac{\sqrt{\kappa^2 + 2\varepsilon^2}}{2}. \tag{8.152}$$

Thus,

$$\mathsf{Z}\left(t, y, \bar{t}\right) = e^{\tilde{\mathsf{C}} - \tilde{\mathsf{B}} y}, \tag{8.153}$$

where

$$\tilde{\mathsf{C}} = \frac{\chi \kappa T}{\varepsilon^2} - \frac{2\chi}{\varepsilon^2} \ln\left(\frac{-\lambda_- \mathsf{E}_+ + \lambda_+ \mathsf{E}_-}{2\zeta}\right), \qquad \tilde{\mathsf{B}} = \frac{(\mathsf{E}_+ - \mathsf{E}_-)}{(-\lambda_- \mathsf{E}_+ + \lambda_+ \mathsf{E}_-)}, \tag{8.154}$$

which coincides with the standard expressions given by Cox *et al.* (1985).

8.8 European Options with Stochastic Interest Rates

This section shows how to price equity options with stochastic interest rates. While the formulation of this problem may appear straightforward, its solution proves to be tedious. It is assumed that interest rate is governed by the Ornstein–Uhlenbeck–Vasicek processes.

$$d\hat{y}_t = (\chi - \kappa \hat{y}_t)\, dt + \varepsilon d\hat{Z}_t, \quad \hat{y}_t = y, \tag{8.155}$$

where $\hat{Z}_t$ is the standard Wiener processes. The risk-neutral evolution of the foreign exchange is governed by the following equation:

$$\frac{d\hat{S}_t}{\hat{S}_t} = \hat{y}_t dt + \sigma d\hat{W}_t, \quad \hat{S}_t = S, \tag{8.156}$$

or, equivalently,

$$d\hat{x}_t = \left(\hat{y}_t - \frac{1}{2}\sigma^2\right) dt + \sigma d\hat{W}_t, \quad \hat{x}_t = x, \tag{8.157}$$

where $\hat{x} = \ln\left(\hat{S}/K\right)$. In general, $d\hat{Z}_t$ and $d\hat{W}_t$ are correlated, so that $d\hat{Z}_t d\hat{W}_t = \rho dt$.

Consider the familiar backward Kolmogorov problem for European calls and puts:

$$
\begin{aligned}
&U_t + \frac{1}{2}\varepsilon^2 U_{rr} + \rho\varepsilon\sigma U_{rx} + \frac{1}{2}\sigma^2 U_{xx} \\
&\quad + (\chi - \kappa r)\, U_y + \left(y - \frac{1}{2}\sigma^2\right) U_x - rU = 0, \qquad (8.158)\\
&U\left(\bar{t}, y, x\right) = K\left(\phi\left(e^x - 1\right)\right)_+ .
\end{aligned}
$$

As usual, start with the change of the dependent variable:

$$
U = KB_1 V. \qquad (8.159)
$$

where $B = \exp\left(\alpha_1 - \beta_1 y\right)$ is the domestic bond price, given by (8.131), so that

$$
B_t + \frac{1}{2}\varepsilon^2 B_{rr} + (\chi - \kappa r)\, B_y - rB = 0. \qquad (8.160)
$$

Hence,

$$
\begin{aligned}
&V_t + \frac{1}{2}\varepsilon^2 V_{rr} + \rho\varepsilon\sigma V_{rx} + \frac{1}{2}\sigma^2 V_{xx} \\
&\quad + \left(x - \frac{1}{2}\varepsilon^2\beta_1 - \kappa r\right) V_y + \left(y - \frac{1}{2}\sigma^2 - \rho\varepsilon\sigma\beta_1\right) V_x = 0, \qquad (8.161)\\
&V\left(\bar{t}, y, x\right) = \left(\phi\left(e^x - 1\right)\right)_+ .
\end{aligned}
$$

Now, change independent variables $(t, y, x) \to (t, \eta_1, \eta_2)$, where

$$
\eta_1 = y, \quad \eta_2 = -\alpha_1 + \beta_1 y + x. \qquad (8.162)
$$

Thus,

$$
\begin{aligned}
&\frac{\partial}{\partial t} = \frac{\partial}{\partial t} + \left(-\alpha_1' + \beta_1'\eta_1\right)\frac{\partial}{\partial \eta_2}, \\
&\frac{\partial}{\partial y} = \frac{\partial}{\partial \eta_1} + \beta_1 \frac{\partial}{\partial \eta_2}, \quad \frac{\partial}{\partial x} = \frac{\partial}{\partial \eta_2}.
\end{aligned} \qquad (8.163)
$$

so that

$$
\begin{aligned}
&V_t + \left(-\alpha_1' + \beta_1'\eta_1\right) V_{\eta_2} \\
&\quad + \frac{1}{2}\varepsilon^2\left(V_{\eta_1\eta_1} + 2\beta_1 V_{\eta_1\eta_2} + \beta_1^2 V_{\eta_2\eta_2}\right) + \rho\varepsilon\sigma\left(V_{\eta_1\eta_2} + \beta_1 V_{\eta_2\eta_2}\right) + \frac{1}{2}\sigma^2 V_{\eta_2\eta_2} \\
&\quad + \left(\chi - \frac{1}{2}\varepsilon^2\beta_1 - \kappa\eta_1\right)\left(V_{\eta_1} + \beta_1 V_{\eta_2}\right) + \left(\eta_1 - \frac{1}{2}\sigma^2 - \rho\varepsilon\sigma\beta_1\right) V_{\eta_2} = 0, \\
&V\left(\bar{t}, \eta_1, \eta_2\right) = \left(\phi\left(e^{\eta_2} - 1\right)\right)_+ . \qquad (8.164)
\end{aligned}
$$

Assume that $V(t, \eta_1, \eta_2)$ only depends on t, η_2, $V(t, \eta_1, \eta_2) = V(t, \eta_2)$, which is consistent with the terminal condition. Thus,

$$\begin{aligned}
&V_t + \left(\frac{1}{2}\varepsilon^2\beta_1^2 + \rho\varepsilon\sigma\beta_1 + \frac{1}{2}\sigma^2\right)V_{\eta_2\eta_2} \\
&\quad + \left(-\alpha_1' + \beta_1'\eta_1 + \left(b_1 - \frac{1}{2}\varepsilon^2\beta_1 - \kappa\eta_1\right)\beta_1 - \frac{1}{2}\sigma^2 - \rho\varepsilon\sigma\beta_1 + \eta_1\right)V_{\eta_2}=0 \\
&V\left(\bar{t},\eta_1,\eta_2,\eta_2\right) = \left(\phi\left(e^{\eta_2} - 1\right)\right)_+ .
\end{aligned} \tag{8.165}$$

But

$$\alpha_1' - \beta_1'\eta_1 + \frac{1}{2}\varepsilon^2\beta_1^2 - (\chi - \kappa\eta_1)\beta_1 - \eta_1 = 0, \tag{8.166}$$

so that

$$\begin{aligned}
&V_t + \left(\frac{1}{2}\varepsilon^2\beta_1^2 + \rho\varepsilon\sigma\beta_1 + \frac{1}{2}\sigma^2\right)\left(V_{\eta_2\eta_2} - V_{\eta_2}\right) = 0, \\
&V\left(\bar{t},\eta_1,\eta_2\right) = \left(\phi\left(e^{\eta_2} - 1\right)\right)_+ .
\end{aligned} \tag{8.167}$$

This is the classical Black–Scholes problem with time-dependent volatility:

$$\begin{aligned}
&V_t + \frac{1}{2}\Sigma^2\left(V_{\eta_2\eta_2} - V_{\eta_2}\right) = 0, \\
&V\left(\bar{t},\eta_2\right) = \left(\phi\left(e^{\eta_2} - 1\right)\right)_+ ,
\end{aligned} \tag{8.168}$$

where

$$\Sigma^2 = \varepsilon^2 \mathrm{B}_\kappa^2 + 2\rho\varepsilon\sigma\mathrm{B}_\kappa + \sigma^2. \tag{8.169}$$

Thus, the price is

$$U = B_1 U^{(C,P)}\left(\frac{B_2 S}{B_1}; T, K, \sqrt{\frac{\int \Sigma^2 ds}{T}}\right), \tag{8.170}$$

where $U^{(C,P)}$ are given by (8.20).

A similar technique can be used for the Heston model and the Stein–Stein model with stochastic interest rates. However, there is one significant difference between these two models - the former model works only when volatility and rate innovations are uncorrelated, while the latter model can handle arbitrary correlations.

9 Conclusions

Due to the space constraints, the discussion must be concluded here. It is left to the reader to explore further the application of mathematical tools and techniques based on Kelvin waves in financial engineering. Three particularly compelling problems are

- the pricing and risk management of credit derivatives;
- the exploration of mean-reverting trading strategies, such as pairs trading;
- the examination of affine jump-diffusion and pseudo-differential processes.

References such as Lipton and Shelton (2012), Lipton and Lopez de Prado (2020), and others provide additional insights into these problems.

This Element has established a unified methodology for determining t.p.d.fs and expectations for affine processes through integral representations based on Kelvin waves. This approach has bridged various disciplines, uncovering profound connections between hydrodynamics, molecular physics, stochastic processes, and financial engineering. Both degenerate problems, which possess more independent variables than sources of uncertainty, and their nondegenerate counterparts are covered, showcasing the versatility of the method.

A surprising link is established between the Langevin equation for underdamped Brownian motion and the vorticity equation for two-dimensional flows in viscous incompressible fluids. Utilizing Kelvin wave expansions, the book solves several relevant financial problems, including the deriving convenient formulas for t.p.d.fs and expectations for processes with stochastic volatility, developing an analytically solvable model for path-dependent volatility, pricing of Asian options with geometric averaging, and pricing bonds and bond options by augmenting the short-rate process with its integral process.

The methodology introduced in this book can address a wide spectrum of complex problems, significantly enhancing the comprehension and modeling of stochastic systems across diverse fields.

References

Abramowitz, M. & Stegun, I. A., eds. 1964 *Handbook of Mathematical Functions with Formulas, Graphs, and Mathematical Tables*. Washington, DC: US Government Printing Office.

Aksenov, A. V. 1995 Symmetries of linear partial differential equations and fundamental solutions. *Doklady Mathematics* **51(3)**, 329–331.

Andersen, L. B. G. & Piterbarg, V. 2007 Moment explosions in stochastic volatility models. *Finance and Stochastics* **11**, 29–100.

Angeris, G., Kao, H. T., Chiang, R., Noyes, C. & Chitra, T. 2019 An analysis of Uniswap markets. *Cryptoeconomic Systems Journal.* **1(1)**. DOI: 10.21428/2F58320208.C9738E64

Arnold, L. 1974 *Stochastic Equations: Theory and Applications*. New York: John Wiley.

Bachelier, L. 1900 Théorie de la spéculation. *Annales de l'Ecole Normale Supérieure* **17**, 21–86.

Barucci, E., Polidoro, S. & Vespri, V. 2001 Some results on partial differential equations and Asian options. *Mathematical Models and Methods in Applied Sciences* **11(3)**, 475–497.

Bayly, B. J. 1986 Three-dimensional instability of elliptical flow. *Physical Review Letters* **57**, 2160–2163.

Bayly, B. J., Holm, D. D. & Lifschitz, A., 1996. Three-dimensional stability of elliptical vortex columns in external strain flows. *Philosophical Transactions of the Royal Society A* **354(1709)**, 895–926.

Berest, Yu. Yu. 1993 Group analysis of linear differential equations in distributions and the construction of fundamental solutions. *Differential Equations* **29(11)**, 1700–1711.

Bergomi, L. 2015 *Stochastic Volatility Modeling*. Boca Raton, FL: CRC Press.

Bharucha-Reid, A. T. 1960 *Elements of the Theory of Markov Processes and Their Applications*. New York: McGraw-Hill.

Bick, A. & Reisman, H. 1993 Generalized implied volatility. Preprint. https://www.researchgate.net/publication/228601694_Generalized_implied_volatility

Black, F. 1976 The pricing of commodity contracts. *Journal of Financial Economics* **81(3)**, 167–179.

Black, F. & Scholes, M. 1973 The pricing of options and corporate liabilities. *Journal of Political Economy* **81(3)**, 637–659.

Bluman, G. & Kumei, S. 1989 *Symmetries and Differential Equations.* Berlin: Springer.

Boness, A. J. 1964 Elements of a theory of a stock option value. *Journal of Political Economy* **72(2)**, 163–175.

Boyarchenko, S. & Levendorskii, S. 2002 *Non-Gaussian Merton–Black–Scholes Theory*. River Edge, NJ: World Scientific.

Carr, P., Lipton, A. & Madan, D. 2002 The reduction method for valuing derivative securities. Working Paper, New York University. https://www.researchgate.net/publication/2860358_The_Reduction_Method_for_Valuing_Derivative_Securities

Cartea, Á., Drissi, F. & Monga, M. 2023 Predictable losses of liquidity provision in constant function markets and concentrated liquidity markets (August 15). *Applied Mathematical Finance.* Available at SSRN 4541034: https://ssrn.com/abstract=4541034 or http://dx.doi.org/10.2139/ssrn.4541034

Chandrasekhar, S. 1943 Stochastic problems in physics and astronomy. *Reviews of Modern Physics* **15(1)**, 1–89.

Chandrasekhar, S. 1961 *Hydrodynamic and Hydromagnetic Stability*. Oxford: Clarendon.

Chapman, S. 1928 On the Brownian displacements and thermal diffusion of grains suspended in a nonuniform fluid. *Proceedings of the Royal Society of London. Series A* **119(781)**, 34–54.

Cordes, H. O. 1995 *The Technique of Pseudodifferential Operators*. Cambridge: Cambridge University Press.

Cox, J. C., Ingersoll Jr., J. E. & Ross, S. A. 1985 A theory of the term structure of interest rates. *Econometrica* **53(2)**, 385–408.

Craddock, M. 2012 Lie symmetry methods for multi-dimensional parabolic PDEs and diffusions. *Journal of Differential Equations* **252(1)**, 56–90.

Craddock, M. & Platen, E. 2004 Symmetry group methods for fundamental solutions. *Journal of Differential Equations* **207(2)**, 285–302.

Craik, A. D. D. & Criminale, W. O. 1986 Evolution of wavelike disturbances in shear flows: A class of exact solutions of the Navier–Stokes equations. *Proceedings of the Royal Society of London. Series A* **406**, 13–26.

Dai, Q. & Singleton, K. J. 2000 Specification analysis of affine term structure models. *Journal of Finance* **55(5)**, 1943–1978.

Davis, M. H. A. 2004 Complete-market models of stochastic volatility. *Proceedings of the Royal Society of London. Series A* **460**, 11–26.

Derman, E. & Kani, I. 1994 Riding on a smile. *Risk Magazine* **7(2)**, 32–39.

Devreese, J. P. A., Lemmens, D. & Tempere, J. 2010 Path integral approach to Asian options in the Black–Scholes model. *Physica A* **389(4)**, 780–788.

Di Francesco, M. & Pascucci, A. 2004 On the complete model with stochastic volatility by Hobson and Rogers. *Proceedings of the Royal Society of London. Series A* **460(2051)**, 3327–3338.

Di Francesco, M. & Pascucci, A. 2005 On a class of degenerate parabolic equations of Kolmogorov type. *Applied Mathematics Research eXpress* **3**, 77–116.

Dragulescu, A. A. & Yakovenko, V. M. 2002 Probability distribution of returns in the Heston model with stochastic volatility. *Quantitative Finance* **2(6)**, 443–453.

Duffie, D., Filipovic, D. & Schachermayer, W. 2003 Affine processes and applications in finance. *Annals of Applied Probability* **13(3)**, 984–10053.

Duffie, J. D. & Kan, R. 1996 A yield-factor model of interest rates. *Mathematical Finance* **6(4)**, 379–406.

Duffie, D., Pan, J. & Singleton, K. 2000 Transform analysis and asset pricing for affine jump-diffusions. *Econometrica* **68(6)**, 1343–1376.

Duong, M. H. & Tran, H. M. 2018 On the fundamental solution and a variational formulation for a degenerate diffusion of Kolmogorov type. *Discrete & Continuous Dynamical Systems: Series A* **38(7)**, 3407–3438.

Dupire, B. 1994 Pricing with a smile. *Risk Magazine* **7(1)**, 18–20.

Ebeling, W., Gudowska-Nowak, E. & Sokolov, I. M. 2008 On stochastic dynamics in physics: Remarks on history and terminology. *Acta Physica Polonica B* **39(5)**, 1003–10017.

Egorov, M. 2019 StableSwap: Efficient mechanism for Stablecoin liquidity. White paper.

Fabijonas, B., Holm, D. D. & Lifschitz, A. 1997 Secondary instabilities of flows with elliptic streamlines. *Physical Review Letters* **78(10)**, 1900–1903.

Feller, W. 1951 Two singular diffusion problems. *Annals of Mathematics* **54(1)**, 173–182.

Feller, W. 1952 The parabolic differential equations and the associated semigroups of transformations. *Annals of Mathematics* **55**, 468–518.

Feller, W. 1971 *An Introduction to Probability Theory and Its Application*, vol. 2, 2nd ed. New York: John Wiley.

Filipovic, D. 2009 *Term-structure models.* Berlin: Springer.

Fokker, A. D. 1914 Die mittlere Energie rotierender elektrischer Dipole im Strahlungsfeld. *Annalen der Physik* **348(5)**, 810–820.

Fourier, J. B. 1822 *Théorie Analytique de la Chaleur*. Paris: Firmin Didot, Père et Fils.

Friedlander, S. & Lipton-Lifschitz, A. 2003 Localized instabilities in fluids. In *Handbook of Mathematical Fluid Dynamics* **2**, 289–354. North-Holland: Amsterdam.

Friedlander, S. & Vishik, M. 1991 Instability criteria for the flow of an inviscid incompressible fluid. *Physical Review Letters* **66**, 2204–2206.

Friz, P. & Keller-Ressel, M. 2010. Moment explosions in stochastic volatility models. *Encyclopedia of Quantitative Finance*, 1247–1253.

Fukasawa, M., Maire, B. & Wunsch, M. 2023 Weighted variance swaps hedge against impermanent loss. *Quantitative Finance* **23(6)**, 1–11.

Gatheral, J., Jaisson, T. & Rosenbaum, M. 2018 Volatility is rough. *Quantitative Finance* **18(6)**, 933–949.

Geman, H. & Eydeland, A. 1995 Asian options revisited: Inverting the Laplace transform. *Risk Magazine* **8(4)**, 65–67.

Gershon, D., Lipton, A., Rosenbaum, M. & Wiener, Z. eds. 2022 *Options-45 Years Since the Publication of the Black–Scholes–Merton Model: The Gershon Fintech Center Conference*. Singapore: World Scientific.

Gihman, I. I. & Skorohod, A. V. 1972 *Stochastic Differential Equations*. New York: Springer.

Giorno, V. & Nobile, A. G. 2021 Time-inhomogeneous Feller-type diffusion process in population dynamics. *Mathematics* **9(16)**, 1879.

Guyon, J. 2014 Path-dependent volatility. *Risk Magazine* **27(10)**.

Hagan, P., Kumar, D., Lesniewski, A. & Woodward, D. 2002 Managing smile risk. *Wilmott Magazine* **9**, 84–1008.

Hänggi, P., Talkner, P. & Borkovec, M. 1990 Reaction-rate theory: Fifty years after Kramers. *Reviews of Modern Physics* **62(2)**, 251–341.

Hanson, F. B. 2007. *Applied Stochastic Processes and Control for Jump-Diffusions: Modeling, Analysis and Computation*. Philadelphia, PA: Society for Industrial and Applied Mathematics.

He, C., Chen, J., Fang, H. & He, H. 2021 Fundamental solution of fractional Kolmogorov–Fokker–Planck equation. *Examples and Counterexamples* **1**, 100031.

Heston, S. L. 1993 A closed-form solution for options with stochastic volatility with applications to bond and currency options. *Review of Financial Studies* **6**, 327–343.

Hobson, D. G. & Rogers, L. C. G. 1998 Complete models with stochastic volatility. *Mathematical Finance* **8(1)**, 27–48.

Hörmander, L. 1967 Hypoelliptic second order differential equations. *Acta Mathematica* **119**, 147–171.

Hull, J. & White, A. 1990 Pricing interest rate derivative securities. *Review of Financial Studies* **3**, 573–592.

Ibragimov, N. H. 1985 *Transformation Groups Applied to Mathematical Physics*. Dordrecht: D. Reidel.

Ivasishen, S. D. & Medynsky, I. P. 2010 The Fokker–Planck–Kolmogorov equations for some degenerate diffusion processes. *Theory of Stochastic Processes* **16(1)**, 57–66.

Jacob, N. & Schilling, R. L. 2001 Lévy-type processes and pseudodifferential operators. In *Lévy Processes: Theory and Applications,* O. E. Barndorff-Nielsen *et al.* (eds.), (pp. 139–168). Boston, MA: Birkhäuser.

Janek, A., Kluge, T., Weron, R. & Wystup, U. 2011 FX smile in the Heston model. *In Statistical Tools for Finance and Insurance* (pp. 133–162). Berlin, Heidelberg: Springer.

Jex, M., Henderson, R. & Wang, D. 1999 Pricing exotics under the smile. *Risk Magazine* **12(11)**, 72–75.

Kelvin, Lord 1887 Stability of fluid motion: Rectilinear motion of viscous fluid between two parallel planes. *Philosophical Magazine* **24**, 188–196.

Klein, O. 1921 Zur statistischen Theorie der Suspension und Lösungen. Inaugural-Dissertation. Uppsala: Almqvist & Wiksells.

Kolmogoroff, A. 1931 Über die analytischen Methoden in der Wahrscheinlichkeitsrechnung. *Mathematische Annalen* **104(1)**, 415–458.

Kolmogoroff, A. 1933 Zur Theorie der stetigen zufälligen Prozesse. *Mathematische Annalen* **108**, 149–160

Kolmogoroff, A. 1934 Zufallige Bewegungen (Zur Theorie der Brownschen Bewegung), *Annals of Mathematics* **35(1)**, 116–117.

Kovalenko, S., Stogniy, V. & Tertychnyi, M. 2014 Lie symmetries of fundamental solutions of one (2+ 1)-dimensional ultra-parabolic Fokker–Planck–Kolmogorov equation. *arXiv preprint* arXiv:1408.0166.

Kramers, H. A. 1940 Brownian motion in a field of force and the diffusion model of chemical reactions. *Physica* **7(4)**, 284–304.

Kuptsov, L. P. 1972 The fundamental solutions of a certain class of elliptic-parabolic second order equations. *Differential Equations* **8**, 1649–1660.

Lanconelli, E., Pascucci, A. & Polidoro, S. 2002 Linear and nonlinear ultra-parabolic equations of Kolmogorov type arising in diffusion theory and in finance. In Michael Sh. Birman, Stefan Hildebrandt, Vsevolod A. Solonnikov, and Nina N. Uraltseva, eds., *Nonlinear Problems in Mathematical Physics and Related Topics*, vol. II, 243–265. New York: Kluwer/Plenum.

Langevin, P. 1908 Sur la théorie du mouvement brownien. *Comptes rendus de l'Académie des Sciences* **146**, 530–533.

Lewis, A. 2000 *Option Valuation under Stochastic Volatility with Mathematica Code.* Newport Beach, CA: Finance Press.

Lewis, A. 2001 A simple option formula for general jump-diffusion and other exponential Lévy processes. Available at SSRN: https://ssrn.com/abstract=282110 or http://dx.doi.org/10.2139/ssrn.282110.

Lifschitz, A. 1991 Short wavelength instabilities of incompressible three-dimensional flows and generation of vorticity. *Physics Letters A* **157(8–9)**, 481–487.

Lifschitz, A. 1995 Exact description of the spectrum of elliptical vortices in hydrodynamics and magnetohydrodynamics. *Physics of Fluids A* **7**, 1626–1636.

Lifschitz, A. & Hameiri, E. 1991a A universal instability in fluid dynamics. In 1991 International Sherwood Fusion Theory Conference.

Lifschitz, A. & Hameiri, E. 1991b Local stability conditions in fluid dynamics. *Physics of Fluids A* **3**, 2644–2651.

Lipton, A. 1999 Similarities via self-similarities. *Risk Magazine* **12(9)**, 101–1005.

Lipton, A. 2000 *Pricing and Risk-Managing Exotics on Assets with Stochastic Volatility*. Presentation, Risk Minds, Geneva.

Lipton, A. 2001 *Mathematical Methods for Foreign Exchange: A Financial Engineer's Approach.* Singapore: World Scientific.

Lipton, A. 2002 The volatility smile problem. *Risk Magazine* **15(2)**, 61–65.

Lipton, A. 2018 *Financial Engineering: Selected Works of Alexander Lipton.* Singapore: World Scientific.

Lipton, A. 2023 *Kelvin Waves, Klein–Kramers and Kolmogorov Equations, Path-Dependent Financial Instruments: Survey and New Results. arXiv preprint* arXiv:2309.04547.

Lipton, A., Gal, A. & Lasis, A. 2014 Pricing of vanilla and first-generation exotic options in the local stochastic volatility framework: Survey and new results. *Quantitative Finance* **14(11)**, 1899–1922.

Lipton, A. & Hardjono, T. 2021 Blockchain intra- and interoperability. In *Innovative Technology at the Interface of Finance and Operations: Volume II* (pp. 1–30). Cham: Springer International Publishing.

Lipton, A. & Lopez de Prado, M. 2020 A closed-form solution for optimal Ornstein–Uhlenbeck driven trading strategies. *International Journal of Theoretical and Applied Finance* **23(08)**, 2050056.

Lipton, A. & Reghai, A. 2023 SPX, VIX and scale-invariant LSV. *Wilmott Magazine* **2023(126)**, 78–84.

Lipton, A. & Sepp, A. 2008 Stochastic volatility models and Kelvin waves.*Journal of Physics A: Mathematical and Theoretical* **41(34)**, 344012 (23pp).

Lipton, A. & Sepp, A. 2022 Automated market-making for fiat currencies. *Risk Magazine* **35(5)**. www.risk.net/cutting-edge/investments/7948106/automated-market-making-for-fiat-currencies.

Lipton, A. & Shelton, D. 2012 Credit default swaps with and without counterparty and collateral adjustments. *Stochastics: An International Journal of Probability and Stochastic Processes* **84(5–6)**, 603–624.

Lipton, A. & Treccani, A. 2021 *Blockchain and Distributed Ledgers: Mathematics, Technology, and Economics*. Singapore: World Scientific.

Lipton-Lifschitz, A. 1999 Predictability and unpredictability in financial markets. *Physica D: Nonlinear Phenomena* **133(1–4)**, 321–347.

Masoliver, J. 2016 Nonstationary Feller process with time-varying coefficients. *Physical Review E* **93(1)**, 012122.

Merton, R. C. 1973 Theory of rational option pricing. *Bell Journal of Economics and Management Science* **4(1)**, 141–183.

Merton, R. C. 1976 Option pricing when underlying stock returns are discontinuous. *Journal of Financial Economics* **3(1–2)**, 125–144.

Morse, P. M. & Feshbach, H. 1953 *Methods of Theoretical Physics, Part I.* New York: McGraw-Hill.

Olver, P. J. 1986 *Applications of Lie Groups to Differential Equations*, 1st ed. New York: Springer.

Orr, W. McF. 1907 The stability or instability of the steady motions of a perfect fluid. *Proceedings of the Royal Irish Academy A* **27**, 9–69.

Ovsiannikov, L. V. 1982 *Group Analysis of Differential Equations.* New York: Academic Press.

Pascucci, A. 2005 Kolmogorov equations in physics and in finance. In Elliptic and Parabolic Problems, C. Bandle, et al., eds. *Progress in Nonlinear Differential Equations and Their Applications*, **63**, 313–324. Basel: Birkhäuser.

Piessens, R. 2000 The Hankel Transform. In A. D. Poularikas, ed., *The Transforms and Applications Handbook: Second Edition*. Boca Raton, FL: CRC Press.

Planck, M. 1917 Über einen Satz der statistischen Dynamik und seine Erweiterung in der Quantentheorie. *Sitzungsberichte der Königlich Preussischen Akademie der Wissenschaften*, 324–341.

Reghai, A. 2015 *Quantitative Finance: Back to Basics*. New York: Palgrave MacMillan.

Risken, H. 1989 *The Fokker–Planck Equation: Method of Solution and Applications.* New York: Springer.

Rogers, L. C. G. & Shi, Z. 1995 The value of an Asian option. *Journal of Applied Probability* **32(4)**, 1077–10088.

Rubinstein, M. 1994 Implied binomial trees. *Journal of Finance* **49(3)**, 771–818.

Samuelson, P. A. 1965 Rational theory of warrant pricing. *Industrial Management Review* **6**, 13–32.

Schachermayer, W. & Teichmann, J. 2008 How close are the option pricing formulas of Bachelier and Black–Merton–Scholes? *Mathematical Finance: An International Journal of Mathematics, Statistics and Financial Economics* 18(1), 155–170.

Schmelzle, M. 2010 Option pricing formulae using Fourier transform: Theory and application. Preprint, https://pfadintegral.com/articles/option-pricing-formulae-using-fourier-transform.

Schöbel, R. & Zhu, J. 1999 Stochastic volatility with an Ornstein–Uhlenbeck process: An extension. *Review of Finance* **3(1)**, 23–46.

Sepp, A., 2007. *Affine Models in Mathematical Finance: An Analytical Approach*. Tartu: University of Tartu Press.

Stein, E. M. & Stein, J. C. 1991 Stock price distributions with stochastic volatility: An analytic approach. *Review of Financial Studies* **4**, 727–752.

Terakado, S., 2019 On the option pricing formula based on the Bachelier model. Available at SSRN 3428994.

Uhlenbeck, G. E. & Ornstein, L. S. 1930 On the theory of Brownian motion. *Physical Review* **36**, 823–841.

Vasicek, O. A. 1977 An equilibrium characterization of the term structure. *Journal of Financial Economics* **5**, 177-188.

Weber, M. 1951 The fundamental solution of a degenerate partial differential equation of parabolic type. *Transactions of the American Mathematical Society* **71**, 24–37.

Wong, M. W. 2014 *Introduction to Pseudo-Differential Operators*. Singapore: World Scientific Publishing Company.

Zhang, Y., Chen, X. & Park, D. 2018 Formal specification of constant product ($x \times y = k$) market maker model and implementation. White paper. https://pdfcoffee.com/uniswap-formulas-pdf-free.html

Acknowledgments

I am grateful to my ADIA colleagues Majed Alromaithi, Marcos Lopez de Prado, Koushik Balasubramanian, Andrey Itkin, Oleksiy Kondratiev, Arthur Maghakian, Dmitry Muravey, Adil Reghai, other Q-team colleagues, my ADIA Lab colleague Horst Simon, and a former Bank of America colleague, Artur Sepp, for their encouragement and council. The kind invitation by Riccardo Rebonato to contribute to Cambridge Elements in Quantitative Finance is much appreciated. I am grateful to Drs. Nicola Ghazi and Piergiorgio Neri from Cleveland Clinic Abu Dhabi for saving the vision in my left eye, thus allowing me to finish this Element. Last but not least, the help of my wife, Marsha Lipton, especially her editorial suggestions and financial insights, has been critical in producing this Element.

About the Author

Alexander Lipton is a Global Head of Research & Development at Abu Dhabi Investment Authority, an Advisory Board member at ADIA Lab, a Professor of Practice at Khalifa University, and a Connection Science Fellow at MIT. He is a Co-Founder of Sila, a company providing digital wallet & ACH payment services, and an advisory board member at several companies worldwide. From 2006 to 2016, Alexander was Co-Head of the Global Quantitative Group and Quantitative Solutions Executive at Bank of America. Before that, he held senior managerial positions at several leading financial institutions. Additionally, Alexander held visiting professorships at EPFL, NYU, Oxford, and Imperial College. Earlier, Alexander was a Full Professor at the University of Illinois and a Consultant at the Los Alamos National Laboratory. Risk Magazine awarded him the Inaugural Quant of the Year Award in 2000 and the Buy-side Quant of the Year Award in 2021. Alexander has authored/edited thirteen books and over a hundred scientific papers on nuclear fusion, astrophysics, applied mathematics, financial engineering, distributed ledgers, and quantum computing. He holds several US patents.

Cambridge Elements

Quantitative Finance

Riccardo Rebonato

EDHEC Business School

Editor Riccardo Rebonato is Professor of Finance at EDHEC Business School and holds the PIMCO Research Chair for the EDHEC Risk Institute. He has previously held academic positions at Imperial College, London, and Oxford University and has been Global Head of Fixed Income and FX Analytics at PIMCO, and Head of Research, Risk Management and Derivatives Trading at several major international banks. He has previously been on the Board of Directors for ISDA and GARP, and he is currently on the Board of the Nine Dot Prize. He is the author of several books and articles in finance and risk management, including *Bond Pricing and Yield Curve Modelling* (2017, Cambridge University Press).

About the Series

Cambridge *Elements in Quantitative Finance* aims for broad coverage of all major topics within the field. Written at a level appropriate for advanced undergraduate or graduate students and practitioners, *Elements* combines reports on original research covering an author's personal area of expertise, tutorials and masterclasses on emerging methodologies, and reviews of the most important literature.

Cambridge Elements

Quantitative Finance

Elements in the Series

Machine Learning for Asset Managers
Marcos M. López de Prado

Advances in Retirement Investing
Lionel Martellini and Vincent Milhau

A Practitioner's Guide to Discrete-Time Yield Curve Modelling: With Empirical Illustrations and MATLAB Examples
Ken Nyholm

Girsanov, Numeraires, and All That
Patrick S. Hagan and Andrew Lesniewski

Causal Factor Investing: Can Factor Investing Become Scientific?
Marcos M. López de Prado

The Behavioral Economics and Politics of Global Warming: Unsettling Behaviors
Hersh Shefrin

Hydrodynamics of Markets: Hidden Links between Physics and Finance
Alexander Lipton

A full series listing is available at: www.cambridge.org/EQF

Printed in the United States
by Baker & Taylor Publisher Services